# PUTINOMICS

# PUTINOMICS

## Power and Money

# IN RESURGENT RUSSIA

## CHRIS MILLER

THE UNIVERSITY OF NORTH CAROLINA PRESS   CHAPEL HILL

Designed and set in Arno by Rebecca Evans
The University of North Carolina Press has been a
member of the Green Press Initiative since 2003.

Cover illustration: The front of a Russian 5,000-ruble banknote, 2010 version

Library of Congress Cataloging-in-Publication Data
Names: Miller, Chris, author.
Title: Putinomics : power and money in resurgent Russia / Chris Miller.
Description: Chapel Hill : University of North Carolina Press, [2018] |
Includes bibliographical references and index.
Identifiers: LCCN 2017042863 | ISBN 9781469640662 (cloth : alk. paper) |
ISBN 9781469663913 (pbk. : alk. paper) | ISBN 9781469640679 (ebook)
Subjects: LCSH: Russia (Federation)—Economic policy—1991– |
Russia (Federation)—Economic conditions—1991– | Russia (Federation)—
Politics and government—1991– | Elite (Social sciences)—Russia (Federation) |
Putin, Vladimir Vladimirovich, 1952– | Presidents—Russia (Federation)
Classification: LCC DK510.76 .M56 2018 | DDC 330.947—dc23 LC record
available at https://lccn.loc.gov/2017042863

TO LIYA

# CONTENTS

# FIGURES AND TABLE

## Figures

## Table

# PREFACE / THE STRONGMAN ECONOMY?

"There are two absolutely very well-known historical experiments in the world—East Germany and West Germany, and North Korea and South Korea. Now these are cases that everyone can see!"[1] So spoke Vladimir Putin, president of the Russian Federation, in an address to the Duma in 2012. As a former KGB operative in communist East Germany, Putin knew of what he spoke. Communism, he later explained, was a "historic futility. Communism and the power of the Soviets did not make Russia a prosperous country." Its main legacy was "dooming our country to lagging steadily behind economically advanced countries. It was a blind alley, far away from the mainstream of world civilizations."[2] Putin is not widely known as a critic of communist economics. The collapse of the Soviet Union, he famously declared, was "the greatest geopolitical catastrophe of the century."[3] "Whoever does not miss the Soviet Union has no heart," Putin said on a different occasion. Less well known, he also warned: "Whoever wants it back has no brain."[4]

The Kremlin's wars in Ukraine and Syria and its attempt to reconstruct the "sphere of privileged interests" that Russia lost when the Soviet Union collapsed have only heightened the popular sense that Vladimir Putin and the Russian elite are dead set on building the Soviet empire anew. In economic terms, many people think, Russia's failings since Putin came to power in 1999 mirror the dysfunctions of the Soviet economy. Ask a typical person their impressions of Russia's economy and words such as *corruption, kleptocracy,* and *petrostate* come to mind.

These descriptions get much right. The policy failures and missed opportunities of the past two decades are plentiful. Whole books are devoted to exposing the corruption of Russia's rulers—and indeed they are corrupt.[5] One U.S. senator has described Russia as "a gas station masquerading as a country"—and indeed, oil and gas play as large a role as ever.[6] Other analysts call Russia a "neo-KGB state"—and indeed, former spies and secret agents dominate not only the government but business, too.[7] These critiques of contemporary Russia's political economy are levied by foreigners and Russians alike, and not only by those Russians who support the opposition. The economic problems Russia faces are real, and many are self-inflicted.

Yet neo-Soviet it is not. Today, Russia's state plays a large role in the economy, but unlike in the Soviet period, the Kremlin only dominates certain sectors, leaving others alone. Nor is the story solely of mistakes and failures: things could well have been worse. Indeed, from the perspective of 1999, when Putin came to power and began forging the centrally managed political system that governs the country today, Russia's economic performance has exceeded most expectations. There was some optimism about the independent Russia that emerged from the wreckage of the USSR in 1991, but during the subsequent decade everything seemed to go wrong. The country's agricultural sector sank into depression. Much of the consumer goods industry went bankrupt. Industry did relatively better only because it was sustained by government subsidies that fueled inflation, wiping out many Russians' savings. By the end of the 1990s, the optimistic expectations that Russia would develop a new, capitalist middle class seemed, to most observers, naive. The most visible new class was that of the oligarchs, whose corrupt business dealings were the main news story of the 1990s.

By the time of the 1998 financial crash, when Russia defaulted on its debt and the ruble collapsed, foreign and domestic observers alike had downgraded their expectations of what Russia could achieve. In 1991, some analysts hoped Russia could become a normal European country. In 1999, the most optimistic interpretation was that Russia had become a normal emerging market.[8] That was not a compliment. The news in 1999—the year that Putin took power—was depressing. "In general, the Russian economy is a mess," began one story in the *Washington Post*.[9] "Doubts Riddle Optimism of Young Russians," reported *USA Today*.[10] Looking on the bright side, a headline in Britain's *Independent* noted, "Russia is down but not out; her economy has shriveled but Russia still has a mountain of horrendous weapons."[11] And that was the good news!

Perhaps the post-1998 gloom was unduly negative, unrepresentative of what realistically should have been expected from Russia? Perhaps a better metric would be to find a country that looked like Russia in 1999 and compare its development. A middle-income country. A country in which oil rents constituted at least 10–15 percent of GDP and all natural resource rents constituted around 20 percent of total output.[12] A country in which a young lieutenant colonel took power in 1999, committed to using the security services to bolster his power. A president who claimed the mantle of democratic legitimacy in part based on his ability to force big business and oligarchs to follow his rules, whether by means fair or foul.

One need not invent a country that in 1999 looked so like Russia. It exists in Chavista Venezuela: still governed by an autocratic regime, still dependent on declining oil revenues, still failing to build an economy based on rules rather than political whim. The difference is that the Chavistas spent recklessly during the oil boom while presiding over a mismanagement-induced collapse in oil production and, now, painful shortages of consumer goods created by poorly conceived price controls.[13] According to World Bank estimates, Venezuela was wealthier on a per person basis than Russia in 1999. No longer.[14]

Surely no one could have reasonably expected Russia to turn out like Venezuela today? In fact, in 1999, some observers thought Venezuela was better placed to prosper. At the time, credit rating agencies judged it safer to lend to Venezuela's government than to Russia's.[15] The economic problems we currently associate with Venezuela—consumer good shortages, runaway inflation, and military-enforced food requisitions—were the story of Russia's twentieth century. There was little reason in 1999 to think that this sorry history would not persist into the twenty-first century. Today few people compare Russia and Venezuela. That is because the two countries' lieutenant colonels had very different methods. The Chavista experiment is widely recognized as a failure, but under Putin the Kremlin has consolidated power at home and abroad.

The aim of this book is to explain the Kremlin's economic strategy and to assess whether it has succeeded in achieving its aims. Since the beginning of the Putin era, Russia's leaders have had the following goals, in order of priority: maintaining power, expanding Russian influence abroad, and developing Russia's economy at home. To achieve these goals, the Kremlin has implemented a three-pronged strategy:

1. Strengthen central authority, ensuring the Kremlin has the power and the money to enforce its writ.
2. Prevent popular discontent by guaranteeing low unemployment and adequate pensions.
3. Rely on private business to improve efficiency, but only where it does not contradict the previous two strategies.

These are the three pillars of Putinomics. In instances where these principles do not conflict, the Kremlin's decision making is easy. Where Russia's government faces a choice, it consistently prefers to safeguard central authority even at the expense of incomes or efficiency. The political elite, as well as many ordinary Russians, thinks this prioritization makes sense. Most Russians believe that the decline of state authority during the country's traumatic 1990s contributed to its economic problems. The maintenance of a decisive and unified central government is therefore widely seen in Russia as a precondition for achieving all other economic goals.

The Kremlin's skill in mustering and distributing resources explains why the Russian elite has maintained power for nearly two decades, and how it has deployed power abroad with some success. Many oil-fueled dictatorships squander their oil revenues on Ferrari sports cars and Fendi handbags. Russia's ostentatious oligarchs have accumulated their share of English football teams and hundred-million-dollar yachts armed with missile defense systems.[16] But unlike its own spendthrift 1990s, Russia during the 2000s saved hundreds of billions of dollars during the good years, stowing resources in reserve funds for use when oil prices fell. If the Kremlin's economic policy was as simplistic as is often portrayed—as a series of thefts and errors lubricated by oil revenue—its rulers would not still hold power even as they wage two foreign wars.

The three-pronged strategy that defines Putinomics explains much about Russian economic policy making. The government's consistently conservative fiscal and monetary policy—avoiding large deficits, foreign debts, and rapid inflation—is an expression of the Russian elite's commitment to stable government finances. The role that oligarch-dominated state-owned firms play in energy and other key sectors is justified in part by their willingness to support the Kremlin in managing the populace by keeping unemployment low, media outlets docile, and political opposition marginalized. Much of the country's pro-Putin media, for example, is owned not by the government directly but by oligarchs or by state-owned energy firms. The government's social strategy—underfunding health and education but keeping pensions steady—is evidence that the Kremlin values pensions' contribution to social stability more than it regrets the extent to which poor schooling impairs medium-term growth. The government's emphasis on low unemployment, even at the expense of higher average wages, illustrates the emphasis on social stability. Where private businesses have succeeded, it is in sectors that do not conflict with the Kremlin's more important economic and political goals.

Has this strategy worked? Russia's political elite has achieved its goals. Putin is still in power, and the groups and individuals that have supported him have done well. Russia plays a bigger, if not necessarily friendlier, role on the world stage today. Meanwhile, until recently, the country's elite and populace have flourished. Average Russians saw rapid income growth during the 2000s, and though wages have been roughly stagnant since then, low unemployment and stable pensions have kept average Russians from complaining. Putin has overtaken Leonid Brezhnev as the second-longest-serving Russian leader since the time of the tsars, behind only Joseph Stalin. From the perspective of the individuals who crafted Putinomics, as well as from the elite groups and social classes that backed it, these achievements represent a success. Putinomics was a coherent response to the dilemmas of the 1990s: persistent budget deficits and inflation, financial instability, and a weak central state. Macroeconomic stability, underwritten not only by higher energy prices but also by a new elite political consensus that supported low deficits and low inflation, made possible the boom in investment and consumption of the 2000s. The political preferences of the Russian elite corresponded with sensible macroeconomic policy making. The problems that the Putin coalition wanted to solve were many of the key issues that impaired economic growth in the 1990s.

On other policy questions, however, including issues such as market competition, regulation, and the rule of law, the pillars of Putinomics are conducive to political control but not to economic growth. Oligarchs and state-owned firms write the rules in their favor. They can do so because of their crucial political role. The economic effects of this political system are negative: lower investment and reduced efficiency. At the same time, the government's investment strategy focuses on politically useful vanity projects rather than productive investments in health or education. This explains both why Russia's elite has held on to power and why Russian economic growth has slowed. The political consensus that provided sensible macroeconomic policies in the 2000s persists. But the dilemmas Russia has faced since the 2008 crisis are different than those of Putin's first decade in power. Then, Russia needed fiscal and monetary stabilization. Today, Russia needs better rules to encourage investment coupled with efforts to prepare workers for higher-skilled jobs. Since the protests that accompanied his return to power in 2012 and the annexation of Crimea in 2014, however, Putin's political coalition has shifted away from the groups most likely to support this type of economic change. Instead, the Kremlin has doubled down on the politics of stability—meaning that living standards will continue to stagnate for the foreseeable future, but Russia's political elite will have the resources needed to retain power at home and to play a resurgent role on the world stage.

# NOTE ON TRANSLITERATION

Where possible, I have followed the Library of Congress's system for transliterating Russian words and names, except that I do not denote hard and soft signs, which will be obvious to Russian speakers and irrelevant to non-Russian speakers. Where Russian names already have a commonly used English transliteration that contradicts the Library of Congress system, I use the more common version. Thus readers will normally see Alexei, but I will transliterate the name of the former minister and central banker as "Alexey Ulyukaev," for example. Confusingly, some of the names of individuals discussed have been published in English with multiple spellings.

# PUTINOMICS

# CHAPTER 1

## Putin's Economic Inheritance

President Boris Yeltsin was on vacation when the crisis smashed into Russia in mid-August 1998. Storm clouds had been gathering for months. Russia's government was debt-ridden and nearly bankrupt, reliant on short-term loans to pay pensions and fund basic public services. The Kremlin spent too much and raised too little in taxes, filling the difference by borrowing at extortionate interest rates or by printing money, which fueled inflation. By the summer of 1998, as Russia's borrowing rates spiked ever higher, everyone knew that a painful adjustment was inevitable. The only question was when it would come—and how traumatic it would be.

On July 13, the International Monetary Fund (IMF) led a coalition of international lenders in announcing $22.6 billion of financial support for Russia.[1] In exchange, Russia's government promised sharp tax hikes and spending cuts, a package that was political suicide. But Russia's leaders had no choice but to agree. Yeltsin cut short his summer vacation to assemble parliamentary support for the necessary legislative changes. By early August, however, the political process in Russia had ground to a halt. The government and the Duma disagreed over how to resolve the country's budgetary imbalance. Everyone in Yeltsin's government and in the Duma believed that Russia had time to debate, to discuss, and to play political games. They underestimated the speed with which debt investors were losing faith in Russia's ability to repay—and losing interest in repeatedly rolling over Russia's short-term debt. Yeltsin himself was disengaged. After failing to broker a solution to the political impasse, the president returned to his summer vacation just as the situation was beginning to spin out of control.[2]

Speculative attacks on emerging market currencies had sparked chaos in Thailand, Indonesia, and South Korea earlier that year, and many investors—including those whose loans funded Yeltsin's government—were nervously asking whether Russia would be next. The victims of crisis in Southeast Asia had all been forced to devalue their currencies, a move that amounted to a tax on consumers. When the Indonesian rupiah and Thai baht crashed in 1997 and 1998, those countries' citizens were made poorer in dollar terms, and in response they drastically cut back on purchases of imports, bought with dollars. This restored these countries' financial balance at the cost of impoverishing consumers.

Russia appeared on the brink of a similar fate. The currency was overvalued, and the central bank was spending huge sums to prop it up, keeping it pegged at a set rate against the dollar. The overvalued ruble not only made Russian exports less competitive but also created a dilemma for the central bank, which had a limited quantity of dollars with which to buy rubles.[3] Yet Russians and foreigners alike were looking to sell rubles and get their hands on a more stable currency. Unless the situation turned, the central bank would run out of dollars and be forced to abandon the ruble's peg. Economists refer to such a move as floating the currency. This was the wrong metaphor: if the central bank stopped supporting the ruble, it would sink like a rock.

Yeltsin "loudly and clearly" declared that Russia would not devalue the ruble. Prime Minister Sergey Kiriyenko promised that "there will be no changes in the monetary policy of the central bank."[4] But talk is cheap, and the Kremlin did not back it up with actions. The more the government insisted that it would stand by the currency and repay its debts, the more investors concluded that it was time to sell. On August 13, markets began to panic as investors raced for the exit. Foreigners and Russians alike dumped rubles and bought dollars, forcing the Russian central bank to spend down its dollar reserves to dangerously low levels. New lending to the Russian government all but stopped, as interest rates on one-month government bonds reached 160 percent. The Moscow stock exchange plummeted so rapidly that trading was repeatedly suspended.[5]

Something had to give. Prime Minister Kiriyenko appealed for more foreign aid but was turned down. He was left with no choice but to surrender. The central bank let the ruble fall against the dollar. Starting at six rubles per dollar, the ruble fell to twenty-five. Consumer prices more than doubled.[6] Russians paid the cost of adjustment as they discovered that their wages suddenly bought only half as many goods as before.

At the same time, the government announced it would default on its debts, forcing bond holders to bear some pain, too. Russian banks that held government bonds teetered on the brink of bankruptcy, a trend that was exacerbated by depositors rushing to withdraw their money and stuff it under the mattress.

As the ruble plummeted, demand for dollars was so high that currency exchange booths ran out of cash.[7] "Russia," grumbled one disillusioned investor, "now ranks somewhere between Nigeria and Kenya."[8]

## The Roots of the Crisis

The financial crash of 1998 was widely interpreted as the first crisis of Russian capitalism. In fact it was the last gasp of Soviet socialism. The disagreements about economic policy that divided Russia during the 1990s—conflicts so sharp that they led Yeltsin to shell parliament in 1993, as the country teetered on the brink of civil war—gave way to a new and unexpected elite consensus. During the late 1980s and early 1990s, political disputes over taxes and spending caused the government to run massive budget deficits. By 1999, political conflict had been replaced by a surprising new consensus in favor of cautious fiscal and monetary policy. The new consensus solidified the role of market mechanisms in most sectors of the economy but recognized the need to strengthen the state, especially in the resource-rich energy sector.

The rise of an elite consensus in favor of balanced budgets and low inflation was unexpected, particularly after a decade of economic disbalances driven by political clashes. Beginning in the late 1980s, USSR general secretary Mikhail Gorbachev's program of perestroika sought to create markets to replace Soviet-style command methods of organizing industry and agriculture. Gorbachev soon discovered that a shift toward market economics brought short-run pain before any long-run gain. The Soviet system had long coupled command methods with a system of exorbitant subsidies for politically favored groups. These subsidies had to be unwound if the Soviet economy was to be modernized. But doing so required a complicated and dangerous negotiation with the powerful groups that benefited from them.

The USSR's vast military-industrial complex, for example, faced few constraints on its demands for funds. By the late 1980s, the Red Army and the industries that supplied it consumed around a fifth of Soviet output.[9] The USSR's system of collective and state farms wasted tractors and fertilizer on a vast scale, yet farmers' incomes were propped up by the largest farm subsidy program in human history.[10] Many other industries received similar handouts. If market economics meant subsidy cuts that reduced their well-being, why should industries, farmers, or the military support market reform?[11]

As Gorbachev began pushing the Soviet economy toward a market system, powerful interest groups demanded compensation. Gorbachev would have preferred to force change. But though the Soviet Union was an authoritarian state, the general secretary was far from an absolute dictator. Many groups had the clout to obstruct Gorbachev's efforts, so Gorbachev had to "buy off" those who were made worse off by change, providing reparations for the cost of reform. Because the Kremlin had to cut deals in exchange for reforms, it faced a growing mismatch between its ever-growing spending promises and the painful reality of declining revenues.

The problem of higher budget deficits was easy to diagnose, but it proved impossible to control. In exchange for legislation that unwound collective farms and privatized agriculture, for example, the farm lobby extracted debt write-offs and financial help. The military budget—little of which improved citizens' well-being—escaped cuts throughout the late 1980s. Capital investment in industry spiked upward in the first years of perestroika, despite evidence that such funds were spent as inefficiently as ever, with little return on the billions of rubles "invested." Capital investment was in large part a means for distributing funds to powerful industrial groups, which demanded support in exchange for tolerating Gorbachev's move toward a market economy. The result was a paradox: even as Soviet legislation demanded that the economy be organized along market lines, Soviet enterprises and consumers faced incentives that—thanks to subsidies—had nothing to do with markets at all.

The expansion of subsidies stressed the Soviet budget, but they might have been survivable were it not for a sharp decline in revenue. An ill-conceived war on alcohol consumption slashed the tax take from drink sales just as sliding world oil prices squeezed profits on oil exports. The combination of rising spending and declining revenue pushed the Soviet Union toward fiscal crisis. The Kremlin tried borrowing to bridge its deficit, but no one was willing to lend the Soviet government the vast sums it needed. Gorbachev could not hike taxes or cut spending without threatening his hold on power. The only option was to print money.

In a market economy, expanding the money supply causes prices to increase. But in the Soviet Union, prices in state-run stores were set by the government, though on the black market prices floated freely. As the money supply expanded, workers and businesses found that producing and selling goods at officially decreed prices was increasingly less lucrative. Many enterprises moved their production into the black market; many others stopped producing entirely. As production and distribution of goods froze, shortages spread across the country. Even staple goods were in short supply. Consumers stood in line for hours waiting for bread or milk as supply lines froze and distribution networks dissolved. By 1991, officials in local governments across the Soviet Union had no choice but to introduce food rationing. In Moscow, officials feared that food supplies might run out.[12]

The economic crisis degraded Soviet power. Combined with nationalist agitation and a loss of faith in communism, the failing economy sapped Gorbachev's control over the apparatus of government. Over the course of 1990 and 1991, local leaders began to usurp power, at first in the Baltics and the Caucasus and eventually in Russia itself. Boris Yeltsin, the elected president of the Russian republic, soon realized he had few reasons to support the continuation of Soviet rule over Russia. In late 1991, Yeltsin met secretly with the leaders of Ukraine and Belarus in a forest lodge, where they declared the end of the Soviet Union. Gorbachev, powerless, had no choice but to resign.

The emergence of fifteen independent states in the place of the Soviet Union was a political revolution, as new forces jockeyed for power and as countries forged new governments. Yet the economic realities of the Soviet system did not change overnight. How could they have? Factories and farms, stores and supply chains, payouts to pensioners—this economic infrastructure persisted, though everything was jolted by the collapse of the political system. The most painful reality that newly independent Russia faced at the end of 1991 was the budget deficit that the USSR bequeathed it. The chasm between the government's revenue and expenditure was not reduced by the collapse of the USSR. It was probably made worse, as tax collection all but ceased even as demands on the government budget grew. The IMF estimated that the USSR's deficit reached an astonishing 30 percent of GDP in 1991.[13] Without painful changes, independent Russia's deficit in 1992 would probably have been larger.

Upon taking charge of independent Russia, new president Boris Yeltsin's sought to eliminate the shortages that paralyzed the Russian economy and threatened food supplies. Yeltsin and his economic team, led by Prime Minister Yegor Gaidar, chose to attack shortages by freeing prices on nearly all goods, including food, on January 2, 1991. Yeltsin knew that "shock therapy"—the policy of rapidly shifting toward market prices—would cause pain as prices skyrocketed. But he also knew that there was no other path to eliminate shortages. The choice was between low prices on nonexistent goods and high prices on plentiful goods. Yeltsin concluded that the second option was best. He removed controls, prices skyrocketed, and shortages evaporated. The wave of inflation forced upon Russians the realization that the money in their bank accounts was worth far less than they had hoped. The real value of Russia's savings had collapsed because of the late 1980s financial crisis—but by letting prices rise, Yeltsin made this visible. Many Russians blamed him, rather than the Soviet leadership, for their losses. Lacking money, and politically unable to tax business, Yeltsin's government did little to cushion the blow of higher prices on Russia's vulnerable households.

The main driver of inflation was the ever-expanding supply of money. There were two reasons that the money supply kept expanding: the decision by Russia to share its currency with other post-Soviet countries, and the central bank's policy of loose credit. When the Soviet Union collapsed, the Soviet ruble—which connected the post-Soviet economies—persisted. Central banks of several countries jointly controlled the post-Soviet ruble. Lacking enforceable rules about money creation, this structure allowed smaller countries to print post-Soviet rubles while forcing other countries to bear part of the burden of inflation. Take Turkmenistan as an example. Its central bank could print rubles and lend them to Turkmenistani firms, which could in turn use them to buy goods in Russia. The benefits of this ruble creation accrued to Turkmenian firms, which received Russian goods. The costs of ruble creation—in terms of higher inflation, which reduced the value of all rubles—were felt not only by Turkmenistan but by anyone who held rubles. Because Russia was the biggest country in the post-Soviet ruble zone, it suffered disproportionately from the higher inflation.[14]

The design of the post-Soviet ruble zone incentivized inflation, punishing Russians above all, because Russians held the most rubles. Yet it took Yeltsin's government several years to dismantle the ruble zone and to establish its own currency. The Kremlin hesitated because it feared that abolishing the ruble zone would disrupt trade among post-Soviet countries. International experts such as the IMF also cautioned that rapid reforms might destabilize the economy yet further.[15] But so long as the ruble zone existed, the zone's multiple central banks kept printing money, and inflation galloped higher.

The second cause of inflation was the Russian central bank. The bank's chief from 1992 to 1994, Viktor Gerashchenko, kept credit loose, hoping to stimulate production and investment. But the central bank's credit issuance expanded the supply of money, creating further inflation. Gerashchenko eventually came to see the necessity of tightening credit conditions. But industries that benefited from cheap loans—many of which were prominently represented in the Duma—continued to lobby for loose monetary policy.

Through the early 1990s, President Yeltsin and the Communist-dominated Duma clashed repeatedly over industrial subsidies, with Yeltsin arguing that subsidies caused inflation, and the Communists insisting that cutting subsidies would destroy the country's industrial base. Both arguments were right. In 1993, the dispute turned violent and Moscow teetered on the edge of civil

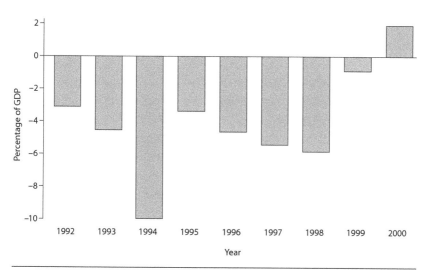

**FIGURE 1**  Russian government budget balance as percentage of GDP, 1992–2000. Rosstat.

war, as Yeltsin's army shelled the Duma to force out opposition lawmakers. The conflict was defused by a referendum and fresh parliamentary elections, in which voters both expressed confidence in Yeltsin and simultaneously returned an anti-Yeltsin parliament to the Duma. Faced with painful economic choices, Russian voters were themselves unsure what to do. Riven by conflicts and divergent interests, Russia's political class could not forge a consensus on how to stabilize the economy.

## St. Petersburg's First Capitalist Government

In St. Petersburg no less than in Moscow, chaos followed the Soviet Union's collapse. Just as Yeltsin struggled to bring order to Russia—or even to control his own government—so too newly elected mayor Anatoly Sobchak found postcommunist St. Petersburg all but ungovernable. Like Moscow, St. Petersburg suffered painful shortages of many foods during the winter of 1991; like Moscow, the dissolution of Communist rule opened space for mafias and criminal gangs to seize profitable businesses. Hyperinflation wiped out family savings. Military factories, which employed thousands of St. Petersburg's workers, were closing their doors, starved of funds.[16] The entire city seemed on the brink of social collapse.

St. Petersburg's mayor quickly concluded that his allies from the liberal intelligentsia were of little use in his effort to restore order. He needed aides who knew how to get things done, and who had the backbone and the connections to enforce his rules. Sobchak did not abandon the city's democratic institutions, but after his election, the former law professor focused his efforts on strengthening law enforcement and tax collection. He turned to his former student in the law faculty at Leningrad State University, Vladimir Putin, for help.[17] Sobchak knew that Putin had just returned from a five-year stint working for the KGB in Dresden, East Germany. After the Communist government of East Germany collapsed, Putin returned home to St. Petersburg and sought work in the new Russia.[18] Sobchak found Putin useful both because of his connections in the security services and for his understanding of foreign economies—a mix of old skills and new.

In August 1991, Sobchak appointed Putin head of the St. Petersburg Committee for External Relations, tasked with managing ties with foreign business.[19] Putin says that his job was to work with firms looking to invest in St. Petersburg, including Coca-Cola and Procter & Gamble.[20] Yet his responsibilities were far broader. St. Petersburg was a commercial hub. Around 20 percent of Russia's trade flowed through the city's ports and pipelines.[21] Putin's position astride this vast flow of money and goods gave him serious clout. One important lever for managing trade—and exerting power—was the regulation of foreign exchange, which was closely controlled during the hyperinflation of the early 1990s. Without Putin's approval, St. Petersburg businesses faced difficulties moving funds abroad.[22]

Putin's influence in St. Petersburg, however, did not stem solely from his regulatory authority. These powers were amplified, allege investigative journalists who have researched the subject, by Putin's ability to maneuver between the city government, the security services, and the mafias that controlled many of the country's leading export industries. From metals to minerals, alcohol to automobiles, the mafias' export businesses gave them ready access to hard currency at a time when the country was all but bankrupt.[23] If public order was to be reestablished, in St. Petersburg or in any other city, government had to find a way to "tax" businesses in the shadow economy, whether by formal or informal means.

KGB connections were crucial in extracting tax revenue from these black-market businesses. For one thing, the KGB had tracked mafias and corruption schemes throughout the Soviet period, so some of Putin's former colleagues had personal knowledge of how corruption rackets worked.[24] At the same time, Putin's background in the security services facilitated his use of the law-enforcement apparatus. In his autobiography, Putin emphasized the unity of

St. Petersburg's law-enforcement agencies during the early 1990s, a unity that he had helped to forge.[25]

The third use of a KGB background was as a source of ideas for "encouraging" businesses to pay taxes. In one incident that sparked a minor scandal, Putin demanded that St. Petersburg companies register with the Committee for External Relations to turn over data on their finances. Working with the tax inspectorate, Putin's analysts examined firms' tax payment records. This went far beyond the formal authority of Putin's committee, but it appears to have produced substantial tax revenue.[26] One St. Petersburg city council member fumed that the scheme utilized "secret service methods" to extract payments.[27] True: that was the point.

Yet even a KGB background was no guarantee of political success. The heirs of the Soviet secret services were powerful, but they were not the only force in the new Russia. On Sobchak's instruction, Putin joined the political party called Our Home Is Russia in 1995, and was named the party's regional head for St. Petersburg. But despite Putin's efforts, the party performed poorly in the 1995 Duma elections, finishing third behind two liberal parties.[28] The following year, Sobchak stood for reelection as mayor, naming Putin his campaign manager. Based on the Duma election results, Putin assumed Sobchak's main challenge would come from the reformist liberals. He underestimated the support obtained by Vladimir Yakovlev, a former Sobchak staffer. Despite the benefits of incumbency, Sobchak and Putin were outmaneuvered by their former ally. Influential Moscow powerbrokers were bent on toppling Sobchak, and they funneled money to the opposition. Putin discovered that his sources of financing had dried up, even as St. Petersburg's mafia bosses collected pots of money for Sobchak's opponents.[29]

When the votes were counted, Sobchak lost the mayoralty, and Putin lost his job. The consequences were worse for Sobchak, who faced not only the end of his political career but also an array of corruption investigations. As prosecutors questioned the former mayor about real estate deals on St. Petersburg's Vasilevsky Island, Sobchak's enemies circled. His chief of staff and several former aides in the city's planning department were arrested.[30] Putin watched nervously. On October 3, 1997, Sobchak complained of heart problems during a police interrogation and was sent to the hospital. He was then transferred to a different hospital, this one managed by a friend of Putin's. Four days later, Sobchak was whisked out of his hospital room onto a private jet, which flew him to Paris. Putin is said to have organized the escape to ensure that his "friend and mentor" was safe from punishment.[31] Putin had dodged a bullet, too.

# The Rise of the Oligarchs

Sobchak's escape from his St. Petersburg hospital bed might seem like a scene from a Cold War spy novel. Political intrigues, assassinations, and the black arts of the secret services continued to plague Russian politics. In other spheres, however, Russia was moving beyond the Soviet period. By the mid-1990s, new businesses were beginning to emerge. Analyst Igor Bunin published an influential book in 1994 that profiled forty entrepreneurs working in spheres from insurance to ports to juice sales. Bunin's point was that Russia was slowly casting off the legacies of central planning and developing entrepreneurs. "It happened," Bunin began his book. "In post-communist Russia there are normal capitalists living and working. Ours. Russians."[32]

As this new entrepreneurial class emerged during the 1990s, many consumers were made better off. If you look at headline GDP figures, which show a production decline far steeper than America's during the Great Depression, you might suspect that household incomes fell by a similar amount. But the GDP data obscure a complicated reality. In fact, much of the sharp fall in industrial output resulted from factories cutting production of goods that consumers had never wanted. As a result, the fall in living standards was significantly less than the collapse that GDP figures suggest.

The military-industrial complex, for example, made up 10–20 percent of the Soviet economy. When defense spending was cut to just several percent of GDP—the normal amount for European countries—this pushed GDP down sharply. Yet cutting wasteful production of unnecessary rockets and tanks made Russians no worse off. Survey data show that, despite the collapse of many Soviet-era industries, Russians on average ended the 1990s with far more material goods than they started with. The average household living space increased by around 20 percent during the 1990s. More Russians acquired more consumer electronics—from radios to refrigerators, TVs to tape recorders—than ever before. Car ownership doubled.[33] The complicated reality of the 1990s was industrial collapse and social instability coupled with nascent consumer affluence.

The fruits of a consumer society, however, were obscured by the chaos unleashed by Russia's lack of a functioning government. In the Soviet period, political power rested not with the state but with the Communist Party. When the Communist Party collapsed in 1991, state institutions lacked the capacity for effective governance. Mafias had grown in influence throughout the final years of Soviet power, expanding to meet rising demand for black market goods as state-run firms stopped functioning. In independent Russia, mafia groups consolidated their influence, supplanting many local police forces. They collected "taxes" in exchange for guaranteeing businesses' security, and operated according to their own laws.

The security services also expanded their influence in the early years of independent Russia. In theory, their powers were restricted by the formal dismantling of the KGB and legislation providing for greater oversight. In reality, current and former agents retained enormous clout. With powerful friends and knowledge of underhanded methods, former spooks were a step ahead in the struggle for property amid the wreckage of the Soviet state. Some provided security for leading businessmen. Alexei Kondaurov, a former KGB general, was hired by banker-turned-oilman Mikhail Khodorkovsky. Others, such as Alexander Lebedev, built business empires spanning from telecoms to textiles. A third group, which included Vladimir Putin, worked directly in the government.[34]

The greatest beneficiaries of the chaos of the Soviet collapse, however, were those who acquired state property. Many people participated in looting the state, and a handful managed to parlay these talents into billion-dollar fortunes. There were two main methods of theft that provided such enormous riches. The first was to seize control of factories, businesses, mines, and oil wells. In theory, the Soviet Union began turning over control of its enterprises to cooperatives in the late 1980s, and—also in theory—independent Russia began privatizing business in the early 1990s. The reality was quite different. Some firms were indeed privatized by law. But the most valuable assets were seized using illegal or underhanded methods.

Rem Vyakhirev served as deputy minister of gas in the Soviet Union. Even his first name—an acronym for Revolution, Engels, and Marx—demonstrated his parents' devotion to the communist cause. After being appointed chief of Gazprom, the firm that inherited the Soviet gas industry, Vyakhirev continued to advocate a muscular state role in the economy, including government ownership of his firm. But state ownership was a fig leaf. Regardless of who "owned" Gazprom, Vyakhirev controlled it. In the absence of effective law enforcement and with powerful allies in the Kremlin, Vyakhirev and other Gazprom executives bought shares in the company through rigged auctions. They exported gas through intermediaries owned by their relatives, selling gas to shell companies at below-market prices and allowing the company to resell gas at the full price, pocketing the difference. In theory, the company was partially private and partially state-controlled. But the legal structure barely mattered as executives stuffed the company's profits into their own pockets. Vyakhirev accumulated a personal fortune estimated at $1.5 billion.[35]

Vyakhirev was not the only owner of an ostensibly state-owned firm to accumulate great wealth. Managers of many other state-owned firms grabbed state property on the cheap. Some of this happened legally. The government's initial privatization plans were criticized for proposing to sell assets to foreigners, even though foreigners were most likely to pay a high price. Under pressure from the Duma, privatization laws were rewritten to give employees and managers the right to buy shares in their own firm at a discount. This cut the revenue the government received from privatization, taking funds that could have been used to bolster social welfare programs and distributing it instead to selected factory managers.[36] Such stipulations rigged the privatization auctions in a legal manner. Other schemes rigged privatization illegally. Oligarchs bribed and blackmailed officials and judges to ensure that auctions were decided in their favor. In one particularly scandalous auction known as the "loans-for-shares" scheme, a $355 million bid for Russia's largest nickel miner was rejected on a technicality, leaving a $170.1 million bid the winner. The legal minimum bid price for the auction was $170 million.[37] By rigging the auction, the winner—Vladimir Potanin's Oneksim Bank—siphoned millions of dollars from the state.

The second means of building a fortune through theft was to take advantage of sky-high inflation rates. Politically connected banks competed to attract government deposits in the early 1990s. For example, a bank might accept a billion-ruble deposit from the government that it knew the government would not withdraw for six months. With the inflation rate running at double and triple digits, the value of the rubles the bank was obligated to return to the government decreased substantially every month. Borrowing rubles, converting them into dollars, and paying back depreciated rubles several months later provided banks with substantial profits. The model was simple, but the returns were enormous, allowing oligarchs such as Mikhail Khodorkovsky and Vladimir Potanin to accumulate vast fortunes. By using their political clout to pay interest rates far below inflation, these banks' early "profits" derived from money skimmed from the state budget.[38]

How did the oligarchs get away with it? The state was too weak to hold the oligarchs to account. Yeltsin's government was divided, as factions representing various oligarchic groups vied for the president's ear. Banker Boris Berezovsky was thought to be close to Yeltsin's daughter Tatiana, while the gas sector was represented by Prime Minister Viktor Chernomyrdin, formerly Soviet minister of gas. At times, some oligarchs even served as officials in Yeltsin's government. While he struggled to corral the diverse interests represented in his government, Yeltsin was fighting a decade-long struggle with the Communists in parliament. This meant that both the president and the Duma were looking for allies against the other. The oligarchs purchased support from Duma members to ensure that legislation favored to their interests. Yeltsin, meanwhile, relied on the oligarchs to bankroll his political campaigns.

Most famously, Yeltsin made a pact with the oligarchs before the 1996 presidential election. Communist leader Gennady Zyuganov, who looked likely to defeat Yeltsin, threatened to reverse privatizations that constituted the basis of the oligarchs' fortunes. "If Zyuganov wins the Russian presidency . . . he will undo several years of privatization and this will lead to bloodshed and all-out civil war," thundered longtime Yeltsin aide Anatoly Chubais in 1996.[39] Chubais convinced the oligarchs to set aside their disputes and mobilize against the Communists. They poured millions into Yeltsin's campaign and—to everyone's surprise—Yeltsin won a second term. In return, the oligarchs were assured that the legality of their dealings in the early 1990s would not be questioned.

It is easy to overestimate the oligarchs' power in Yeltsin's Russia. True, the oligarchs' privatization schemes, and especially the "loans for shares" deal, eroded the rule of law, scared away foreign investors, and sapped Russians' confidence in free markets. In a macroeconomic sense, however, inflation—caused by the government's inability to raise revenue and control spending—was far more damaging to Russians' incomes than privatization. Yet despite some bankers' financial interest in keeping inflation levels high, for example, the government managed to reduce money supply growth in 1994 and 1995, and price increases slowed.[40] The oligarchs stole vast sums, but their influence was not absolute, as their power was checked at times by government and by public opinion. The oligarchs were also divided among themselves. Gas mogul Rem Vyakhirev, for example, had very different interests from media magnate Vladimir Gusinsky.

Even so, combined with Yeltsin's weakness vis-à-vis a fractious Duma and the country's far-flung regional governments, the oligarchs' power grated on Russian public opinion. Berezovsky boasted that a group of seven oligarchs controlled half of Russia's economy. "Russia is undergoing a redistribution of property unprecedented in history," Berezovsky crowed. "No one is satisfied."[41] In the early seventeenth century, a group of seven boyars—Russian aristocrats—deposed Tsar Vasily and invited Polish armies into Moscow, a dark period known as the "Rule of the Seven Boyars," or *semiboyarschina*. One journalist described Yeltsin's Russia as the "Rule of the Seven Bankers," or *semibankirshchina*. The power of the bankers, most of whom were Jewish, was seen as no less humiliating as when the traitorous boyars had turned the country over to Polish armies. Most Russians wanted nothing more than to see Berezovsky and his fellow banker-oligarchs cut down to size. This feeling was widespread not only among average Russians, who felt like they had lost out from the collapse of the USSR. Russia's political elite was also concluding that Russia's government budget could only be balanced if the country's oligarchs began to pay more tax.

## Putin Moves to Moscow

As Anatoly Sobchak was fleeing to Paris on a private jet, Vladimir Putin was planning his own escape. Making use of connections from St. Petersburg, Putin was appointed deputy chief of the Kremlin's Property Management Department, beginning his rapid ascent in Moscow.[42] Though Putin relished his proximity to power, he found that the problems the central government faced were similar to those he wrestled with in St. Petersburg. State authority had eroded. Mafias and oligarchs rewrote or ignored laws they did not like. Regional governments bucked the Kremlin's demands, facing no punishment for doing so. The weakness of central authority was most painfully evident in Chechnya, where from 1994 to 1996 Russia had fought a painful and inconclusive war with separatists. The Kremlin's failure to defeat ragtag militias in Chechnya underscored the widely held view that the government was inept.

Yet even more than the war, the government's effectiveness was degraded by its persistent lack of money. The mismatch between revenue and expenditure that the Soviet Union bequeathed to independent Russia proved difficult to close. The government managed to cut the budget deficit from 20 percent of GDP in 1992 to 7.2 percent by 1996, when Putin first arrived in Moscow.

Fiscal stabilization was accomplished not by raising revenue but by cutting spending. In part, spending was reduced by cutting waste leftover from the Soviet period. Military procurement, for example, was slashed by 60 percent in 1992 alone. Yet many of the spending cuts inflicted serious pain. In inflation-adjusted terms, government health spending fell by a third between 1990 and 1995; education spending was cut by almost half, and pensions fell substantially during those five years. Clinics were closed and schools were shuttered, even as nominal prices skyrocketed.[43]

Harsh spending cuts were the result of the central government's chronic inability to collect taxes. The problem was partly administrative—Russian bureaucracy has never been known for its efficiency—but the root issue was politics. Regional governments and powerful oligarchs did not want to pay higher taxes, and together they were strong enough to thwart collection efforts. As in so many spheres, Russia's tax dilemma had Soviet roots. In the early 1990s, many unprofitable but politically influential industries were kept alive by cheap loans from the central bank. But as Russia tightened monetary policy in 1994 and 1995, these firms and their influential backers in the Duma and the government had to find new sources of funds.

To do so, Russia's massive gas and electricity monopolies were used to fund dying industries. In 1996, Yeltsin established a commission designed, its chairman explained, "to redistribute energy resources at the disposal of government bodies and of enterprises, regardless of their form of ownership."[44] Translated from the Bureaucratese, this meant that the government would coerce energy firms, public or private, to provide gas and electricity to failing factories at below-market prices. At times energy was provided for free. In exchange for this generosity, the government quietly let energy companies avoid paying tax.

Energy made up a sizeable share of the economy, so exempting energy firms from taxation hobbled the government budget. But it served a crucial political purpose. By early 1996, the fuel and energy sector had provided net credit of 42 trillion rubles ($8.3 billion) to struggling industries. In exchange, the energy firms ran up "arrears"—unpaid taxes—of 13.7 trillion rubles, which partially compensated them for lost profits. As more firms, including railroads, were roped into similar schemes, industry began to breathe easier. Only 469 bankruptcies were declared in 1995, as loss-making firms obtained sufficient credit to continue operations.[45] That was good news for the government, which was desperate to stave off factory closings and layoffs that could devastate its political fortunes.

The scheme to keep bankrupt industries alive by tolerating an expansion of energy firms' tax arrears had a big downside. Energy firms were among Russia's largest companies. If they weren't paying taxes, the Kremlin had no hope of plugging its budget deficit. The deficit increased sharply as this strategy was ramped up, reaching 7.6 percent of GDP in 1996.[46] With the Kremlin committed to a policy of low inflation, it could no longer simply print money. It had no choice but to issue an increasing amount of debt to make up for insufficient tax collection.

In 1996 and 1997, the Kremlin knew that something had to be done. But how could Yeltsin take on regional governors and big oligarchs simultaneously? Both obstructed efforts to raise revenue, yet both had immense clout within Yeltsin's own government as well as the Duma. In October 1996, the Kremlin established the Temporary Extraordinary Commission to boost tax revenue. The name was chosen to remind tax cheats of the Extraordinary Commission (Cheka), a brutal Soviet secret police service. The deputy premier responsible for the security services was tasked with overseeing tax collection, and the tax enforcement agency regularly dragged in businessmen for "meetings" during which they were "encouraged" to pay taxes.[47]

Yeltsin's tax collection effort in 1996 and 1997 was reminiscent of Vladimir Putin's revenue-boosting schemes in St. Petersburg—except that it did not work. Tax revenues did not substantially increase. In December 1997, the Temporary Extraordinary Commission declared it would seize the two firms with the largest tax debts. But each of these firms was owned by a powerful oligarch—one by Berezovsky, the other by Potanin. Both oligarchs put up a fight, using their media assets and political clout to push back against the government's tax claims. The government succeeded in bringing in some revenue, but only after a bruising battle and a long delay.[48]

Yeltsin's struggle for tax revenue was marked by more defeats than victories. When the Kremlin proposed tax changes in 1998 to centralize revenue collection, its plans were attacked by regional governments. Alexander Lebed, the former presidential candidate who now governed Siberia's Krasnoyarsk region, threatened to stir up separatist feeling by declaring that he considered Moscow nothing more than a "neighbor from beyond the Urals."[49]

In response, the Kremlin escalated its battle for tax revenue by naming as the new tax chief the hard-charging Boris Fedorov, who promised a take-no-prisoners approach. Yeltsin also fired Prime Minister Viktor Chernomyrdin, the former Soviet gas minister who was widely believed to defend Gazprom's interests. The president replaced Chernomyrdin with little-known Sergey Kiriyenko, a political neutral who was inclined to take on powerful interests.[50] The stage seemed set for a crackdown on influential energy firms and the oligarchs who ran them.

Yeltsin's new team pounced, tearing up existing agreements with Gazprom. The government wanted Gazprom to pay taxes when gas shipped rather than when it received payment from customers—a method of ensuring that Gazprom paid taxes according to a predictable schedule. On July 2, 1998, Kiriyenko ordered the tax service to begin seizing Gazprom assets and threatened to use the government's stake in Gazprom to change the company's management. The firm's share price fell by 14 percent. Yet Gazprom had a powerful arsenal with which to respond. It began by cutting the amount of gas it supplied to industries, hoping to force factories to close and thus spark a political crisis that would force Yeltsin to negotiate. Then Gazprom mobilized supporters in the Duma to obstruct plans to seize the firm's assets, with

Communist leader Gennady Zyuganov declaring that "splitting up Gazprom is tantamount to splitting up Russia." The Duma voted 307 to 0 to demand that Yeltsin refrain from seizing Gazprom assets. Even oligarchs without ties to Gazprom, such as Boris Berezovsky, backed the gas monopoly's position as a means of sending a message to the government: efforts to increase tax collection would be resisted.[51]

The government had no choice but to settle. A deal signed in late July was described as a compromise. Gazprom agreed to make slightly higher monthly tax payments, though it was alleged to have violated its promises beginning the following month. In exchange, Yeltsin's government publicly stated that there would be no question of seizing Gazprom's property and accounts or replacing its board of directors or chairman Rem Vyakhirev. Gazprom had won. "Who do you think you are?" Vyakhirev had asked Prime Minister Kiriyenko, as the dispute raged. "You're just a little boy."[52]

Try as it might, Yeltsin's government could not increase tax revenue. Russia teetered on the brink of bankruptcy. At one point in June 1997, having poorly managed its spending plans, the Kremlin had to borrow several hundred million dollars from hedge fund magnate George Soros to fund the government for a week between when pensions were paid and when a new bond was issued.[53] Had Soros said no, Russia would have had to postpone payments to millions of pensioners. Chaotic management boded poorly for the stability of state finances, particularly as Russia's debt burden grew, and financial distress spread across emerging markets from Asia to Latin America throughout late 1997 and early 1998. Russia's economy seemed to be recovering from the tumult of the early 1990s, but Yeltsin's government looked scarcely more stable than Gorbachev's—and everyone remembered how disastrously that ended.

### The Great Crash

Vladimir Putin was appointed head of the FSB—the KGB's successor agency—in July 1998 amid a growing financial crisis. His portfolio now included all manner of threats to Russia's security, above all the risk of terrorism from Chechnya, where Moscow was waging a brutal counterinsurgency campaign against separatist forces. But it was impossible to ignore the economy. Warning signs had been visible for months. On October 28, 1997, Russia's stock market plunged by 20 percent, evidence that investors had growing doubts. A series of market crashes and currency crises in Thailand, Indonesia, South Korea, and elsewhere led skittish investors to pull money from emerging markets, dragging assets downward. The price of oil, a major source of Russian tax receipts, declined by over 15 percent in 1997, placing further pressure on the already cash-strapped government. Meanwhile the IMF, unhappy with the slow pace of tax reform, refused to transfer to the Kremlin a $700 million tranche of a promised loan.[54]

Pressure intensified in the summer of 1998, just as Putin was taking the reins of the FSB. In late May, after the government announced that no one had bid in a privatization auction for Rosneft, an oil firm, markets plunged 10 percent in a day, fearing that the failed auction presaged stormy waters.[55] As credit markets tightened, Russia's government had to offer ever-higher interest rates to entice investors to hold its debt. Because much of the government's debt was short term, it had to be rolled over on a regular basis. Higher interest rates meant that the government had to pay more to service its debt, widening its already large budget deficit. This in turn required more debt issuance. Fearing the Kremlin was in an unescapable circle of debt, investors took flight.

The ballooning debt paralyzed the government. Yeltsin's ministers had tried every trick to increase tax revenue, with little success. Spending was already low in comparative terms, and attempts to cut spending further would anger the Duma, threatening a political crisis. That was the last thing Yeltsin needed. He turned again to the IMF, dispatching aides to Washington to request $35 billion needed to avert default. Hoping to stave off yet another emerging market financial collapse, the fund transferred $4.8 billion to the Kremlin in early July.[56]

But even that massive sum was not enough. Financial markets had lost faith that Russia could ever pay its debts. Investors suspected that the government would have no choice but to default and devalue the ruble—so they had to get their money out of Russia immediately, selling rubles and buying dollars. As foreign investors and the country's own oligarchs rushed out, markets swooned. This put pressure on the country's banks, whose capital was tied up in Russian assets. As asset prices fell, these banks faced insolvency. The final straw was a letter published by Soros warning that "the meltdown in Russian financial markets has reached the terminal phase."[57]

Despite Yeltsin's public promise that "there will be no devaluation of the ruble," the show was over. As the Kremlin's reserve ran dry, Russia's leaders had only two options—printing money and inviting hyperinflation, or defaulting on the debt and devaluing the ruble against foreign currencies. Soros's letter publicly urged the government to choose the latter option. Yeltsin's ministers, their backs against the wall, concurred. Russia declared that it would not pay its debts, nor would it defend the ruble at its current peg against the dollar. On August 17, Sergey Kiriyenko announced that the ruble was being devalued. By the end of 1998, the ruble had fallen to a third of its precrisis value.[58] As the ruble slumped, inflation peaked at over 100 percent in mid-1999, devastating Russians' purchasing power.[59] The new middle class was hard hit. Whatever optimism remained about the prospects of capitalism in Russia had been extinguished.

### The Return of the Old Guard?

The crash of 1998 discredited Russia's liberal reformers even among the small share of the population that retained faith in them. Throughout the 1990s, liberals had warned of a Communist revanche. The Communist Party remained the largest faction in the Duma. Its leader, Gennady Zyuganov, nearly defeated Yeltsin in the 1996 presidential election, and Yeltsin was saved only by a flood of shadowy campaign cash from the oligarchs. Now, two years later, the liberals were humiliated and impotent. At the darkest moment since the Soviet Union collapsed, the Communist old guard seemed poised to retake power.

In Russia's far-flung regions, politicians began rolling back markets and reinstituting state control. In the Far East, authorities in Vladivostok were reported to have reintroduced administrative control over food distribution networks. Alexander Lebed, the populist governor of Krasnoyarsk, announced that the government would begin controlling prices on consumer goods. Kaliningrad, the small exclave on the Baltic Sea, declared it would no longer remit taxes to Moscow.[60] The basic institutions of Russia's nascent capitalist system were at risk.

The Kremlin, too, seemed ready to revert to Soviet ways. As the liberals' credibility collapsed, Yeltsin tacked desperately to the left, seeking a deal with the Communists in the Duma. Yeltsin purged his government of leading liberals and tapped a group of old Soviet bureaucrats to replace them. Yuri Maslyukov, who headed the central planning agency in the final days of the Soviet Union, was named deputy prime minister with responsibility for the economy. Russia's central bank, meanwhile, was handed back to Viktor Gerashchenko, the Soviet banker who presided over a disastrous hyperinflation when he ran the central bank in the early 1990s.

These appointments sparked fear in financial markets. One economist labeled Gerashchenko "the worst central banker in the world" after his first, calamitous stint as head of the Bank of Russia. Maslyukov was little different, with one IMF official recounting that he operated like "a Soviet manager," had "no feel for the market," and was "economically illiterate."[61] The Kremlin's new Soviet tilt was confirmed by Yeltsin's choice of Yevgeny Primakov as prime minister. Primakov had served as an adviser to several Soviet leaders. With Soviet cadres back in charge, many analysts reasoned, surely Russian capitalism's days were numbered.

Yet Primakov's government did the opposite of what most observers—including many of the prime minister's supporters—expected. He tackled the budget deficit, not primarily by hiking taxes, as many in the Duma wanted, but by slashing spending. Consolidated government spending fell from 48 percent of GDP in 1997 to 34 percent by 2000.[62] The budget that Primakov passed in February 1999 was coupled with pressure on oligarchs and regional governments to pay taxes.[63] By 2000, the combination of harsh spending cuts and aggressive tax collection jolted the budget into surplus. The liberal reformers of the 1990s may have been discredited—but the Soviet-style politicians who led the government after the 1998 crisis maintained many of their most controversial policy goals: balanced budgets, reduced inflation, and a market-based private sector.

The IMF may have thought that Russia's new leaders were "economically illiterate," but it was impressed with the results. The IMF's official history of its relations with Russia notes that though the fund feared the new government would adopt inflationary policies, "in fact, the authorities pursued reasonably tight monetary and fiscal policies."[64] Gone were the days when Yeltsin was the only Russian leader who opposed double- or triple-digit inflation. Now even the Communists seemed resigned to tight monetary policies. On the central question in Russian politics in 1998—whether to adopt policies that would exacerbate inflation—Primakov bucked the demands of many in the Duma. He stuck to his line even as inflation quickly ate away the real value of wages and pensions.

Russians were surprised to discover that Primakov, the former deputy chairman of the KGB, intended to implement policies that won IMF approval. Yet Primakov's background was not as hostile to policies of austerity as his Communist Party links might suggest. The Soviet Union had stood for state control, not for vast deficits or hyperinflation. Primakov and others like him associated deficits with Gorbachev's disastrous tenure as Soviet leader, when the Soviet Union collapsed under the weight of unpaid bills—not a period that anyone wanted to repeat. In addition, the memory of the painful hyperinflation of the early 1990s was fresh. Inflationary policies had been backed by many industrial bosses and ex-Soviet bureaucrats at the time, but loose money proved no panacea. Across the Russian elite, a new consensus was emerging, favoring tighter monetary policy and lower deficits. Primakov's pairing of former Communists with orthodox economic policy may have seemed counterintuitive. But it was as good evidence as any that the crash of 1998 marked a watershed in how Russia's elite thought the economy should be governed.

Primakov was not the only official in Yeltsin's government with former KGB ties to embrace this new fiscally conservative consensus. Vladimir Putin, who managed the FSB throughout the economic crisis, grew steadily in Yeltsin's estimation. In 1999 Yeltsin moved to thwart Primakov's political ambitions by sacking him as prime minister. Dissatisfied with Primakov's replacement, Yeltsin promptly fired him, too. Yeltsin then asked Putin to serve as prime minister. On August 9, 1999, Putin was confirmed in the position. Given how quickly Yeltsin cycled through prime ministers, Putin may not have assumed he would stay in the role for long. But on December 31, 1999, at the end of the millennium, Yeltsin shocked Russia by announcing his resignation and turning over the Kremlin to Vladimir Putin.

Even for a politician as ambitious as Putin, this was a rapid ascent. Just four years earlier he was a behind-the-scenes politico in St. Petersburg. Upon moving to Moscow he had rapidly won the trust of Yeltsin and his colleagues. Yet Putin also appeared to represent a new political era. He was relatively untainted by the political battles of the 1990s, since he spent most of the decade outside of Moscow. To most Russians he represented a breath of fresh air.

In political terms, then, Putin took power with a clean slate, unencumbered by the legacy of a decade-long bare-knuckle brawl between Yeltsin and the Communists. Moreover, the 1998 crisis had forged a stronger elite consensus on economic policy, so Putin did not face as stark a choice between the policies advocated by liberal technocrats and those backed by Communists and industrial bosses in the Duma. Yet the structures that defined Russia's economy remained. Oil and gas revenues continued to play a major role in funding the government. The tax system barely functioned. The country's industrial base was comatose; its small firms were mired in corruption and red tape. For a decade the government had funded its budget deficit by printing money, causing high inflation, as the economy lurched from crisis to crisis. This was Vladimir Putin's economic inheritance.

# CHAPTER 2

## Reforging the Russian State

"Dear citizens of Russia!" declared President Vladimir Putin in his first address to the Federal Assembly on July 8, 2000. It was Russia's equivalent of the State of the Union, a chance to set priorities and explain his goals to Russians, who knew little about him. Putin began his address not with grand claims or promises of prosperity, but with tax policy. From income tax rates to deductions, from the total tax burden to its effect on the shadow economy. It was a technocratic start to a speech that, many expected, would be used to set out broader goals.

Putin could see no greater priority. The tax issue, he explained, was the country's most pressing problem. The introduction of tax reforms, he promised, "will become a reference point of a new era in building the state, and in the rules of behavior in the economy." The entire state and social structure depended on a new set of economic rules, which would bring in more revenue and stabilize the country's budget. "We must ensure that all of us—entrepreneurs, authorities, citizens—strongly feel our responsibility to the country, so that strict fulfillment of the law becomes the deliberate choice of all citizens of Russia. Policies built on open and honest relations of the state with society will protect us from repeating past mistakes. They are the basic conditions of a new social contract." The key to economic stabilization, he asserted, was a stronger, functioning, capable government. Putin promised that stronger government finances would boost the economy. The word Putin used most frequently in his address, however, was not *economy* but *state*.[1]

### Strong State, Strong Economy

American political scientist Mancur Olson famously argued that government by bandits is tolerable only if the bandits stay in one place. Roving bandits simply seek to pillage, Olson explained. After seizing resources from one town, they pillage the town down the road. Stationary bandits, however, face different incentives. Thuggish though they may be, such bandits can even act responsibly, enacting policies that foster economic growth. The reason, Olson explained, is that rather than killing chickens, stationary bandits prefer to take eggs. A smart stationary bandit will encourage economic growth, to pillage (tax) even more in the future. In the end, Olson believed, the policies adopted by a stationary bandit could improve the lives of bandit and populace alike.[2]

After the corruption and violence of the 1990s, few Russians at the turn of the millennium would have objected to describing their political leaders as bandits. More often they used cruder language. Olson's notion—that rule by a single strong power was better than diffuse local mafias—made sense to many Russians. The idea that Russia needed a stronger central government was embraced by both market liberals and statist conservatives alike.

Market liberals saw a stronger state, which would effectively collect taxes, enforce the rule of law, and defend property rights, as crucial to economic growth. Statist conservatives appreciated the focus on law and order. Russia's new president understood the logic. The link between rebuilding state authority and economic growth was a central plank in Vladimir Putin's political campaigns. It let Putin assemble a new coalition between business and security elites that continues to undergird his power today. Russia's oligarchs and its business class backed Putin's efforts to strengthen state authority because they believed this would facilitate economic growth. Conservative, law-and-order nationalists cheered the restoration of centralized power and found Putin's orderly capitalism far more appealing than the chaotic capitalism of the Yeltsin era. Influential Russian economists argued that "macroeconomic stabilization hinges on a strengthening of political institutions."[3]

Reforging Russia's state and rebuilding its economy were two sides of the same coin, many believed. In many countries, business leaders want less government intrusion. After the chaotic 1990s, Russia's business classes generally believed that the key to stability was a stronger state. This provided the basis for a sturdy coalition between business and security services, whom Putin satisfied both by strengthening the government and providing stable macroeconomic management.

## Power Vertical

The first step toward rebuilding the government's authority, Putin concluded, was to strengthen Moscow's power over the provinces. After moving to Moscow, Vladimir Putin had initially served as first deputy to the chief of staff of Yeltsin's presidential administration. He was put in charge of supervising contacts with the governors of Russia's far-flung regions, a job he says was the most interesting work he ever had.[4] Managing relations between Moscow and the regions was key to resolving many of Russia's problems: the Kremlin clashed repeatedly with regional elites. After the Soviet Union collapsed, Russia became a federation, with each province granted its own elected leader and tax system. Yeltsin famously told regional elites in 1990 to "take as much sovereignty as you can swallow." They happily obliged. The collapse of central authority during the final months of the Soviet Union gave regional power-brokers a chance to seize power. The Kremlin decided there was little point in trying to control everything in the provinces given how little authority the government exercised even in Moscow. The provinces got a free ride for most of the 1990s, with little central supervision.

But however many thousands of miles separated Russia's far-flung settlements from the Kremlin, many Russians wished that their new tsar—President Yeltsin—would do more to establish order. The reality was that decentralization caused as many problems as it solved. Russia was not the only territory to declare its sovereignty as the Soviet Union dissolved. So too did Tatarstan, Karelia, and other provinces within Russia that had large non-Russian ethnic groups.[5] In Chechnya, the province in Russia's southern Caucasus border region, disputes about sovereignty led local leaders to declare independence, launching a brutal civil war that still smolders today. By contrast, Yeltsin resolved conflicts with oil-rich Tatarstan and other provinces peacefully, preventing them from leaving the Russian Federation. The cost, however, was formal recognition of these provinces' special rights, and the surrender of further power to local elites.

Well-devised federalism is no bad thing, as residents of Canada, Germany, the United States, or any other federal state can attest. Yet newly independent Russia suffered the downsides of federalism with few of the benefits. In many countries, federalism is justified by the notion that smaller units of government are more responsive to their peoples' interests and more accommodating of local differences. On certain issues, such as Tatarstan's support of the Tatar language, this may have happened in Russia during the 1990s.

On balance, however, Russian-style federalism made the country worse off. Regional governments were no more effective than the Kremlin, but they used their power to obstruct the central authorities.

Russian federalism's most serious fault during the 1990s was that it obstructed tax collection at a time when the central government was desperately short of cash. During the 1990s, the revenue from Russia's taxes was shared between central and regional governments. The Kremlin's inability to enforce rules meant that regions regularly confiscated revenue that was owed to the center. Regional authorities helped businesses hide from tax collectors. Firms benefited from a lower net tax bill, while regional leaders acquired political capital. The federal government, which was struggling with massive budget deficit, lost out.[6]

Vladimir Putin was not the only Russian to conclude that the government needed to strengthen central authority, but he had a clearer plan than most Russians of how the problem should be fixed. In his work as Yeltsin's aide responsible for relations with the regions, Putin recounted, he "developed relationships with many of the governors." It was clear, he came to realize, "that work with the regional leaders was one of the most important lines of work in the country." His diagnosis of the problem was straightforward as his solution. "The *vertikal*, the vertical chain of government had been destroyed," Putin concluded. "It had to be restored."[7]

In an interview in 2000, Putin suggested that restoring a vertical power—a hierarchical system in which each level of government followed instructions from the level above it—would be a straightforward task. "After all," Putin explained, "the governors are part of the country, and they also suffer from management weakness," so they would benefit from more efficient government. "You can't please everybody, but you can find common approaches," Putin insisted. He was right that the country's broken system of dividing power made both center and regions worse off. But Putin's vision of fixing Russia's broken federalist system by replacing it with a vertical hierarchy not only contradicted Russia's constitution but also challenged the authority of the regional elites whose clout undergirded Russia's federal system.

To rebuild central authority—to enforce tax laws, create a regulated market, and provide the sort of public goods that are a precondition of economic growth—Putin spent his early years in power appointing new officials to key positions. He chose people he could trust, either because he knew them personally or because their backgrounds were like his. As it happened, Putin's own background made him well-suited for reestablishing a "vertical of power" in Russia. His former employer—the KGB—was the institution that had enforced order during the Soviet period. Most of the KGB's alumni were keen to see such order restored.

Putin began by creating seven new federal districts, which were tasked with mediating between the regions and the Kremlin. Of the seven officials initially appointed to head these new federal districts, two were former KGB officers, two were army generals, and one was a police general. Only two of the seven were civilians, and one of these civilians was alleged to have KGB ties.[8] This was the first step in a vast expansion of the role played by security officials in Russian politics. Each of the seven heads of the federal districts was also appointed to Russia's Security Council. The territory of the new federal districts corresponded precisely with the territorial division of the Interior Ministry's troops. Several other security agencies soon created their own divisions based on the federal districts.[9] Many governors concluded that the new federal districts were less about coordinating policy and more about enforcing the Kremlin's writ. They sensibly kept their heads down in response.

The federal districts were the first of many changes that strengthened the Kremlin's authority by expanding the remit of the security services. Chief federal inspectors in each region, for example, were drawn from the ranks of the *siloviki*—former employees of the KGB or army who had transitioned into politics.[10] Putin also solidified his personal control over the security services, firing the ministers of defense and interior, both holdovers from the Yeltsin era, and nominating Sergei Ivanov and Boris Gryzlov in their places. Meanwhile, Mikhail Fradkov was put in charge of the tax police. Both Ivanov and Fradkov are believed to have a background in the KGB, while Gryzlov was a St. Petersburg politician and a former classmate of FSB director Nikolai Patrushev.[11]

Putin's strategic appointments—and his willingness to tap long-standing KGB networks to buttress his formal authority with informal networks—facilitated the consolidation of power. He continued to trim gubernatorial authority, refashioning the balance of power in favor of the Kremlin. In 2001, the rules governing the appointment and dismissal of judges were rewritten, strengthening the Kremlin's ability to interfere in court decisions while decreasing local elites' influence on the judiciary.[12] Putin also gained new powers that let him remove governors and dissolve regional legislatures.[13]

These changes drove a remarkable reversal of fortune in Russian politics. Regional elites, who had been the greatest beneficiaries of the fragmentation of the 1990s, struggled to respond to Putin's aggressive recentralization of power. Gubernatorial elections were replaced by presidential appointment. The new federal districts chipped away at gubernatorial authority by shifting power to officials dependent on the Kremlin.[14] The shake-up of the security forces and the appointment of Putin allies to leading positions broke the bonds between regional elites and the police, prosecutors, and the Interior Ministry—bonds that, under Yeltsin, had undermined the central government's monopoly on violence and diluted presidential authority.[15] Now, the security forces answered solely to the Kremlin. And at the top of the new vertical power sat Vladimir Putin.

### The Gref Program

Even as Putin centralized power by appointing KGB allies to key posts, he also sought to make the government more effective. Here, too, Putin's goals appealed both to law-and-order conservatives, who feared that the government was incompetent, and to business-oriented economic liberals, who wanted to cut red tape. German Gref, who, like Putin, had served in the St. Petersburg city government before moving to Moscow in 1998, was tasked with devising a strategy to make the Russian state work better. Gref assembled many of Russia's leading economists and public policy experts to provide advice to the new government. The goal, Gref declared, was to boost GDP growth to 8 percent per year.[16]

Gref's recommendations, which were presented in a major report, touched nearly every aspect of Russian life, from education to employment, infrastructure to industry. The report's broad conclusion—driven by the liberal-minded economists who served as Gref's expert advisers—was that Russia's government should do less but do it more effectively. In the social sphere, for example, Gref's team recommended moving away from universal government-provided benefits. Instead, they argued that the government should target financial assistance at the poorest Russians, while fostering a system of retirement savings accounts and health insurance to provide for the middle class. Monopolies should be subject to competition. The government's main task in the industrial sphere was to provide a stable investment climate by securing property rights and establishing an effective judicial system. Subsidies to industry should be phased out, the report argued, to reduce the budget deficit and inflation.

Gref's proposals were as controversial as they were ambitious. They amounted to a full restructuring of the Russian government, as many commentators realized.[17] Gref supported many of the least popular policies from the Yeltsin era, including cutting social programs, ending industrial subsidies, and withdrawing the state from economic life. Gref promised that his proposals would increase efficiency. But many people benefited from programs that Gref thought were holding the country back.

Regional elites were particularly opposed. Yegor Stroyev, the chairman of the Federation Council, the upper house of Russia's parliament, attacked Gref's plan at the annual St. Petersburg Economic Forum in June 2000. Stroyev argued that Gref's proposals lacked mechanisms to "stimulate domestic production, without which serious economic growth is impossible." Stroyev emphasized that "the government needs to understand: if regions don't work in this direction, there won't be any economic development."[18] Stroyev's criticism was echoed by many other regional leaders. Kursk Oblast governor Aleksandr Rutskoi growled that Gref's program is "rubbish that cannot be implemented."[19] Journalist Mikhail Delyagin, meanwhile, argued that the plan's "main instrument of transformation is social default" through cuts to welfare programs.[20] Delyagin suggested that Putin "is increasingly reminiscent of Gorbachev" in his inability to cope with the contradictory forces that buffeted the Kremlin.

To counter Gref's plan, a committee of regional leaders and economists was assembled under the leadership of Viktor Ishaev. The economic advisers who worked with Ishaev were sharp critics of the Gref proposals. Abel Aganbegyan and Leonid Abalkin had been prominent economists in the USSR and had advised Soviet leaders such as Mikhail Gorbachev. None believed that Gref's recommendations would benefit Russia.

Abalkin, for example, alleged in a leading newspaper that the Gref report contained false claims and dubious calculations. More important, Abalkin argued, it misunderstood the mechanism by which Russia's economy could return to growth. The eminent academic slammed Gref's "questionable conclusion that in the long run only private investment could drive production."[21] The government also needed to invest, he argued, echoing a common criticism of Yeltsin-era investment cuts. Indeed, almost all Ishaev's colleagues had been critics of Yeltsin during the 1990s. As Ishaev explained in an interview, Russia during the 1990s, "implemented the IMF's strategy, but it was not beneficial for us."[22]

The general trend under Yeltsin—encouraged by the IMF but driven primarily by Russian economists and political leaders—was to shift away from the Soviet style of managing the economy by government decree and toward a system in which the government focused on a small number of macroeconomic indicators such as inflation and GDP growth, while leaving most other decisions to private actors. Ishaev rejected that approach. "The regulation of the economy on the level of macro-indicators has no effect," he argued. "The most effective is micro-regulation on the level of the regions, regional politics." Ishaev and his coauthors advised that government play a more active role in allocating and funding investment. This had been a constant debate throughout the 1990s, as economic liberals sought to unwind the Soviet-era connections between industries and the central bank, while their opponents argued that ending the flow of cheap credit to Russian firms would cause mass bankruptcies and unemployment. Under Yeltsin, the government had steadily reduced financing for industrial investment. But the adjustment happened slowly, over the course of a decade, giving businesses time to adjust.

Putin's arrival to power, however, offered an opportunity to reverse this trend by reinstating the government's role in subsidizing and directing investment. Ishaev argued that the government should embrace its role as a guiding hand for the industry, without which, he believed, Russia was unlikely to achieve the economic growth needed to alleviate social challenges. "We need to set strict requirements for economic growth rates. The tempo should be no lower than 5–6 percent per year," Ishaev advised—a bold change for an economy that had shrunk for much of the previous decade. The only way to guarantee such growth rates, Ishaev posited, was through an "investment breakthrough" that saw investment levels increase on average by 8–9 percent per year over the subsequent decade. This was possible, Ishaev argued, only by expanding government investment.[23]

How could he be sure that government-backed investments would make money and not be siphoned off into Cypriot bank accounts? Ishaev downplayed the threat of corruption, arguing that Russia had sectors that could become competitive exporters, such as agriculture and electricity. There were many reasons why an increase in capital investment would unlock broad-based economic growth, Ishaev argued. Existing built capital—infrastructure and buildings—were being underutilized, he believed, due to the economic crash of the 1990s. A burst of investment could put these resources back to productive use—"a practically free source of economic growth." Second, the crisis of the 1990s made production within Russia relatively inexpensive compared with other centers of global manufacturing, giving Russia a cost advantage, at least when compared to Western Europe or the United States.

On top of funding investment, Ishaev believed the state should manage firms. "The government has to be an effective owner in certain industries," he argued. Privatization is not necessarily better than state control. "Russian economics research of the past century has shown that a change of ownership does not adequately improve production efficiency. . . . The government has management, the defense industry, part of the credit system, licensing, and finally, the law enforcement system. . . . In short, there are plenty of levers for managing the economy."[24] Perhaps most important, Ishaev's report suggested, was to use the central bank's monetary reserves to make direct loans to businesses, a policy that offered theoretically endless funds but risked reigniting inflation.[25]

Ishaev's proposals seemed perfectly pitched for a young president seeking to bolster his government's authority, and for a society that believed that Yeltsin-era capitalism had failed ordinary Russians. The government, Ishaev argued, should seek to "strengthen and expand the middle class," as the country's "deeply divided society remains a key impediment to the strengthening of Russian statehood." And Ishaev's recommended methods corresponded with those that many Russians—including many in the Duma—supported. "One of the illusions of the 1990s," Ishaev argued, "is the belief that liberalization and privatization are themselves sufficient prerequisites for the development of a market economy." The reality was the opposite. The key task, Ishaev believed, was "to form a strong and effective state."[26]

## Putting Reform into Action

U.S. president Franklin Delano Roosevelt was once given two contradictory proposals, one to raise tariffs on imports, the other to lower them. "Weave the two together," Roosevelt asked, leaving his aides stupefied.[27] But daft policy can be deft politics. Roosevelt sought to chart a middle path, keeping even his aides guessing about his intentions. Putin took a similar approach with the Ishaev and Gref plans. Presented with two opposing viewpoints about how Russia's government and economy should be organized, the president asked his aides to weave them together.

There were significant overlaps between the Gref and Ishaev proposals—and between the political groups that they represented. This made "weaving together" a not completely unrealistic goal.[28] Despite the political conflict of the 1990s, Russia's governing class agreed on several key principles. The possession of private property by individuals and businesses was legitimate. The accumulation of vast fortunes was acceptable in theory, so long as the fortunes were acquired at least somewhat legally. Markets must be competitive in order to be fair and effective. The government had an obligation to provide pensions and health care, but it would do so only at a very low level and would not welcome labor unions' participation in the political process. These basic principles were accepted across the Russian political spectrum in the early 2000s, from the Union of Right Forces party to the ostensibly left-wing Communists.

Political disagreement focused on several questions. What should be done with fortunes that were not acquired legally or were built up in legal grey zones? How should government address monopolies, particular in instances in which market competition was not feasible? The most important dispute, though, was how the government should bolster economic growth. Should it invest directly in Russian firms? Could the central bank directly fund investment? Are budget deficits justified when caused by investment spending? Putin might have asked that his aides find the best of all approaches—but on some issues decisions had to be made.

Indeed, from the very beginning of the process of weaving together the Gref and Ishaev plans, there was a twist. The person charged with combining the two proposals was German Gref. In the spring of 2001, the "Strategy for the Development of Russia through 2010" was formally adopted by the government. In theory it was a mix of the Gref and Ishaev plans. In reality, one of Gref's aides told a newspaper, only 10 percent of Gref's initial proposals were adjusted to take into account Ishaev's criticisms. A section was added on science, and proposals for the government's role in regional politics was reworked.[29] But most of Ishaev's main differences with Gref—above all, his demand for more direct government financing of industry—was ignored. Government staffers referred to Ishaev's plan as a backward "state-Soviet" proposal and joked that when asked to combine the two proposals, all they did was add a meaningless line taken from Ishaev's introduction: "The most important function of the supreme power of the country is strategic goal setting."[30] Whatever that means.

The debate over the government's economic strategy took over a year. It was ostensibly marked by ups and downs as different perspectives and political groups vied for the president's ear. At times, it looked as if Gref's liberal vision might lose out. At one point, the Gref plan's fate looked so dim that Kommersant, a leading business newspaper, ran an article titled "The Life and Death of the Gref Plan."[31] But in retrospect, the entire debate seems to have been determined from the start. "In economics," wrote Yevgeny Yasin, a leading economist and liberal intellectual, "President Putin has been a stealthy reformer yearning for consensus."[32]

But even if the government formally adopted a policy of liberal reforms, did this affect bureaucratic practice? Many Russian journalists were skeptical.

Many people "still haven't realized that approval of the Gref Program does not mean readiness to implement it," wrote one columnist, who saw the program's approval not as evidence of real intent to reshape government but rather as a "wave from deep-water clashes of several elite clans."[33] Economic policy in the early 2000s may well have been shaped by elite groups—what political question is not?—but many of the policies had real effects. On the tenth anniversary of the report's release, one of Gref's former top aides issued a report card that found that about one-third of Gref's initial recommendations had been implemented.[34] In several spheres, especially during the early 2000s, the government rapidly adopted many of Gref's key recommendations, above all in the sphere of regulation and tax.

Few in Moscow doubted that the Russian bureaucracy imposed too many rules and enforced them too capriciously. Many branches of the government, from health inspectors to traffic police, seemed to exist primarily to collect bribes. In a 1999 survey, for example, 70 percent of Russian firms said it was a rarely possible to appeal a regulatory decision without a bribe.[35] Inspectors visited businesses less to examine their operations than to threaten and collect payments in exchange for leaving the targeted firm alone. Industrial inspections varied drastically by region, with an average of 6.5 inspections per month in Krasnoyarsk but only 1.1 per month in Tver. There was no evidence that Krasnoyarsk factories were safer than Tver's. The difference between the two provinces had less to do with factories than with inspectors, who were apparently more venal in Krasnoyarsk.[36]

Rates of inspection varied between Russian provinces, but there was little doubt that the whole country suffered from an infestation of bribe-extorting officials. In 2000, a typical small company received dozens of inspector visits each year, many of which required a bribe after the official identified violations real or imaged.[37] One study found six times as many inspections in Moscow than in Warsaw, Poland, a city with a comparable level of economic development and that, like Moscow, also previously had a centrally planned economy.[38]

To cut the burden that bribes and regulatory compliance placed on Russian firms, the Gref reforms sought to slash business regulation. Legislation passed in the early 2000s restricted the number of activities requiring a license, for example.[39] Registering a business was made simpler, and the time required was reduced from a month to just five days.[40] License requirements for certain professions were removed.[41] Foreign exchange rules were liberalized.[42] Certain product markets were deregulated.[43] Laws governing land sales were loosened. The government began efforts to join the World

Trade Organization (WTO), which would simplify trade procedures and lower tariffs.[44] Putin was personally involved in some of these reforms.[45] As political analyst Nikolai Petrov noted at the time, "President Putin is serious about civil service reform. . . . He is offering the Russian people more than philippics."[46] Yet Russia's bureaucracy remained difficult and costly to navigate. Surveys conducted by the World Bank found that the investment climate improved during the early 2000s, but the rate of change was slow, and problems remained widespread.[47]

The most successful reform, in the eyes of many Russian leaders, was taxation. Collecting tax revenue had been an insoluble problem throughout the 1990s. The main problem was getting Russians to pay the taxes they owed. Tax collectors faced a nearly hopeless task. They were resisted violently at the regional level. In 1996, one study reported, "26 tax collectors were killed, 74 were injured in the course of their work, 6 were kidnapped, and 41 had their homes burnt down."[48] Only 8 percent of large businesses paid taxes in cash, while the rest paid in kind or not at all.[49]

Because of this, IMF estimates suggest, during the late 1990s government coffers received only half of the taxes due.[50] The structure of the tax system did not help. The tax code was a jungle of different levies that individuals and businesses struggled to understand. Official tax rates were high, encouraging laborers and businesses to stay in the shadow economy and pay no tax at all. But even though headline rates were high, average tax rates were low, due to an array of credits and deductions. The result was a system that simultaneously raised little revenue while discouraging legal work and business activity.

Putin's first government tackled taxes immediately. Corporate taxes, which on certain industries had been as high as 43 percent, were reduced to 24 percent, with no exceptions. Other inefficient taxes, like the Soviet-legacy turnover tax, were phased out entirely. A system that had previously relied on a total of fifty-two taxes now collected only fifteen types of tax. The change was most drastic at the local government level, where a patchwork of twenty-three taxes was replaced by two, on land and on personal property. Provinces were limited to collecting three taxes, on corporate property, transport, and gaming. The most significant change, however, was to personal income taxes. Prior to 2001, the top marginal tax rate was 30 percent, but the average effective tax rate was 13.5 percent. Many people avoided tax by receiving their salary in an envelope of cash at the end of every month. To push employment out of the shadow economy, the individual income tax system was replaced with a single flat tax of 13 percent—roughly the same average rate as before, but with less incentive to cheat.[51]

In terms of its stated aims of capturing revenue and cutting the cost of compliance, the new tax policy worked. Central government revenue increased by 3 percent of GDP between 1998 and 2002, a third of which came from personal income taxes.[52] There was much, of course, that the tax reform did not do. The government made no attempt to raise the magnitude of revenues that would have been necessary to rebuild a welfare state, for example, or to hike investment in health and education. In 2000, Russia's government spent only 2.9 percent of GDP on education, compared with the European Union average of 4.8 percent. Health spending was 5.4 percent of GDP, compared to 8.4 percent in the European Union. As Russia's economy grew in the 2000s, public and private investment in health and education increased, but it remains below the European average. The tax hikes of Putin's early years in office made no effort to raise the magnitude of revenue that would have been necessary to meet European average spending on health and education.

Indeed, in the medium term, the flat tax functioned as a cap on the government's revenue-raising capabilities. Hiking the personal income tax rate has thus far proven politically impossible, because urban upper middle classes have become accustomed to relatively low taxes, and the government is wary of angering them. Yet as a solution to the problems of the 1990s, the tax reforms of the early 2000s worked reasonably well. The budget was balanced.[53] The government sorted out its relations with 99 percent of taxpayers. But the oligarchs at the top also represented a lucrative source of revenue. Ordinary taxpayers might burn down the tax collector's house. In their pursuit of lower tax rates, the oligarchs had far more powerful, and more damaging, cards to play.

### Taming the Oligarchs

On July 28, 2000, in the Kremlin's ornate Ekaterininsky Hall, President Putin met with twenty-one leading Russian businessmen. Kremlin officials told some journalists that the meeting was intended to calm the country's nervous oligarchs, who looked worriedly at the legal proceedings that threatened some of their peers with fines, jail time, or worse.[54] One suspects that the businessmen—from banker Vladimir Potanin to oilman Mikhail Khodorkovsky to industrialist Kakha Bendukidze—did not leave feeling reassured. "No clan, no oligarch, should come close to regional or federal authorities," Putin declared. "They should be kept equally far from politics."[55]

The need for oligarchs to stay out of politics was a frequent theme of Putin's. "I don't really like the world 'oligarch,'" he explained. "An oligarch is a person with stolen money, who continues to plunder the national wealth using his special access to bodies of power and administration. I am doing everything to make sure this situation never repeats in Russia."[56] The oligarchs, many of whom feared that their businesses would be "de-privatized"—that is, seized by the state—sought assurances from Putin that no such confiscation would occur. Potanin, whose nickel firm was being harassed by prosecutors, asked Putin about the security of his property. "Are you sure you will be able to prove your case in court?" asked Putin. When Potanin answered affirmatively, Putin said, "So prove it. What do you have to fear?"[57]

Other oligarchs faced pressure from Putin over their tax payments. After Lukoil head Vagit Alekperov told Putin that the existence of large vertically integrated companies strengthens the state, Putin attacked him for paying insufficient tax. Lukoil pumped more oil than any company in Russia, Putin said, but its tax payments per ton of oil were only the seventh highest. Sibneft president Evgeny Svidler also received a personal rebuke from the president. Both oligarchs meekly claimed that the data Putin cited were inaccurate. "The main goal of the meeting was to put the oligarchs in their place," explained one presidential aide.[58] Mission accomplished.

It was easy to see why the government wanted to pressure the oligarchs. New tax laws and better tax collectors would only make a difference if businesses paid taxes. Small and medium-sized firms had little choice. But Russia's biggest enterprises, controlled by its class of unaccountable oligarchs, had a history of not paying taxes or of rewriting tax laws to suit their own purposes. Putin's government set out to change that—and to send a message that oligarchs no less than average citizens were responsible for following the government's orders. Just months after Putin took power, Vladimir Gusinsky, a banker-turned-media magnate, was arrested in a takedown widely presumed to be linked to Gusinsky's NTV television channel, which had been critical of Putin. Gusinsky was later released on the condition that he sell the TV station and leave Russia. He has not returned.

Four months later, a second oligarch fell. Boris Berezovsky, whose businesses spanned automobiles to airlines, announced while traveling abroad that he would not return to Russia, fearing that the government would press charges against him, too. The exile of Gusinsky and Berezovsky was a devastating blow for Russian media, as the oligarchs had each invested heavily in newspapers and TV stations which, though far from independent (they usually parroted their owners' opinions), at least provided a point of view different from the government's. From a business perspective, however, the exile of Gusinsky and Berezovsky did not appear to be a turning point. Both oligarchs were extensively involved in politics, making many enemies and few friends. Berezovsky had a knack for insulting Russians by insisting that his self-interested lobbying was the only thing preventing Communists from returning to power.[59] By 2000, most Russians—whether in the security services, the business elite, or the public at large—saw him as a problem rather than as a solution. Few were sad to see him go.

Both Berezovsky and Gusinsky had played fast and loose with the law, and when the government described their exile as part of an attempt to rebuild the rule of law, many Russians found that explanation compelling. The Russian public wanted to see the oligarchs cut down to size and their political influence reduced. That was a tall order—but the oligarchs as a class were indeed changing. Those who had acquired assets in the 1990s wanted to see those assets defended, so they tended to support efforts to reduce the power of mafias and criminal organizations—groups that use their power to seize others' businesses.

The oligarchs' business model was changing, too. In the early 1990s, most of the great fortunes were made in banking, by taking advantage of high inflation or otherwise stealing from the state. But the 1998 crash had driven many of the oligarchs' banks out of business. Some owners lost their fortunes, while others survived only by abandoning finance and turning to other lines of business instead. The greatest change was the increasing importance of commodities to Russia's leading businessmen, not only oil but also aluminum, nickel, and steel.[60]

The oligarchs' shift toward physical assets, the government hoped, would make their businesses easier to tax. The government made no secret of its desire to collect more revenue from business. "The state has the right to expect entrepreneurs to observe the rules of the game," Putin explained in July 1999. "The state announced that it would act more vigorously towards the environment in which business operates. I am referring first and foremost to the tax sphere and the restoration of order in the economy."[61] Levying heavier taxes on big business was a popular policy among most Russians. Though the oligarchs were understandably opposed, cracking down on oligarch-owned businesses also fit the preferences of Putin's political coalition. Statists appreciated the focus on law and order and the boost to government revenues. Liberal officials in the Finance and the Economy Ministries saw potential benefits from more stable public finances and a reduction in oligarchs' ability to rig markets. Many average Russians were happy to see the country's billionaires brought down a notch.

Putin was not unsympathetic to the needs of business, but he saw higher tax revenue as key to restoring central authority and announced that he would brook no opposition to his campaign to raise revenue. "These people who fuse power and capital: there will be no oligarchs of this kind as a class," Putin threatened, alluding to Stalin's promise to eliminate kulaks—rich peasants—as a class. Stalin's antikulak campaign caused many thousands of violent deaths. Putin wanted the oligarchs to understand: he was tough, too. "The state has a club, the kind that you only need to use once: over the head," Putin explained. "We haven't used the club yet. But when we get seriously angry, we will use this club without hesitation."[62] The oligarchs had been warned.

# CHAPTER 3

## Rise of the Energy Giants

As the price of oil surged during the 2000s, the oligarchs who owned energy assets became even richer—at least at first. It quickly became clear, however, that despite accepting private business in most spheres of the economy, Russia's oil industry would be dominated by Putin and his allies. This policy had clear costs in terms of deterring foreign investment and reducing efficiency. But other goals took precedence, above all the need to ensure central political control. More than any other industry, oil demonstrates Putin's desire for dominance of the biggest revenue streams and patronage networks. Yet Russia's energy sector is not a simple story of consolidation and centralization. Even as most oil production returned to state hands, Gazprom's monopoly on natural gas was steadily weakened, thanks to competition from other oligarchs aligned with the president. Where competition does not threaten political control, it has persisted. But the hierarchy of goals—first, ensuring the Kremlin's political and financial strength and only second, improving efficiency—has been clear. The oil and gas magnates who retained ownership of their energy assets have done so by ensuring that they satisfy the Kremlin's political goals before pursuing their own financial self-interest.

This was an easy balance to strike when the energy sector boomed during the 2000s, thanks to productivity increases and higher prices. Higher prices were a matter of luck, but productivity improved in part because of decisions made in the 1990s. The Soviet energy industry had pumped millions of barrels of oil per year, enough to keep the country's economy afloat during the 1970s and 1980s. Yet although its output was impressive, its productivity was not. A 1992 report conducted by a U.S. energy consulting firm found that because of aging equipment, poor management, and inefficient extraction practices, the oil infrastructure that the USSR bequeathed to independent Russia was only 10 to 30 percent as productive as Western levels. In some

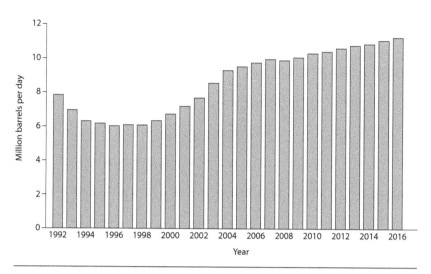

**FIGURE 2** Russian oil production, 1992–2016 (million barrels/day).
U.S. Energy Information Agency.

spheres, technology lagged a half century behind. Some oil fields still used
equipment donated to Russia through the World War II–era Lend-Lease
agreement.[1]

The years immediately after the dissolution of the USSR were not, however, a period of rapid turnaround. Because ownership rights were unclear,
managers preferred to take profits rather than invest in new production. By
1998, annual investment in oil production was $3 billion, less than a third
of the 1990 level. This figure probably exaggerates the decline, as a sizeable
portion of Soviet "investment" was wasted or stolen.[2] But investment did fall
sharply in the early 1990s, causing oil production to fall by over 20 percent
from 1992 to 1996.[3]

The years after 1998, however, marked a reversal of fortune for Russian oil
firms. Oil investment and production spiked higher, beginning a decade-long
boom. Capital investment in the sector tripled between 1998 and 2004. The
world oil price hit a low point in 1998, bottoming out at $12 per barrel that
year. By 2005, however, the oil price was over four times higher, at $51 per bar-
rel. Russian firms' production costs, meanwhile, fell sharply in 1998 because of
the devaluation of the ruble.[4] These two factors made oil production far more
profitable than in the 1990s. No less significant, however, was that many in
the industry believed that ownership rights were becoming clearer.[5] As firms
that owned oil fields began to feel confident that they would benefit from the
proceeds of their investments, they plowed billions of dollars into modern-

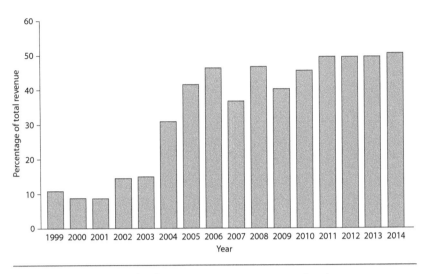

**FIGURE 3** Russian oil and gas tax revenue as percentage of total government revenue, 1999–2014. Ministry of Finance; Andrei Illarionov.

izing existing fields. New companies such as Yukos and Sibneft doubled their production between 1999 and 2004, with other oil majors not far behind.[6]

During Putin's first two years in power, the government took steps to foster confidence in property rights in the energy sector. Unlike in the early Yeltsin years, when the government lurched from near civil war in 1993 to controversial elections in 1996, the years that immediately followed Putin's ascent were marked by new confidence in Russia's political institutions. Putin himself publicly emphasized the importance of political stability to energy investment. "I worked in Saint Petersburg on a great many different projects," Putin explained in an interview in 2000. "If we're going from one putsch to another, and no one knows when the next putsch is coming and how it will end, then who will invest? There will be no large-scale investment until we have a steady political system, stability, and a strong state that protects market institutions and creates favorable investment conditions."[7] Putin's initial actions appeared to match his words. Oil sector privatizations continued during his first years in office, in a more organized fashion than before.[8] Foreign oil majors were convinced that conditions had improved. BP announced a $6 billion investment in oil firm TNK, evidently with the government's full support.[9]

The oil boom reshaped Russian politics by injecting huge sums into the economy. Oil and gas export revenues amounted to $28 billion in 1998; by 2005 the figure was $143 billion.[10] For a government that had struggled through the 1990s to pay its bills, higher oil prices and surging output seemed like a gift from the gods. Russia's political leaders were determined to get what they perceived as the government's fair share. By the mid-2000s, oil and gas taxes were providing roughly half of government revenue, up from 10 percent at the beginning of the decade. Yet extracting revenue from the oligarchs who controlled Russia's oil majors remained a serious political challenge. The oil boom buoyed the wealth of Russia's richest men, and some of them hoped to turn this wealth into political power. In the struggle over the taxation of Russia's oil riches, however, Russia's oligarchs discovered how exactly Putin intended to govern.

### Khodorkovsky versus the State

After Putin's scripted public meetings with Russia's oligarchs, most of the billionaires assured the government that they would diligently follow the rules. After all, they had lobbied heavily in the late 1990s for beneficial tax changes, many of which were implemented in Putin's first years in office.[11] The profits tax was cut from 35 percent to 24 percent, for example.[12] Natural resource producers were major beneficiaries. Several different resource taxes were consolidated into a new "resource extraction tax," which benefited businesses with the lowest costs and the best assets—in other words, firms owned by the oligarchs.[13]

Even with the new tax regime, oligarchs had recourse to other tricks for reducing their tax burden, many of debatable legality. The provinces of Chukotka and Kalmykia were backwaters far from the center of business activity. Kalmykia is located north of the Caspian Sea, best known for having the only predominantly Buddhist populace in Europe, where even today many people look to the Dalai Lama for religious guidance. In Chukotka, a frozen arctic territory across the Bering Strait from Alaska, there are more reindeer than people.[14] Businesses flocked to register their operations in both provinces to take advantage of tax discounts these territories offered.[15] According to Russia's Ministry of Finance, the top three provincial tax avoidance schemes cost the government $1.5 billion in revenue in the early 2000s.[16]

Given these backdoor methods of tax relief, most oligarchs were content to cut deals with Putin, assuring the Kremlin that they were contributing to state coffers while doing their best to minimize their obligations. Some oligarchs, however, demanded even more. The most aggressive was Mikhail Khodorkovsky. Khodorkovsky had always stood out for his supreme self-confidence and his lack of political tact. He founded his first major business venture, Menatep Bank, in the late 1980s, taking advantage of connections forged in the Communist Youth League.[17] In the early days after the Bolshevik Revolution of 1917, the Youth League was filled with ardent Communists, but by the final decades of the Soviet Union its primary use was providing networking opportunities for ambitious young adults. It was an environment in which Khodorkovsky thrived. He used the Communist Youth League's official status to obtain seed capital for his bank, which grew rapidly into a business worth many millions of dollars.[18]

In the early 1990s, Khodorkovsky made a fortune by attracting government deposits to his bank and speculating against the collapsing ruble. His bank, Menatep, was the largest holder of government funds, and much of the profit he made as a banker came at the government's expense.[19] Khodorkovsky used his banking business to expand into other sectors, purchasing the Yukos oil company at a knock-down price in 1995 through a scandal-plagued privatization scheme.

Khodorkovsky celebrated the bare-knuckle capitalism that symbolized to many Russians what was wrong about the 1990s. In a manifesto he produced along with business partner Leonid Nevzlin, Khodorkovsky exhorted his fellow citizens "to stop living according to Lenin!" The laws of capitalism should guide behavior, Khodorkovsky and Nevzlin explained. "Our guiding light is Profit, acquired in a strictly legal way. Our Lord is His Majesty, Money, for it is only He who can lead us to wealth as the norm in life."[20] Even setting aside Khodorkovsky's dubious claims about leading a "strictly legal" life, his capitalist manifesto suggested just how out of touch he was with the Russian mainstream. Khodorkovsky saw himself as a prophet of capitalism; many Russians saw him as a crook.

In Khodorkovsky's defense, however, he proved an efficient if ruthless manager. Russia's bloated enterprises needed aggressive leadership if they were to improve productivity, which lagged far behind international benchmarks. In April 1996, Khodorkovsky appointed himself first vice president of Yukos and began to recast the Soviet-style behemoth as a modern energy company. He asserted control over Yukos with military rigor, sending security guards to seize oil wells and refineries and implementing a strict monitoring regime overseen by former KGB officers.[21]

Khodorkovsky identified and fired mafia-linked employees who siphoned off Yukos's oil.[22] He slashed Yukos's workforce, ordering his security service to keep a list of employees who came to work drunk—a persistent problem in desolate Siberian oil towns—and ordered that 90 percent of them be fired.[23] Yukos also cut "social payments" to oil towns, which in lieu of a functioning tax system funded social services from subsidized housing to child care.[24] His methods were merciless, and they provoked violent pushback from mafias and oil towns, which were harmed by benefit cuts and demands that wages be tied to productivity. But Khodorkovsky was undeniably effective. In the first three years that Khodorkovsky controlled Yukos, the firm's production costs fell by two-thirds.[25]

Khodorkovsky devoted similar attention to cutting Yukos's tax bill. The tax reduction effort combined Khodorkovsky's maximalist personality with his belief in "His Majesty, Money." Just as Putin was consolidating power in the Kremlin, Khodorkovsky was ramping up a campaign to lower his company's taxes. His most important ally in this effort was Vladimir Dubov, a Yukos executive who was elected to the Duma and named chairman of the tax sub-committee.[26] Dubov helped Khodorkovsky score two key antitax victories. The first was to beat back government attempts to hike taxes on dividends.[27] Dubov's second Duma victory, known as the Yukos amendment, capped export duties on refined oil at Yukos's request.[28] What was good for Yukos was bad for the budget, but Khodorkovsky did not relent. Yukos continued to use regional tax minimization schemes more aggressively than any other oil firm.[29]

Aggressive tax minimization was not Khodorkovsky's only sin. He began talks to build an oil pipeline to China, directly against the government's wishes. He was seemingly unfazed by opposing the Kremlin on an issue central to Russia's foreign policy. In contrast to Khodorkovsky's vision, Putin wanted a pipeline that stretched all the way to the Pacific rather than de-livering oil directly to China. The president repeatedly made his views on the subject known, pointedly declining to endorse Khodorkovsky's pipeline plan while on a state visit to Beijing. In a meeting of the national Security Council, meanwhile, Putin underscored his belief that Russia was better off with a pipeline to the Pacific, for reasons that were geopolitical as much as economic.[30]

Khodorkovsky's response was to mock the government. He declared that if the government built a pipeline to the Pacific, then Yukos would not supply it with oil. He accused Putin of "beating the dragon on the tail" by refusing to deliver oil to China, warning the government that China "has a GDP three or four times larger than ours, its growth rates are two to three times greater, and its population is ten times ours." The conclusion, Khodorkovsky believed, was that Russia should accommodate China by building his preferred pipe-line. Putin, by contrast, concluded that Khodorkovsky was meddling in Rus-sia's foreign policy in pursuit of personal financial gain. Khodorkovsky won few allies in this fight. His contempt for government officials was alienating, as were his demands that the government fire officials on the sole grounds that he found them incompetent. At a public meeting with Putin and other oligarchs, for example, Khodorkovsky openly accused Putin's ally Sergey Bogdanchikov, the chairman of Rosneft, of corruption.[31]

As Khodorkovsky's affronts to presidential power multiplied, his list of allies shrank. Khodorkovsky knew he was under threat. To defend his assets, he redoubled efforts to sell a stake in Yukos to a Western oil firm, which he thought would protect him from expropriation. Talks with Chevron and Exxon accelerated, but the threat to his property grew. In June, the release of a report titled *The State and the Oligarchs*, which claimed that Khodorkovsky and others were planning a coup against Putin, incited calls for clipping Khodorkovsky's wings. The report was designed to spark action against Khodorkovsky, and the response to it showed that many in Russia's elite believed that the oligarch had overstepped his bounds. Putin, meanwhile, warned in June 2003 that "the large oil companies are actively opposing the tax on mineral resources, arguing that the government is putting too heavy a burden on them. . . . We must not allow certain business interests to influence the political life of the country in their narrow group interests."[32]

Even as the noose tightened, Khodorkovsky charged ahead. In the summer of 2003, Khodorkovsky's deputy in the Duma, subcommittee chairman Dubov, doubled down on efforts to shape energy legislation. Dubov brought a group from Yukos's legal department to the floor of the Duma to lobby for special provisions. One Duma member stood at the rostrum with a cell phone pressed to his ear as he recited words fed to him by Yukos staffers. Even for a group of legislators used to the most venal corruption, this was one step too far. The Duma member-turned-Yukos shill was shouted down by the body's speaker, who screamed, "Sergei Ivanovich, have you no fear of God?"[33] The member had faith in Khodorkovsky's god: "Our Lord, His Majesty, Money."

## Putin Springs the Trap

Even as Russia's oligarchs exalted "His Majesty, Money," an increasing number of Russian citizens were asking tough questions about the oligarchs' own money—which they extracted from Russia's natural resources. In the early 2000s, one Russian political analyst noted, every candidate for the Duma was repeatedly asked, "What is your stance on the oil rent issue?"[34] Rents—the payments that Russia's energy tycoons received beyond what was necessary to bring oil out of the ground—were widely perceived to be a major injustice in postcommunist Russia. As many political leaders noted, natural resource riches were also a potentially lucrative means of funding government.

Much of the agitation about oil rents came from the political opposition. Gennady Zyuganov, the Communist leader, estimated the value of oil rents expropriated by the industry at $100 billion. This was likely far above the real value that could be extracted from Russia's oil firms, but many Russians had estimates in the tens of billions. Sergey Glazyev, an economist whose political career skyrocketed in the early 2000s in part due to his advocacy of hiking taxes or even nationalizing the country's oil giants, put the number at $12 billion. United Russia, the governing party, was forced to respond to public demand for action, holding a conference on the subject of oil rents in 2003. Putin himself sharply criticized oil firms' "superprofits"—profits that came at the expense of the state.[35] In his annual press conference in 2003, for example, Putin explicitly called for a transfer of oil rents from firms to the government.[36]

This was the political context in which Khodorkovsky lobbied for more tax breaks and for looser tax enforcement. It was hard to imagine a less conducive climate for an oil tycoon to buy off Duma members in pursuit of his own financial interest. The memory of 1998, when a budget crisis forced swinging cuts in real wages, was fresh in Russians' minds. Everyone understood the need for more revenue, and many Russians thought that the oil tycoons—some of whom had benefited from the 1998 devaluation, as their ruble-denominated costs plummeted faster than dollar-denominated export revenue—ought to pay more. Putin had threatened that the state had a club with which it could discipline oligarchs. Many Russians thought it was high time the club was used. One poll in July 2003 found that 88 percent of Russians believed that all large fortunes were accumulated illegally, while 77 percent wanted privatization results fully or partially reversed, and 57 percent supported criminal investigations against oligarchs.

When Khodorkovsky's private jet landed to refuel in the Siberian city of Novosibirsk on October 25, 2003, it was surrounded by troops from the FSB's Alfa brigade, the country's most elite security force. Khodorkovsky was arrested and thrown in jail. Berezovsky and Gusinsky—the oligarchs that Putin took down immediately after assuming power—had been granted an honorable exile in Europe. Khodorkovsky faced a more painful fate. Along with his top associate, Platon Lebedev, and many low-level Yukos employees who were caught in the crossfire, Khodorkovsky would spend a decade behind bars.

Prosecutors charged that Yukos had evaded billions of dollars of taxes. It was a claim that, on one level, everyone knew was true. Like most oligarch-owned corporations, Yukos had used methods fair and foul to reduce its tax bill. Yet rather than a real court case, the prosecutors set up a show trial. The size of Yukos's alleged bill for back taxes plus fines was fabricated. It fluctuated over time, even as the prosecutors' witnesses contradicted each other.[37] Yukos management pointed out that government calculations suggested that Yukos should have paid taxes equivalent to 100 percent of revenue in 2001 and 105 percent of revenue in 2002—in other words, that the firm should have paid more in taxes than it made in profits.[38] Prosecutors and the courts were less interested in due process of law than in dismembering the company, punishing its executives, and dividing its assets. In the end, the firm was presented with a $28 billion tax bill, a sum it could not pay.[39] Yukos's managers, meanwhile, were convicted of tax evasion.[40] Khodorkovsky was condemned in May 2005 to nine years in a Siberian prison.

Khodorkovsky's jailing brought forth vultures who circled his oil empire, knowing that the oligarch's downfall would lead to a redistribution of his assets. Many of the juiciest pieces of Russia's oil infrastructure, and the best managed, were suddenly up for grabs. To settle Yukos's tax bill, the government announced an auction of Yuganskneftegaz, the crown jewel of the Yukos empire, which produced roughly 60 percent of the firm's oil. On December 19, 2004, the auction for Yuganskneftegaz was won by Baikal Finance Group, an obscure shell company founded just weeks beforehand in Tver, a provincial town. Baikal Finance Group had nonetheless managed to raise $9.3 billion to pay the auction bill, gaining control of one of Russia's best oil assets. (A German firm had estimated the market value at between $14.7 billion and $17.3 billion, meaning that the mysterious Baikal group received a below-market rate.)[41] Days later, Baikal Finance Group was purchased by Rosneft, the state-owned oil firm headed by Igor Sechin. In a single deal Rosneft transformed itself from a minor player in Russia's oil industry to an energy behemoth.

### Yukos and the Budget

The fall of Yukos was a watershed in Russian politics. Khodorkovsky was not only cut down and stripped of his assets, he was imprisoned for a decade. A serious political threat to Putin was neutralized. Oligarchs and Duma members realized that it was time to fall in line. Opposition to Putin was neutered. The business classes learned to keep their noses out of politics. And the clique around Igor Sechin, meanwhile, gained control of the remnants of Yukos, a cash cow whose resources amplified the influence of Putin's former KGB colleagues. Russian and foreign investors had long feared expropriation from mafias and unscrupulous oligarchs. Now they added the government to the list of threats. Khodorkovsky's bleak existence in a Siberian penal colony was a constant reminder of the hard edges of Putin's rule.

Khodorkovsky spent his time in prison atoning for his sins as Russia's robber-baron-in-chief. He established ties with intellectuals across the world, tried to run for the Duma, and attempted to convince Russians that, though he was best known as a prophet of capitalism, he had now become a convinced social democrat. He published essays in Russia's leading newspapers calling for a "left turn" in Russian politics. He presented himself—from his jail cell—as a future president. He continued to command surprising sympathy from otherwise cynical members of Russia's business elite.

Vladimir Putin's economic team, however, saw the Yukos affair in a different light. The officials who might have been expected to oppose the dismantling of Yukos because it scared off investment were in fact vocal supporters of the prosecution's case. Finance Minister Alexei Kudrin explained that the Yukos affair was inevitable, "not in the personal sense, but in the sense of a clarification of the rules of the game."[42] Speaking to the American Chamber of Commerce in Russia, Igor Shuvalov, then a top Putin economic aide, concurred, describing Yukos as a case of "indicative justice," which underscored the need to follow tax rules.[43] Shuvalov's honesty startled his audience. But no one doubted that Shuvalov's logic was the best explanation of the Yukos affair. Khodorkovsky's downfall was "the beginning of the road in the relationship with other taxpayers," Shuvalov explained.[44] If Yukos's tax schemes were illegal, Shuvalov suggested, "companies would be better off not waiting for the courts to examine their tax history and making extra payments into the budget."[45] Finance Minister Kudrin agreed, insisting that "business must not aggressively take advantage of the shortcomings of our legislation. I stress 'aggressively,' that is, when billions of dollars are deliberately removed from being subject to tax."[46]

The Duma heeded the Kremlin's warnings. Duma members who had previously been in oil firms' pockets suddenly emerged as proponents of higher taxation. After a decade of carving out special exemptions for oil companies, the Duma promptly closed many of the tax schemes that oil firms exploited. A month after Khodorkovsky's arrest, Duma members voted to reverse the "Yukos amendment" that capped export duties.[47]

Russia's big oil firms got the message, too. After Khodorkovsky's arrest,

Sibneft paid the maximum profit tax rate of 27.5 percent, in 2004, compared to only 7 percent several years earlier. Lukoil, meanwhile, paid 24.7 percent of its profits in tax in 2004, while Surgutneftegaz paid 20 percent. Putin's economic team had little doubt as to why this extra revenue emerged. Anatoly Serdyukov, who oversaw tax collection, openly attributed much of the increase in revenue after 2003 to Khodorkovsky's imprisonment.[48] It is easy to see why. Russia's oil firms fell over each other to prove their willingness to pay taxes. At one point, Lukoil sent $200 million to the government without being asked. The firm's vice president, Leonid Fedun, explained that he believed "the fact that the state is domineering now is good." "Oil is a strategic thing," he added. "Of course the state should participate."[49]

### The Takeover of Gazprom

Russia's oil industry had been carved up during the Yeltsin-era privatizations, but in theory Russia's gas industry remained owned largely by the state. The reality was quite different. Rem Vyakhirev ran the company as if it were his personal fiefdom. Vyakhirev's family dominated the company despite only owning a small portion of the shares. His son Yuri managed Gazprom's export division, Gazeksport, while his daughter Tatiana owned a large share of Gazprom's pipeline builder, Stroitransgaz.[50] His cousin Viktor managed Gazprom's primary drilling contractor, Burgaz. Many of Gazprom's most lucrative supply contracts were negotiated between different members of the Vyakhirev family.

This system promoted Vyakhirev's interests at the expense of shareholder interests. Gazprom began to lose control of its assets to other companies, many of which were alleged to be controlled by allies of Vyakhirev and other Gazprom managers. What was once a unified state monopoly was breaking apart into dozens of little pieces, as Vyakhirev and his crew in effect privatized the company by putting the most valuable pieces in their own pockets.[51] They succeeded because they had strong support from regional governments and had bought, according to one estimate, a hundred allies in the Duma.[52]

Putin saw Vyakhirev's dismemberment of Gazprom as a roadblock in his plan to recentralize Russia. Gazprom was not only a potentially lucrative source of tax revenue. It was also a threat. If the riches of Russia's gas reserves fell under the control of competing political forces—especially those in Russia's regions, which had formed powerful alliances with the gas industry through the 1990s—it could undermine Putin's ability to strengthen the central government.

Putin did not immediately sack Vyakhirev upon assuming power. He let Vyakhirev continue to lead Gazprom throughout 2000 and the first half of 2001, focusing his political capital on taming politically involved oligarchs such as Boris Berezovsky and Vladimir Gusinsky. It took Putin a full year and a half in power to move against Vyakhirev, who was eventually fired after a personal meeting in the Kremlin in May 2001. Vyakhirev's ostensible infraction was to have participated in an oligarch protest against Putin's decision to exile Gusinsky. In fact, Putin had been searching for an excuse to sack Vyakhirev and to assert control over Gazprom.[53]

Putin replaced Vyakhirev with Alexey Miller, an official who had served under Putin on the Committee on International Relations in St. Petersburg during the early 1990s. Miller remained in St. Petersburg through most of that decade, working with the city's port and the Baltic Pipeline consortium, experience that gave him some familiarity with Gazprom's business. Miller was said to have ties to liberal economists such as Anatoly Chubais. He was respected as a capable technocrat, if not a visionary leader. He had never previously worked for a gas company. That, however, was the point. There were few people with a background in gas without close ties to Vyakhirev, but Miller had none.[54]

Miller's background gave Putin confidence that he could be trusted to return control of Gazprom to the Kremlin. As chief executive officer, Miller purged Gazprom's senior management of Vyakhirev loyalists. The gas experts remained, but many of the officials associated with finance, accounting, contracts, and procurement were replaced with new officials who answered to Miller alone. Many were brought in from St. Petersburg, leading to a widespread impression that this was in part a takeover by St. Petersburg forces.[55]

Whatever Miller's method, it succeeded in regaining control of Gazprom assets. Take Itera, a company headquartered in Jacksonville, Florida, which at one point was said to have been Russia's second-largest exporter of natural gas.[56] By the late 1990s, Itera was buying natural gas fields from Gazprom. Over the course of the decade it purchased majority stakes in gas fields that yielded 18 billion cubic meters (bcm) of gas per year. Combined with the transit of Central Asia gas, the firm's sales amounted to 85 bcm in 2000, slightly less than a fifth of Russia's overall gas production. This was a lucrative business, and it was widely alleged to have been made more lucrative by the fact that many of Itera's transactions with Gazprom were not at arm's length. Many Itera trustees were alleged to be "relatives or mistresses of senior Gazprom executives."[57] It does not take a great leap of imagination to suggest that the sale of Gazprom's assets to Itera's Jacksonville-based leadership might have taken place at below-market prices.

When Miller began to assert control over Gazprom, cracking down on Itera was one of his first goals. Miller launched an array of investigations into the transactions between Gazprom and Itera, searching for evidence of corruption. These investigations were part of a complicated negotiation as the old Gazprom elite was pushed from control of lucrative revenue streams. Gazprom's board of directors, led by Boris Fyodorov, a former finance minister, appointed German Gref to analyze the Itera transactions. The auditing firm PricewaterhouseCoopers was brought in to scrutinize the deals' pricing and accounting standards.

These investigations were intended to show the old guard at Gazprom the downsides of failing to cooperate with Putin's new rules. Having cowed Vyakhirev-era executives into submission, new CEO Miller began repurchasing many of the gas fields that Gazprom had sold to Itera in the late 1990s. Soon many of the main fields were back in Gazprom's hands, their revenue no longer being siphoned off by a shadowy firm in Jacksonville.[58] By 2003, Itera's gas sales to former Soviet states were a third of their 2001 peak.[59] In 2004, putting further pressure on the firm, Gazprom cut off Itera's access to the pipeline network, prohibiting the firm from moving gas. Under increasing pressure, Itera was eventually "persuaded" to sell most of its remaining assets to Gazprom.[60]

### The Return of the State

The reestablishment of state control over Gazprom could have been the first step in modernizing Russia's gas industry and ensuring that it was regulated in a way that maximally benefited its major shareholders, the Russian public. The previous model—whereby the government was Gazprom's largest shareholder, but the Vyakhirev family and its allies expropriated most of the profits—was hardly in the public interest. Some on Putin's economic team hoped to use their new control over Gazprom to push the giant toward good governance, either by insisting on transparent governance or by privatizing the company completely.

German Gref, for example, backed breaking up the firm, perhaps by creating multiple gas producers and treating the pipeline system as a government-regulated utility. In such a case, private shareholders would have an incentive to cut waste at gas producers, while competition would keep costs down. Gas industries in many countries are highly regulated, but Gref and his allies in the presidential administration believed that a regulated private system would be less corrupt and more efficient than government ownership. "Next year," Gref declared in 2004, "we will break up Gazprom."[61]

Today, a decade later, Gazprom remains firmly in the government's hands. A new clique of oligarchs has replaced the Vyakhirev elite, but corruption remains widespread. There are three main reasons why. First, the government feared privatizing such a valuable asset, lest it be used to fund political opposition. Second, Gazprom was not simply a domestic concern—it was central to Russia's foreign policy, too. Unlike oil, which is easily transportable and sold at transparent market prices, gas is shipped primarily through pipelines at negotiated rates. Gazprom's business deals with Russia's neighbors were a key facet in the Kremlin's foreign policy, especially its efforts to influence countries in Eastern Europe. The government feared that breaking up and privatizing Gazprom would herald a return to the days when Khodorkovsky threatened to contradict the government's foreign policy plans and build his own pipeline to China.

The third and perhaps decisive issue was that state ownership of gas assets created vast opportunities for corruption. Once political elites had dipped their hands in the honeypot, turning control over to the private sector became all but unthinkable. At Gazprom, the reestablishment of government control and the ejection of Vyakhirev led the company to expand yet further. In the same year that the government established a majority stake in Gazprom, guaranteeing its control, the firm spent $13.1 billion to enter the oil business by purchasing Sibneft from oligarch Roman Abramovich.[62]

The logic that prevented the breakup of Gazprom and drove its empire-building was visible not only in gas. The oil industry—which in productivity terms was one of the great success stories of privatization—also began a slow but steady renationalization. The Yukos expropriation had not been intended to end private ownership of oil assets. But by showing how nationalizing oil firms could enrich political patronage networks, the demise of Yukos set in motion a decade of consolidation in Russia's oil industry, in which the main beneficiary was Russia's state ownership—and therefore Russia's political elite.

Indeed, by the mid-2000s it was already clear that Gazprom's new management was little better than the Vyakhirev-era elite.[63] The company was widely alleged to facilitate corruption through its procurement deals. Many companies that supply Gazprom are owned by long-time friends of Putin's, including Gennady Timchenko and Arkady Rotenberg.[64] Allegations that the company overpays on its pipeline business, owned by Rotenberg, for example, are widespread.[65]

For a time, corruption at Gazprom did not appear to harm the firm's commercial goals. The price of gas spiked in the mid-2000s, and Gazprom's valuation peaked at $367 billion in 2008, making it the third-most-valuable firm in the world, behind only Exxon Mobile and PetroChina.[66] The firm's leaders promised that, within a decade, Gazaprom would reach a trillion-dollar valuation.[67] Today, however, those claims look like the height of hubris. Mismanagement and the government's repeated willingness to treat the firm as a slush fund rather than a commercially oriented company have led to a precipitous drop in its value: by 2017 it was worth less than a quarter of its pre-2008 peak. There are many reasons why its value has fallen, ranging from wasteful, politically induced spending on the Sochi Olympics, to ongoing procurement corruption, to the government's decision not to raise domestic gas prices to market levels.[68]

The firm's biggest problem, however, was its colossal failure to predict the collapse in energy prices in 2014 and 2015—or to take any steps to hedge against this. Even when prices were high, Gazprom's decision to begin vast new projects to extract natural gas from high-cost fields looked financially risky.[69] These projects were driven, many speculated, less by cost-benefit analysis than by political pressure to keep production high. But the shale revolution in the United States caused a glut in natural gas supplies, driving prices down. Barring a sharp reversal in energy prices, many Gazprom projects now look hopelessly in the red. *Vedomosti*, the leading business newspaper, has estimated that Gazprom may have spent 2.4 trillion rubles on unneeded investment projects.[70] That is roughly equivalent to the decline in the firm's share price since its 2008 peak.

Yet despite—or because of—the corruption at Gazprom, Russia's government drastically expanded the role that the government played in the oil sector. Igor Sechin, the powerful oligarch and long-time Putin associate who controls the state-owned Rosneft oil company, led the charge. Rosneft began its inexorable expansion in 2004 when it purchased the main oil assets of Mikhail Khodorkovsky's Yukos oil company in a rigged auction. Then Rosneft bought TNK-BP, Russia's third-largest oil company, in March 2013, from a group of Russian businessmen and from BP, the British oil company, for $44.4 billion plus transferring to BP a 19.75 percent share of Rosneft's own stock.[71] The government's role in the oil industry strengthened further.

## Russian Gas: Market versus Monopoly

Even as Gazprom's new leadership was busy replacing 1990s-vintage corruption rackets with new schemes to benefit its Putin-era management, a new factor was putting pressure on Gazprom to shape up. Russia's oil industry has followed a steady trend toward greater state control, a process in which the expropriation of Yukos was only the first, if the most important, step. The gas market, however, has gone in reverse. Russian gas production was never demonopolized, so Gazprom made up around 90 percent of the country's gas production throughout the 1990s. But over the past decade, Gazprom's monopoly has steadily unraveled.

The process began in the early 2000s, as powerful oligarchs acquired small gas firms and began pushing for greater market access. The counterintuitive result was that, despite serving as the Kremlin's cash cow, Gazprom today faces a weaker market position than at any point since it was created out of the Soviet Ministry of Gas. Russia's gas industry, therefore, is more competitive than ever, even though Gazprom's legal monopoly on exports mostly remains in place, at least for now. Despite this, Russia's smaller gas producers have strong financial incentives to keep pumping gas. Their success has pushed down gas prices and put financial pressure on Gazprom to shape up. Russia's oil industry may be increasingly dominated by the state, but the gas sector is moving in the opposite direction.

This new competition in Russia gas production stems from what energy analyst Tatiana Mitrova has called Russia's "new deal" on gas.[72] During the first half of the 2000s, government price controls on gas enabled Gazprom to sell to consumers and industries in Russia at prices far below what Europe paid for Russian gas. This policy was only partially deliberate. Domestic prices, which were set in rubles, were driven down to $11 per million cubic meters in 1998 by the ruble's crash, a fraction of international prices. Low prices at home, which amounted to a massive subsidy from Gazprom to consumers and industries, suited political leaders and Russia's populace, who felt that in an era of rising energy prices, the energy industry should share some of its wealth. Thanks to price controls, consumers had lower heating bills, and gas-guzzling industries faced lower production costs.[73]

Because price controls cost Gazprom dearly, the government did not extract high taxes from it during the early 2000s. Instead, Gazprom "paid" its dues to society through low prices and by agreeing to fund various social programs. In exchange, Gazprom had a de facto monopoly in the domestic market and a legally guaranteed monopoly abroad. At home, its position was safeguarded by price controls. Gazprom itself lost money on domestic sales during the early 2000s, and low prices meant that other firms—which were barred by law from the profitable export market—had little incentive to produce much gas at all.[74] Gazprom, by contrast, made most of its money from the export market, as the government engaged in controversial gas diplomacy to defend Gazprom's profitable position as a monopoly supplier to much of Eastern Europe.

By the late 2000s, however, Gazprom's business model had stalled. Export volumes and revenues were falling.[75] The government launched a complete reversal of its gas market policy. Gazprom's biggest gas fields in West Siberia were yielding less gas, forcing the company to invest in more complicated and expensive locations. To ensure that Gazprom remained profitable, the government hiked domestic prices. Over the subsequent six years, domestic prices increased by an average of 15 percent per year in nominal terms. By 2013 gas prices were ten times higher in dollar terms than the low point after the 1998 crash of $11 per million cubic meters.[76] Because Russia consumes about two-thirds of gas at home, these price increases seemed to mark a reversal of Gazprom's fortunes.[77]

Yet although higher domestic prices boosted Gazprom's profits, they also made domestic gas sales profitable for the small independent firms that also produced gas in Russia. When Gazprom was forced by law to sell gas at bargain prices, independent producers struggled to undercut Gazprom's prices. But when prices were increased, independent producers suddenly found themselves able to compete. Their production costs were lower than Gazprom's, both because they had acquired better gas fields and because they were run more efficiently than the state-owned behemoth. Independent producers undercut Gazprom and took many of its best customers. When the economic crisis of 2008–9 caused industrial production—and gas demand—to slump, Gazprom saw its sales fall, too. The independent producers continued to acquire greater market share.[78]

As Gazprom watched its market share decline, it faced a higher tax bill, too. Gazprom's tolerance of low domestic gas prices was a key facet in the social contract that undergirded the firm's low tax bill in the early 2000s. When prices were hiked, transferring wealth from consumers and industries to Gazprom, pressure grew on Gazprom to contribute through higher taxes.[79] Because of price hikes, tax changes, and the expansion of independent producers, Russia's gas market began to look less like a monopoly and more like an arena in which competition and market forces mattered.[80]

Gas market liberalization happened not through legislation but through oligarchic competition, as independent producers muscled in on Gazprom's business. Many of the non-Gazprom producers were linked to powerful oligarchs who lobbied for their firms. By the end of the 2000s, for example, the five largest producers of gas behind Gazprom were all affiliated with powerful oligarchs. Novatek, the largest, had sold a 23.5 percent share to Gennady Timchenko, a former judo partner of Putin's.[81] Rosneft, Russia's state-owned oil giant, was controlled by Igor Sechin, the powerful Putin associate. Rosneft was one of several Russian oil firms that increased gas production in response to price changes. Similarly, by the end of the 1990s, TNK-BP, then owned by BP in partnership with Mikhail Fridman, Viktor Vekselberg, and Leonard Blavatnik, had also become a sizeable gas producer.[82]

The political influence that the independent gas producers wielded let them push their interests at the highest levels of Russia's government. At times, Putin himself has appeared to embrace their aims. In 2009 then–prime minister Putin declared, "We are seeing it as our goal to provide our gas producers with more liberal access to Gazprom's pipeline system," even though a program of low-cost access to Gazprom pipelines benefited the smaller producers at Gazprom's expense. One of the reasons Putin outlined corresponded to arguments made by technocrats such as Gref: more competition would spur efficiency. "In Russia like everywhere we see the negative side of excess monopoly," Putin declared. "Gas is no different." The downsides of monopoly, he argued, include "excess administration, the lack of due flexibility in the market, and restraints on the growth of independent producers. . . . Then there's corruption. It's there at Gazprom too."[83]

Russia's oligarch-backed independent gas producers have used declarations such as this to expand at Gazprom's expense. Some of this expansion may have occurred through negotiations that were as much political as commercial, involving provincial governments and shadowy political networks.[84] Yet the motive that drives these firms to take business from Gazprom is financial: seizing market share from Gazprom puts these companies in control of revenue streams worth billions of dollars. Taken alone, none of the non-Gazprom producers commands a major share of the gas market. In certain regions, however, some of them have displaced Gazprom. Today, producers besides Gazprom supply roughly a quarter of all Russian gas, up from only 10 percent in 2000.[85]

Leading analysts of Russia's gas sector expect this trend to continue. The independent producers have consolidated, with Rosneft purchasing TNK-BP and Itera, which will bolster interest in reducing Gazprom's legal protections yet further. So long as Russia remains oversupplied with gas—and so long as much of the low-cost gas is in the hands of independent producers—the financially optimal policy will be to let the independents continue to eat into Gazprom's market share.[86] While Gazprom faces potentially massive investment costs over the next decade if it is to keep up with demand and develop new fields, Russia's oil firms could expand their gas production at lower cost, if they are given a financial reason to do so.[87]

On top of this, Gazprom's export monopoly is already being whittled away. Legislation passed in 2013 allowed the government to permit other firms to export liquefied natural gas. Novatek received the first such permit in September 2014.[88] Rosneft and Gazprom continue to jostle over competing liquefied natural gas projects on Sakhalin Island, on Russia's Pacific Coast.[89] Gazprom, meanwhile, continues to lose influence in Moscow at the expense of other players in Russia's energy sector.[90] The slump in global energy prices that began in 2014 placed further pressure on Russia to produce its lowest cost reserves, which are not owned by Gazprom.[91]

In the case of the gas market, oligarchs' self-interest combined with technocratic support for a system based on competition and efficiency has brought Russia a new gas policy. An economic system reliant on oligarchs is rarely optimal, but when the status quo is an inefficient monopoly, oligarchic competition can represent an improvement. Since 2000, Russia transitioned away from a system in which Gazprom had a monopoly at home and abroad, charged low prices, and paid low taxes. Now the reverse is true: Gazprom's monopoly at home has all but ended and its export monopoly is slowly being eroded; it charges consumers higher prices now, but it also pays higher taxes.[92] For the government and for the gas market, this is a far more efficient equilibrium.

## Managing the Oil Sector

Putin's government inherited a booming oil sector, thanks both to higher prices and to the tough reforms of the late 1990s. The combination of privatization and ruthless managers such as Mikhail Khodorkovsky caused Russian oil production to begin growing in 1999 after a decade of post-Soviet decline. The new production practices and effective management instituted in the late 1990s continued to bear fruit through the early 2000s, with nearly double-digit annual production growth.[93] The government benefited from higher tax revenue, which it assessed on oil firms' revenues rather than profits, using a sliding scale that imposed higher taxes when oil prices were high.

The tremendous growth rates of the early 2000s could not continue forever, and they declined to the low single digits by the middle of the decade. But the 2008 financial crisis was a shock. In early 2008, the oil price shot up to nearly $150 a barrel before slumping to a fraction of that level by the end of the year. As prices fell, Russia's oil firms began slashing investment.[94] Oil production fell over the course of 2008, a remarkable reversal after nearly a decade of growth.[95]

The problem was that the existing tax system did not adequately incentivize investment in new production. There were two reasons why. First, the government taxed revenue rather than firms' profits. When the new oil tax regime was implemented in the early 2000s, Finance Minister Alexei Kudrin feared that a profit tax system would be easy to cheat. Profit is calculated by revenue minus costs. Yet during the 1990s Russia's oil firms proved adept at maximizing costs by, for example, buying equipment at inflated prices from companies run by relatives. The family would get a sweet deal, while the firm's higher costs would reduce reported profits and, thus, the tax bill.

Kudrin and his allies reasoned that a revenue tax was harder to cheat, and the government opted for taxing the oil sector through two main levies, one on production and the second on export.[96] These taxes worked fine for straightforward oil fields with low production costs. But by failing to take account of the fact that some fields are more expensive to develop than others, the tax provided few incentives to invest the billions of dollars necessary to explore new, often high-cost, fields. The second problem was the relatively heavy dependence on export taxes. Because consumption of oil at home avoided the export duty, the tax system encouraged domestic consumption. Russian oil refineries were a major beneficiary, experiencing far higher profit margins than did comparable firms in Europe.[97] But the government lost tax revenue, and the economy suffered from the inefficient use of the country's oil riches.

The oil price crash of 2008 combined with the slowdown in production spurred the government to act. It began offering incentives for exploration and production in new fields in East Siberia and elsewhere. At the same time, in 2011, the government began a series of tweaks to the oil tax regime designed to make it profitable to invest in new production. Taxes on export were cut while the mineral extraction tax—which is levied on both domestic consumption and exports—was increased.[98] These reforms achieved their goal, as oil export volumes grew steadily.[99] Russian oil production repeatedly hit post-Soviet highs.[100]

The management of the country's energy sector demonstrates again the priorities of Putinomics. When the state's authority was in question—when the Kremlin was unable to tax fully the oil industry, and when Khodorkovsky threatened Putin politically—the government's overriding priority was to reassert central control. Jailing Khodorkovsky was controversial, but both statist conservatives and more liberal technocrats supported the effort to re-establish central authority and rebuild government finances. Once the state's primacy was established, technocrats were given space to use tax incentives to optimize production. In the gas sector, where the state's predominance was never in doubt, the role of private players has increased—though all the non-Gazprom producers remain quick to pledge their loyalty to the Kremlin.

# CHAPTER 4

## Stabilizing Russia's Finances

"They are itching to get their hands on that money," Finance Minister Alexei Kudrin told journalists in 2004, referring to the country's spendthrift Duma members, its grasping industrial bosses, and the new class of security service elites who rose to power under Vladimir Putin. They wanted nothing more than to grab hold of the oil-fueled tax revenue that began flowing by the billions into Russian government coffers in the early 2000s. It was a rich prize for Russia's ruling class, who wanted to spend the windfall on pet projects from roads to rockets to corruption-financed Rolls Royces.

But what would happen when oil prices fell, Finance Minister Kudrin asked them? It was only several years earlier that an oil price slump caused the deficit to explode in 1998, forcing the government to devalue the currency and to default on its debt. Oil prices were volatile, Kudrin reasoned, so Russia should save its budget surpluses to prepare for leaner times. "You can tell them until you're blue in the face that you mustn't spend it," Kudrin moaned. "But even after I've explained all that, they still come after me, crying, 'Hand over the money!'"[1]

The 2000s were boom years for Russia, as oil prices skyrocketed from less than $20 per barrel in 1998 to over $80 a decade later. Russia's government raked in billions, especially as its new energy tax regime transferred an ever-greater share of oil company profits to the government. That Russia got rich as oil prices increased was foreseeable. More surprising is that not all its windfall energy wealth was spent immediately. Many oil-soaked dictatorships waste their petrodollars during good years and face dire consequences when prices plummet. Putin's Russia had its fair share of excess, as the gaudy palaces of his friends and his security chiefs show. Yet what is more surprising is how much of the oil wealth Russia saved. Over the course of the 2000s, over half a trillion dollars was put in reserve funds, defended from the grasping hands of Duma deputies and KGB clans. Putin and his team had lived through the tumult of the 1991 and 1998 crises, and they knew that hard times would come again. They feared debt, made sure that the government lived within its means, and built up a large stock of financial firepower to deal with any contingency.

Putin's government is often accurately described as including many former KGB colleagues and judo sparring partners. These groups have indeed acquired great influence. But they have coexisted, somewhat strangely, with a group of talented, technocratic managers centered in the Finance Ministry, the Economic Development Ministry, and the central bank. Putin selected many of these officials himself, and on issues that he cared about, such as budget deficits and inflation, Russia's economic policy mostly followed their advice. The Duma continued to demand spending hikes and tax cuts; heads of state-run monopolies lobbied for higher subsidies; and Putin's old judo-buddies accumulated vast commercial empires. But despite the push and pull of politics, and the near-constant demands for a couple billion rubles here or there, the Finance Ministry—backed by the president—won many of the battles that it fought. Its main goal was to avoid the deficits that drove Russia to ruin in the 1990s. With the president's support, the government used a large share of its windfall tax revenue during the 2000s to pay down debt and to save for a future rainy day. By the middle of the decade, thanks to this fiscal balancing, Russia had the most stable financial environment it had ever known.

### Paying Down Debt

When Putin became president in 1999, Russia was over its head in debt. Moscow owed money to everyone: to international investors, who had lent Yeltsin's government billions of dollars; to Russians themselves, many of whom held ruble-denominated bonds; to European governments such as France and Germany, who owned debts dating from the Soviet era; and to the IMF, to repay the bailouts of the 1990s. The dollar value of Russia's total external public debt in 1999 was $148.5 billion. That was down slightly from the crisis year of 1998, when Russia owed $158.7 billion to external debt holders. But the 1999 figure was significantly higher than the $134 billion owned in 1997, the year when debt levels drove Russia to financial crisis. More daunting was the ratio of debt to GDP, which measures a country's ability to pay its debts. In 1999 external debts were equal to Russia's GDP. That was a dangerously high level for a country that had just emerged from a financial crisis.[2]

Yet repaying the many foreigners who had lent Russia money was not a major concern of most of Russia's political elite. The Duma, which was responsible for approving government budgets, preferred to raise salaries and spending. During the early 2000s most Russians were still recovering from the 1998 inflation shock, and their incomes were still, in inflation-adjusted terms, lower than before the crisis. Boosting incomes was an understandable concern. Duma Banking Committee chairman Alexander Shokhin, for example, told the government in 2001 that if it wanted to make a $3.8 billion payment due to foreign governments that year, it should borrow money from Russia's central bank rather than divert money from spending plans. Given that the central bank's reserves were only $27 billion, and that such a proposal would reduce the reserves by over 10 percent, that was hardly a recipe for monetary stability.[3] But it represented an understandable impulse to focus spending on Russia rather than its creditors.

Indeed, Shokhin was not alone in urging the government to prioritize current spending over debt repayment. The Communists in the Duma, who realized that the government's decision to spend billions paying off foreign capitalists provided them with an easy political punching bag, jumped on the bandwagon. One Communist-backed petition declared that it was "immoral and unacceptable to pay billions of dollars to save the so-called positive international image . . . at the expense of our country's future."[4] Communist Party leader Gennady Zyuganov attacked the government's debt repayment proposals, arguing that the Kremlin was "continuing to crawl in the rut [dug] by Boris Yeltsin and his cronies."[5] Given how low an opinion most Russians had of Yeltsin's financial management, this was stinging criticism. And $15.2 billion of the debt was due to the IMF—an institution that many Russians blamed for the country's economic problems in the first place.[6]

Yet many Russian economists drew the opposite conclusion. The magnitude of Russia's debt burden, they argued, was a main reason it should be paid down as soon as possible. Yevgeny Yasin and Yevgeny Gavrilenkov, two well-known economists, noted that "spending on the payment and servicing of foreign debt in 1999 will total (if there is no restructuring agreement) approximately 10 percent of GDP, which is comparable to the entire federal budget's share of GDP, and about 30 percent of national savings." That was a massive—and unsustainable—sum. If debt service of such magnitude persisted, it would hobble Russia's economic prospects. Far better, they reasoned, to pay down the debt sooner rather than allow it to hang over the country's economic prospects. "A long-term budget, in which a primary surplus of no less than 3–4 percent of GDP is envisioned," is what Russia needs, they argued. "Such a budget would demonstrate the government's firm intention to pay off its debts."[7]

Despite public animosity toward foreign lenders and the IMF, Putin's government sided with liberal economists and against the Communists. The Kremlin focused relentlessly on reducing its debt burden. Rapid economic growth helped, providing Russia with more resources—and more tax revenue. Russia's GDP grew quickly during the early years of the decade, expanding by 9 percent in 2000 and 5.4 percent in 2001.[8] The debt to GDP ratio fell sharply, from a dangerous level of 100 percent of GDP in 1999 to a manageable 23 percent of GDP just four years later.

Only part of the improvement was due to economic growth. The government also spent billions of dollars reducing its outstanding stock of debt. One reason it did so was that, in the early 2000s, the government faced a steep debt servicing schedule, with billions due each year. The repayments peaked at $17 billion in 2003, a date that motivated the government—and put pressure on the recalcitrant Duma to contain its spending plans and ensure that the government would not default.[9]

Putin's economic team worked vigorously to drum up support for debt repayment. All the government's main economic officials supported rapid debt repayment. This included not only Kudrin, the finance minister, but also Prime Minister Mikhail Kasyanov, whom Putin inherited from the Yeltsin era; German Gref, author of the economic reform program that kicked off Putin's presidency; and Andrei Illarionov, Putin's outspoken economic adviser.[10] These officials used the 2003 peak of debt repayment—which they described as a "doomsday" event—to mobilize the political elite behind reforms to increase government revenue and thereby increase Russia's ability to service the debt. Tax collection efforts, the centralization of revenue, and spending control were all justified by the need to pay off foreign debts and limit financial risk.[11]

Putin himself believed strongly in the need to wean Russia off debt, and he was convinced that the country backed this policy. Once Russia had passed the mountain of debt service due in 2003, Putin bragged, "We paid 17 billion dollars, and the country felt nothing."[12] At his annual dial-in press conference that year, the president underscored the tremendous reduction in the country's debt burden and expansion of its reserves. "When I began working as president of the country, in 2000 the gold reserves of the Central Bank

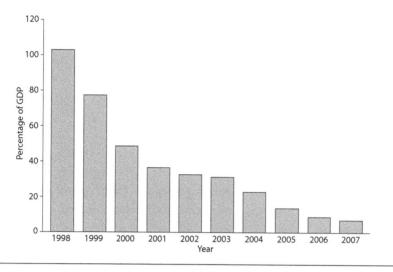

**FIGURE 4** Russian external sovereign debt as percentage of GDP, 1998–2007. International Monetary Fund.

amounted to 11 billion dollars. That is, in ten years [since the Soviet collapse] the country saved $11 billion." Now, though, the country was doing far better. "In 2003, in just one year it grew by $20 billion, and the reserves of the Central Bank are $70 billion." Even as reserves grew, the president boasted, debt levels fell. "Today our ratio between foreign debt and GDP is better than in many Western European countries. And that is one of the most important indicators of the health of an economy."[13]

After Russia met its mammoth $17 billion debt repayment in 2003, it was clear that the country had turned a corner from the 1998 default. The country's economy had improved markedly, making a second default unlikely. In response to the improving economic circumstances, many leading economic officials sought to refocus attention away from debt repayment toward other pressing needs. As early as 2002, for example, Prime Minister Kasyanov proposed abandoning the budget surplus to cut taxes, something that the Finance Ministry vigorously opposed.[14]

Driven by Finance Minister Kudrin, the government remained focused on bringing down its debt burden, prioritizing debt repayment above nearly every other issue. In 2006, Moscow repaid the $21.3 billion it owed the Paris Club of foreign government creditors, handing over an additional $1 billion for the right to pay back the debt ahead of schedule.[15] The debt burden shrank rapidly. Thanks to Russia's budget surpluses, the government did not issue foreign currency debt again until 2010, when it raised $5.5 billion to lock in historically low interest rates. Investors lent to the Kremlin for a ten-year period for only 1.35 percentage points higher than what they charged the U.S. Treasury.[16] The threat of a messy default—which hung over Russia for the first decade and a half of independence—was no more.

### The Savings Funds Debate

As it paid down its debt, Russia soon faced a problem its leaders had never known: what to do with extra money. Having slashed spending and hiked taxes in the early 2000s, and continuing to benefit from high oil prices, the country had a budget surplus. If oil prices stayed at the same level, the budget would be in surplus far into the future. The natural response, many Russian politicians argued, was to spend the extra cash, either by cutting taxes or by increasing spending. After the tax reform of the early Putin years, including the introduction of a flat 13 percent income tax, Russia's tax burden was relatively low, which removed the urgency of tax cuts. But government spending levels were far below those in similar countries, and the quality of health care, education, and infrastructure was mediocre. The case for increasing public investment in these spheres was easy to make.

But to the surprise of most observers—and in contrast to some of its commodity-dependent peers—Russia did not spend its entire oil windfall. During the early 2000s, it put much of the revenue from high oil prices in the bank, saving it for rainy days. The decision to save the budget surplus, first through a fund called the Stabilization Fund, then through the Reserve Fund and the National Welfare Fund, was one of the more controversial economic decisions of Putin's presidency. Yet Putin repeatedly backed Finance Minister Alexei Kudrin, who spearheaded the creation of these savings funds and defended them against demands that they be spent today rather than set aside for the future. Everyone in government had a pet project on which to use the savings—some on infrastructure, some on industry, some on tax cuts. But with Putin's backing, Kudrin fended off most of these attempts to spend Russia's savings. The result was that Russia entered the crises of 2008 and of 2014 with several hundred billion dollars of reserves, a serious cushion for hard times.

The idea of creating a stabilization fund began spreading around Russian economic policy circles immediately after the 1998 crash. Everyone realized that the budget's heavy dependence on taxing the oil industry meant that revenue would rise and fall along with the oil price, a factor over which Russia had no control. Indeed, Putin's effort to hike taxes on the oil sector exacer-

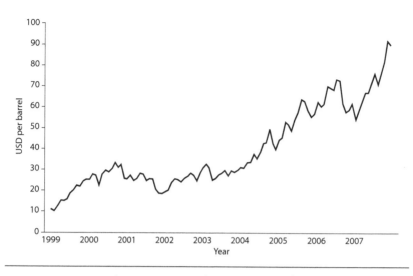

**FIGURE 5** Oil prices, 1999–2007 (U.S. dollars/barrel). Brent crude, nominal terms. U.S. Energy Information Agency.

bated the dependence on oil revenues. Higher oil taxes were justified on the grounds that the oligarchs had won control over energy assets at unjustifiably low prices, and that taxing the energy sector would allow tax cuts for manufacturing and service sector firms. But the more revenue that came from oil, the more the government budget would fluctuate with world oil prices. No one had forgotten that the 1991 collapse of the Soviet Union and the 1998 default both coincided with an oil price slump.

The only way Russia could extract sufficient tax resources from its energy sector while avoiding huge oil-price-driven fluctuations in government revenue was to save money when prices were high in order to spend when prices were low. That may sound easy, but the politics of public spending makes saving a budget surplus extraordinarily difficult. The U.S. budget, for example, has been in surplus only a handful of times over the past half century.[17]

The creation of a durable mechanism for saving Russia's budget surplus, therefore, required a combination of factors. For one thing, the memory of the previous crashes was still fresh—and still painful. Everyone remembered the havoc that an unsustainable budget deficit could cause. At the same time, this memory was backed by ironclad political will to enforce discipline and to defend the savings from would-be raiders. The political decision to save a portion of Russia's oil funds was enforced by the Finance Ministry—but this policy was only enforceable because everyone knew it was supported from the top.

The intellectual work behind the creation of a savings fund began as early as 2000, with several influential think tanks and research institutes publishing papers on the subject. A group of economists from Yegor Gaidar's Institute of the Economy in Transition, for example, prepared a report in 2001 noting that "the average yearly price of oil . . . reached a fifteen- to twenty-year high in 2000." High prices, this research suggested, would not last forever. When prices fell, if Russia was not prepared it would suffer a budgetary collapse, as had happened just three years earlier.

Countries such as Norway and Chile, however, had found savings funds to be a useful mechanism for managing commodity price volatility. Norway is a major oil and gas producer, while Chile is the world's largest copper miner. Both countries were as dependent on commodity prices as was Russia, and both used savings funds to help balance their budget through boom and bust cycles on global commodity markets. Russia could learn from other countries' use of such funds to smooth government spending over the course of boom-bust cycles, the economists reasoned, and thereby counteract the negative effects of commodity price slumps on the country's budgetary position and the broader economy.[18] Given the magnitude of Russia's oil riches, global price trends would inevitably affect the country's economy. A stabilization fund was a sensible means of managing the consequences.

Establishing a savings fund would require higher taxes on oil profits, something that Putin's government was already working hard to accomplish. This move increased the budget's dependence on oil taxes, a point that the government's opponents often note. But the Kremlin had solid political and economic reasons to increase reliance on oil taxation and decrease the role played by other sources of revenue.

The Kremlin wanted to cut taxes on every sector of the economy, from industries to individuals, and hiking taxes on the oil sector would enable such a policy to be budget-neutral. There was a clear political logic at play. Low taxes were a crucial part of the social contract that Putin was forging. Political activism of the sort that had characterized the 1990s, whether by striking coal miners, industrial lobbies, or wily oligarchs, was strongly discouraged. The best way to keep people out of politics was to reduce their interest in government policy. If government took a big percentage of income and profits via taxes, people might start asking questions about how their money was spent. Far better to fund the government not on the backs of potentially rebellious citizens but on the oil companies that Putin's government was bringing to heel.

But the most important rationale for cutting taxes on the nonoil sector was not politics but economics. As oil prices recovered from their late-1990s lows,

Russian economists began to worry about "Dutch disease," a malady named after the deterioration in Dutch industry that had followed the discovery of a large gas field in the country in 1959. Once the Netherlands started selling gas abroad, Dutch companies converted foreign earnings into currency that could be spent at home. This drove up the value of the Netherlands' currency. A more expensive currency meant that other Dutch exports—manufactured goods, say—were less competitive on foreign markets than those of other countries. So the Netherlands manufacturing sector struggled even as the gas sector boomed.

Since the Netherlands' experience with "Dutch disease" in the 1970s, economists have found that commodity windfalls harm other sectors of commodity-dependent economies. One way to counteract Dutch disease is to make nonoil sectors more competitive. In the early 2000s, fearing the emergence of Dutch disease, Russian economists advocated cutting taxes on the noncommodity portion of the economy, and making up the revenue by more heavily taxing the oil industry.[19] This strategy fit with the Kremlin's other goals, and the relative tax burden on industry and services fell over the early 2000s even as oil taxes increased.

Leading Russian officials made these arguments as they reshaped Russian tax and budget policy during the early and mid-2000s. Speaking to the Duma in 2001, Putin argued that "the federal budget should be protected to the highest possible degree from external influences such as a change in world prices for Russian exports." Putin saw two means of doing this. One was to adopt a "conservative macroeconomic prognosis proceeding from a pessimistic appraisal of prices for Russian exports"—in other words, not overestimating future oil prices. A second technique was to set aside "additional revenues which arise under the condition of higher export prices," and to save them in case oil prices fell.[20]

The latter idea pointed toward a stabilization fund. Kudrin and other budget hawks convinced the president that extra money should be placed in a special savings vehicle to guarantee it would not be spent. Support for a stabilization fund gathered steam. Putin himself repeatedly and publicly underscored the need for a stable budget over time. He regularly criticized Duma deputies who "vote for legislation that will ruin the budget."[21] And he declared that "stability of budgetary and tax policy is a very important factor of economic development. . . . Sound macroeconomic policy is needed."[22] With the president's support, the Stabilization Fund was created on January 1, 2004. Revenue earned when oil exceeded a specified price was to be deposited into the fund and invested in high-quality dollar, euro, or British pound–

denominated foreign government bonds.[23] It was a cautious investment strategy designed to ensure that Russia's savings were carefully managed.

The savings fund immediately faced a new challenge. By 2005, the second year of its existence, the fund had already surpassed its limit of 500 billion rubles. Oil taxes were gushing into government coffers, and the oil price kept rising. Russia's government deposited in the fund one-third of the tax revenue it earned that year from taxing oil.[24] Soon the fund was reaching its limit. Per the legislation that created the Stabilization Fund, any money in excess of 500 billion rubles could be spent on other purposes. The government decided to use the surplus to repay debt—a conservative choice. $3.3 billion was spent paying the IMF and $15 billion was set aside to pay off the Paris Club international creditors. Vnesheknombank, a state-owned bank, received $4.3 billion in debt repayments from the government, settling loans that had been made in 1998 and 1999. And $1.04 billion was set aside to close a deficit in Russia's pension fund.[25]

In total $24.8 billion was withdrawn from the Stabilization Fund in 2005—but the fund ended the year with even more resources, $42.9 billion in total.[26] All the investment choices so far were in line with the cautious fiscal policy. But if the fund remained capped at 500 billion rubles, the Finance Ministry would struggle to save the amount it thought necessary. After all, by the mid-2000s, Russia did not have much debt left to pay down. It would not be long, the ministry feared, before other officials would begin demanding spending hikes, thereby counteracting carefully laid plans to prepare for the next wave of low oil prices.

### Putin, Monetarist

Felix Dzerzhinsky, the aristocrat-turned-Bolshevik revolutionary, is best known for founding the Cheka, the Soviet secret police. Like Stalin, Dzerzhinsky had considered becoming a priest before opting instead for a career that would earn him the nickname "Iron Felix" for his ideological devotion and for his brutality. Yet iron is not the only metal by which Dzerzhinsky should be remembered. Amid the hyperinflation that accompanied the founding of the Soviet state, Dzerzhinsky was a key supporter of the "gold ruble," a new currency that finally stabilized the Soviet monetary system after the revolution. Dzerzhinsky was not only a ruthless secret police boss—he was a capable economic policy maker, too.[27]

Dzerzhinsky was not, it turns out, the only Soviet secret policeman to oppose inflation, or to focus on managing the money supply. Putin, too, made

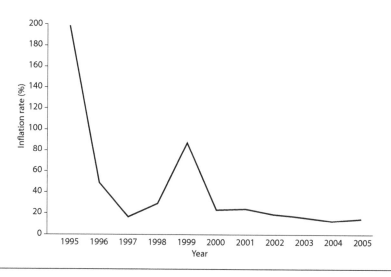

**FIGURE 6** Russian consumer price inflation, 1995–2005. World Bank.

low inflation a key policy goal. The country had struggled with persistent inflation since the late 1980s. A small and stable amount of inflation, many economists believe, supports economic growth. But Russia's experience showed why rapid price increases were so harmful. The inflation of the early 1990s sowed economic chaos, which fell most heavily on the poor. The late 1990s saw another rapid burst of inflation, with prices increasing by 85 percent in 1999 alone. But inflation fell sharply throughout the 2000s, reaching single digits by the middle of the decade.

The slowdown in price increases was surprising for several reasons. For one thing, Russia had long relied on inflation as a form of "tax." The government could not raise sufficient revenue, so it filled the budget deficit by printing money. The subsequent increase in prices—inflation—reduced the real value of money held in bank accounts. This method of funding the government was far from ideal, but few analysts believed that Russia could collect sufficient taxes to balance the budget and reduce inflation. Second, the officials who ran the central bank during the late 1990s and early 2000s were the very same people who had presided over the inflationary surge of the early 1990s, and whose policies contributed to its prolongation. Most famously, Viktor Gerashchenko, who headed Russia's central bank during the hyperinflationary years from 1992 to 1994, was reappointed to the position after the 1998 crisis. Based on his public statements there was little reason to think that Gerashchenko's monetary policy beliefs had changed.

The most important reason to expect continuity was the strength of the proinflation lobby. Much of Russia's manufacturing sector, for example, which inherited inefficient production practices and unnecessarily large workforces from the Soviet period, continued to teeter on the edge of bankruptcy. These businesses were kept alive throughout the 1990s thanks to cheap government loans. A policy of low interest rates helped these firms roll over debt, while inflation eroded the real value of the funds they were expected to pay back.

Russia's influential export industries, including not only the oil and gas sector but also nickel, aluminum, and diamond mines, also supported loose monetary policy. They required large capital investments, so they benefited from cheaper borrowing costs. Nor did they suffer from the downsides of inflation. Because their commodities were sold abroad and priced in dollars, inflation did not devalue their revenue streams. But by driving down the real value of the ruble against the dollar, inflation made these exporters' costs, such as workers' salaries, relatively cheaper, thus boosting ruble profits. Indeed, export firms and the oligarchs who own them have been vocal backers of loose monetary policy, with some, such as aluminum magnate Oleg Deripaska, publicly declaring that the central bank's management was "ridiculous."[28]

Some Russian economists agreed with the critiques levied by the country's business lobbies. These economists believed that an "excessive" focus on reducing inflation deterred economic growth. The government's decision not to increase spending in line with oil price increases—a policy in part designed in order to avoid adding pressure to inflation—"causes underfunding of investments in infrastructure, high technology, and manufacturing," complained one economist from Moscow State University. Rather than single-mindedly seeking to bring down inflation, this economist argued that "the main problem for Russia's monetary policy is to find a way to exponentially increase budget and bank funding of socioeconomic and scientific-technical development." Doing that required "goals, tools, and principles of monetary policy suited to Russian conditions"—not, he implied, monetary policy mindlessly imported from the West.[29]

Such economists argued not that inflation was good but that aggressively fighting it carried high costs. Viktor Polterovich, a well-known academic economist, penned a memo to the government titled "Reducing Inflation Should Not Be the Main Goal of Russia's Economic policy."[30] The benefits of more expansive monetary policy would outweigh the downside of higher inflation. For example, such economists argued, the government and central bank could use a range of policy tools to cut the cost of lending. The central bank could reduce interest rates, expand the types of assets it accepted as collateral, and even provide unsecured loans to banks. These steps would free up room on banks' balance sheets for further lending—and, these economists hoped, new investment. Similar policies might be used to encourage investment by state-owned firms. So long as the companies invested profitably, these economists argued, there was little to fear.[31]

These critiques of anti-inflationary policy, and support for subsidized lending rates, were supported by many Russian political elites. The most outspoken advocate of looser money was Sergey Glazyev, who served as a Communist member of the Duma in the early 2000s, before founding his own left-wing nationalist party, Rodina, in 2003. He ran for president on the Rodina ticket in 2004, promising to raise living standards and purge the oligarchs. His message performed far better than expected, before the Kremlin's media machine moved to silence him. Since then, Glazyev has been coopted as an adviser to President Putin on questions of Eurasian integration. He was also reported to be in the running to be named head of the central bank in 2013, though he was not selected.[32]

If he had been appointed to the central bank role, it would have led to a very different monetary policy. Glazyev is a vocal opponent of the central bank's tight money policy, which he has repeatedly criticized as "absurd."[33] The types of policies that Glazyev advocated—cutting interest rates, expanding the money supply, and restricting foreign banks in Russia—would have increased inflation, despite his claims to the contrary. But Glazyev's main point was that Russia's monetary policy was focused on the wrong goal. Price stability had displaced issues that Glazyev thought were more important, namely employment and economic growth.[34]

The liberal economists around Putin had little time for arguments such as Glazyev's. They attacked inflation aggressively. For one thing, Putin himself backed a policy of low inflation and advocated an inflation target of 3 percent per year, a level far lower than independent Russia had ever experienced—and a goal it has not yet met.[35] With such strong political support, the advocates of low inflation won most of the battles they fought. The appointment of Sergey Ignatiev as head of the central bank in March 2002, where he replaced the old-school Viktor Gerashchenko, was a key step in the solidification of Putin-era monetary policy. Under Ignatiev, the central bank's decisions on regulation and interest rates rarely diverged from what was recommended by the IMF.

Across the economic ministries, most officials believed in keeping inflation low. Without stable prices, they argued, neither Russians nor foreigners would feel confident investing. The combination of capital flight, high borrowing costs, and shallow financial markets had plagued Russian business since the early 1990s, making it difficult to raise capital needed to build factories or expand product lines. Inflation exacerbated all of these problems, the government's financial officials argued. The threat of higher inflation made Russians feel more comfortable saving in dollars rather than rubles, so Russia's rich shipped their money abroad. Russian banks had to charge high interest rates on loans to offset the erosion of the funds' value by inflation. Until inflation stabilized, these officals argued, Russia was unlikely to receive the investment it needed.

Putin's economic advisers believed that loose monetary policy triggered inflation and reduced rather than increased investment. The threat of higher inflation would scare away potential lenders and diminish the supply of loanable funds, thereby driving up borrowing costs. Nor was it wise, Putin's advisers argued, to rely on the government to lend to firms if the private sector would not. Russia's state apparatus did not have a strong track record of investment success, they pointed out, but it did have a history, during the early 1990s, of sparking hyperinflation while supporting industrial investment.[36]

One means of reducing inflation was tight monetary policy and relatively high interest rates. This was the policy that Russia's central bank followed under Sergey Ignatiev, its newly appointed chief. Yet many ministers and advisers also thought that such a policy was insufficient, particularly given the scale of petrodollars flooding into the country. The reality, many of Putin's advisers argued, was that unless a significant portion of the country's petrodollars was invested in foreign currencies, Russia could not reduce inflation. Andrei Illarionov, Putin's personal economic adviser, advocated saving additional funds outside of Russia lest they add to inflation.[37] Alexey Ulyukaev, the deputy chairman of the central bank, meanwhile, voiced fears that Russia's economy was overheating due to oil-funded inflows.[38]

The key figure in the anti-inflation fight—as in the battle over Russia's Stabilization Fund—was Finance Minister Alexei Kudrin. He was a committed inflation hawk, convinced that price increases threatened Russia's economic future. "As inflation increases," he wrote in one article, "so does its volatility," so businesses struggle to make plans and lack the confidence to invest. Inflation also depressed asset prices, since potential investors faced uncertainty about their valuation relative to dollars.[39] Because of this, Kudrin believed, as inflation increases, so does the volatility of economic growth.[40] Hence restraining price increases was crucial to the government's broader effort to foster economic development.

How could inflation be tackled? By carefully restraining the money supply,

Kudrin argued. "Not achieving inflation goals is a sign of the state's inability to control the money supply," he wrote.[41] "In countries with a high inflation rate," he argued, "the rate of inflation becomes directly proportional to money supply growth, with a correlation coefficient approaching 1."[42] If the supply of rubles was reduced, Kudrin believed, price increases would slow accordingly. How, then, to control the money supply? They key was "vesting the central bank with operational independence on the one hand, and with a high degree of responsibility for achieving the set targets, on the other."[43] Such a policy would empower the bank to make unpopular but necessary decisions with regard to interest rates or banking regulation—choices that were needed if money supply growth was not to outstrip economic growth, threatening inflation.

Thanks to Kudrin's influence and to the political elite's openness to a low-inflation policy, price increases slowed during the 2000s. Inflation dipped below double-digit rates for the first time in 2006, a development Kudrin applauded.[44] But he continued to worry that Russia's oil riches threatened financial stability. He advocated using the Stabilization Fund to hold Russia's oil profits in foreign-currency-denominated assets outside of Russia, a move he hoped would limit the inflationary effect of huge inflows.[45]

Absent a significant increase in the Russian economy's productive capacity, distributing oil funds through higher pensions or subsidies would cause the economy to overheat, sparking inflation.[46] "You see," he explained in 2004, "every ruble in the economy circulates several times and drives up prices. Let's say we inject money from the Stabilization Fund into a factory. If that money is not to have an inflationary effect, the factory must generate four times the investment. But our economy is not capable of doing that. That's the arithmetic."[47]

## Saving the Surplus

Even after Russia paid down most of its foreign debt, officials in the Finance Ministry continued to vigorously defend the budget surplus provided by high oil prices. They continued to fear that high oil prices would not last. They also feared that letting oil profits flow back into Russia would expand the money supply without leading to an increase in productive investment, thereby causing higher inflation. Yet as Russia's fiscal situation improved—and as oil prices continued to stay at relatively high levels—it became increasingly difficult for Finance Ministry officials to fend off attempts to spend Russia's oil riches.

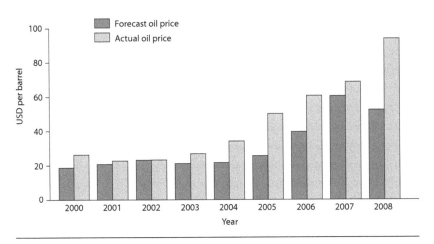

**FIGURE 7** Actual oil prices vs. prices forecast in government budgets, 2000–2008 (U.S. dollars/barrel). Vatansever, *The Political Economy of Allocation of Natural Resource Rents,* 350; media sources.

One technique the Finance Ministry used to prevent spending hikes was to deliberately underestimate the oil price when writing annual budgets. Because the oil price was also the key driver of GDP and tax revenue, underestimating the oil price in budget projections made it seem as if the government would have less money than it did. Throughout the 2000s, with only two exceptions, budget projections underestimated oil prices, often significantly so. But tricks such as these were at best a short-term solution. Kudrin, who served as finance minister until 2011, wanted an ironclad method of defending Russia's oil-backed budget surpluses, and to put away the excess funds as savings for a rainy day.

The policy of saving several percent of GDP per year remained controversial, both because many in Russia's political elite believed the money could be better invested at home, and because many of them wanted to get their hands on it themselves. Sergey Glazyev, the one-time presidential candidate, remained a leading critic of Kudrin's savings policy. Throughout the mid-2000s, he repeatedly took to the media to lambast the Stabilization Fund for failing to invest in Russia's economy and saving money in foreign currency instead. "Instead of using the taxpayers' money for the purposes of the socio-economic development of the country," Glazyev publicly complained in 2006, the government "freezes funds in the Stabilization Fund and exports them abroad."[48]

Kudrin's goal was to protect the budget's finances over the long run. Glazyev, by contrast, wanted to develop the country's economy in the short run. "We have two to three years to put the country on a modern, innovative path of development," Glazyev argued in 2006. The only way to accomplish his goal in such a short time horizon was to boost investment, by "radically changing the structure of the budget in favor of science and education, to transform the Stabilization Fund into a development budget, to create a system for long-term financing of productive investment."[49] Glazyev called for doubling spending on science, tripling spending on education, and quadrupling spending on culture. If the government were to take such a step, there "would be no budget surplus and no Stabilization Fund," Glazyev promised. He saw that as a positive facet of his plan.[50]

Glazyev was the most vocal opponent of the Stabilization Fund, but he was not alone. Opposition focused on two main downsides to the fund. One was that it failed to deal with Russia's existing social problems, mediocre health system, embarrassingly low male life expectancy, underfunded education, and decaying infrastructure, especially outside of the major urban centers. For many Russians, especially those not living in Moscow, St. Petersburg, or other large cities, the consumer boom of the mid-2000s seemed like a distant dream. Yes, living standards were rising, especially when compared with those of the late-1990s. But in agricultural regions and in industrial towns, life for many seemed at least as hard as during the Soviet period, when communism guaranteed jobs, housing, and cheap food. For these Russians, one academic noted, the government's effort to save for a rainy day is "pointless, because the rainy day has already arrived! Russia's social and economic problems have to be tackled now, and not bequeathed to future generations."[51]

Yet Russia during the 2000s mostly ignored its working class, for reasons that will be discussed below. Despite the presence in the Duma of two nominally center-left parties—one of which was the Communists—Russia's poor received relatively little attention from political leaders, who correctly foresaw that given rising wages and pensions, the lower class would remain politically quiescent. The main criticism of the Stabilization Fund and budget surpluses that Kudrin and the Finance Ministry carefully guarded came not, therefore, from the socially minded Left but from Russian business.

Here, too, Glazyev was perhaps the most outspoken participant in this debate, articulating critiques designed both for the working class and for industrialists, the two groups he hoped to assemble in a political coalition to oppose Kudrin's tight budgetary policy. The industrialists were less interested in Glazyev's fiery speeches about social crisis than they were spurred to action by his prediction of a looming industrial collapse.

Russian industry had shrunk since 1991 as the factories of the Soviet-era rust belt were shut. Across the political spectrum, Russia's elite realized that industrial revitalization required new investment. Indeed, those industries that did receive new investment, such as the country's cement plants and steel mills, looked reasonably healthy by the 2000s. Yet Russia's leaders did not agree on how to increase investment. Kudrin and his allies hoped that, given an environment of economic growth, a stable currency, and low inflation, businesses would find it profitable to invest, and funds would naturally flow into Russian industries. To some extent this happened. Yet many others—and not only on the Glazyev-style left—thought that the government should do more to make funds available for investment. If the supply of potentially loanable funds increased, many people reasoned, the cost of borrowing would fall, and it would be easier to invest.

Where to find a large pot of funds to invest? Many Russians looked to the Stabilization Fund. In Moscow's financial community, for example, proposals circulated for mobilizing the government's savings and investing them in the real economy. One challenge would be ensuring that such funds were invested efficiently. Governments in general have a mixed track record of picking investments, and Russia's recent experience was worse than average. Over the past half century, the Kremlin had plowed billions into enterprises with declining returns.

Moscow's financiers proposed various methods of ensuring that investments were carefully targeted. If a portion of the Stabilization Fund was used to create retirement savings accounts for individuals, for example, Russians could make their own investment choices, placing the money in stock or bond funds. Such a proposal would give individuals a strong incentive to invest intelligently, increasing the funds available for firms looking to raise money. This proposal had the added benefit of filling an expected shortfall in Russia's pension system.[52]

But Kudrin and his allies were unimpressed by such proposals. For one thing, many Russians had had negative experiences with investment funds thanks to a series of well-known frauds in the early 1990s such as the MMM pyramid scheme. For another, as in most countries, pension changes are politically toxic. A scheme to supplement pensions with private investments could prove politically disastrous. Most of all, however, proponents of the Stabilization Fund feared that funds earmarked toward investment would be misused and contribute nothing to economic growth. Glazyev's rhetoric, for example, did little to inspire confidence. In his framing of the problem, the only problem was investment. He never addressed how to ensure that investment flowed to profitable projects rather than white elephants. Without effective investment mechanisms in place, Kudrin and his allies feared, what Glazyev described as "investment" could easily turn out to be waste. But Glazyev either saw no need for concern or believed that time was too short to bother with efficiency. Russia had to act immediately if it was to prevent "the degradation of Russia's research and production" potential, he argued. Soon, the decline would be "irreversible," the economic crisis "final."[53] But it was Glazyev's proposed policy of investing without concern for efficiency, liberal economists noted, that had driven Soviet industry into the ground in the first place.

Kudrin and his allies struggled to resist demands for more spending. Russia's economy and its government budget depended heavily on oil prices, and a sharp decline in prices would cause a gaping budget deficit. Taxes on hydrocarbons "provided 30 percent of all revenues," Kudrin noted, with the federal government reliant on the two main levies on oil for 40 percent of its revenue in 2005. The creation of the Stabilization Fund had helped limit the risk of a price shock, but only to a point. Kudrin argued that in 2004 and 2005, only half of the revenue earned from above-average oil prices were deposited in the Stabilization Fund. The rest was spent.[54]

This had predictably negative consequences, Kudrin believed, the same consequences he foresaw when he initially advocated crafting a stabilization fund. For one thing, the influx of oil money drove up the real value of the ruble, making domestic production less competitive. By January 2005, Kudrin calculated, the real value of the ruble had almost reached its level before the 1998 financial crisis. The positive effects of devaluation on domestic production, therefore, were exhausted. "Further increases in the real effective exchange rate," he predicted, "will have a serious negative influence on the competitiveness of the Russian economy."[55]

At the same time, the decision not to set aside all the proceeds of above-average oil prices meant that the budget's dependence on oil was increasing. "Stabilization will be effective if the creation of stabilization funds reduces the reliance of budget expenditures on the price of oil," Kudrin argued in 2006, but the reverse was happening. To cut taxes on the rest of the economy, Russia had hiked taxes—and its dependence—on the oil sector. That was a sensible response to the challenge of Dutch disease, but Kudrin sensed risk.

He wanted Russia both to tax oil heavily and to spend as little of the revenue as possible. "Budget expenditures must rely on revenues that do not depend on temporary price surges," he argued, pointing to oil's volatility. "Countries that upon creating stabilization funds have taken the path of increasing budget expenditure, thereby violating the principle of limiting the money supply, have been unable to finance their growing budgetary obligation."[56] But having already cut taxes on nonoil sectors, if the government saved all its oil revenues, it would have little money to spend. Kudrin was open about what this meant for government spending: "Expenditure must also be reduced." Kudrin and his allies in the Finance Ministry made this argument repeatedly, pointing to the disastrous deficits of the 1990s and to the unpredictability of oil prices. "International experience," Kudrin argued, "shows that positive results in the economy have been achieved by countries that, besides creating [reserve] funds, have also constrained budget expenditure." Russia should adopt a strict budget rule that capped spending increases at the growth rate of the nonoil economy.[57] The only alternative, he believed, was "financial instability" when the next oil price shock arrived.

Yet Kudrin increasingly discovered that his calls for limiting spending fell on deaf ears. In the aftermath of the 1998 financial crash, Russians were poorer, but the memory of the crisis was fresh. So it proved possible to assemble a coalition in favor of limiting spending and building up reserves. In the early 2000s, this policy was backed by a wide range of Russian elites, from the business community to the head of the security services, because the stability of the state appeared to be at stake.[58] The coalition that backed Putinomics understood the link between financial stability and political stability. By the end of the decade, however, after Russia had paid down its debts and stashed several hundred billion dollars in reserves, the need for ultraconservative budgetary policies was less clear.[59] Many Russians had supported macroeconomic stabilization because they believed it was a necessary foundation for economic progress. Kudrin counseled continued caution. But many Russians believed that, because the country had sorted out its finances, it was time to reap the benefits of growth.

# CHAPTER 5

# Restructuring Russian Industry

Sergei Roldugin has expensive taste in musical instruments. Or so one might conclude from the Kremlin's explanation of how the cellist spent the $2 billion that was discovered to have been funneled out of Russia through shell companies and Panamanian bank accounts in his name. The 2016 leak of the Panama Papers, records from a law firm that helped clients hide money from tax authorities, presented a side of Russian business and finance that was widely suspected but rarely so visible. Roldugin, who has been a friend of Putin since the 1970s, is said to be the person who introduced the Russian president to his former wife. He is the godfather of Putin's daughter Maria. These connections, rather than any evident business skill, allowed him to amass a tremendous fortune.[1]

The structure of Roldugin's apparent wealth provides important hints into how Russia's elite manages its money, and how it distributes the perquisites of power. Roldugin—who everyone knows is a friend of the president—is alleged to have received stakes in oligarch-owned companies, a type of tribute to the tsar. He and his companies were granted massive unsecured loans from state-owned banks, including $650 million from the Cyprus branch of VTB, Russia's second-largest state-owned lender.[2] "I am proud of people like Sergei Pavlovich," Putin said when asked about the enterprising cellist. "He spent almost all the money he earned on musical instruments abroad and brought them to Russia."[3]

## Business in Putin's Russia

Not all fortunes in Russia, however, stem from connections with the Kremlin. Corruption is widespread, of course, and some Russian businesses thrive on contracts doled out by bribable bureaucrats. But Russian industry is diverse:

some sectors are inefficient and unreformed; others have boosted productivity and compete internationally. There are several factors that differentiate the better-run Russian firms from their backward peers. The country's big state-run companies remain, on average, corrupt and badly managed. The state-owned energy sector wastes large sums of money, including on corruption schemes. State-owned banks such as VTB and VEB make lending decisions that are shaped as much by politics as by profit. But other sectors function quite differently. Retail has grown quickly, led by domestic chains that expanded across the country and drove down cost. And Russia's tech firms, including Yandex, VKontakte, and Mail.ru, draw on the country's deep well of programming talent to outcompete American giants like Google and Facebook on the domestic market. Has Russian business succeeded under Putin? It depends on where you look. Here, too, the priorities of Putinomics prevail. Banks and energy firms are important politically, so political goals take precedence over economic efficiency. But in industries not closely linked to politics, market incentives tend to dominate decision making.

## Corruption, Property Rights, and Investment

The failures of Russian business are obvious, even when shielded behind shell companies and anonymous bank accounts. Take Sergei Roldugin. No evidence has emerged to support Putin's claim that Roldugin used his oligarch-funded shell companies to acquire a secret stash of Stradivariuses, though he did buy at least a couple.[4] Evidence is plentiful, however, that the system of shell companies and offshore bank accounts that Russia's elite use to hide their financial dealings from prying eyes has shaped Russian financial and corporate life. Every quarter, Russia's central bank publishes data on foreign investment into Russia, listing which countries spend the most money buying Russian assets. Every quarter, sunny islands such as Cyprus, Bermuda, and the British Virgin Islands lead the list, often surpassing countries such as Germany and Britain. Russian economists have shown that "investment" from such tax havens is more likely to be directed to corrupt Russian provinces than well-governed areas, suggesting that some of these flows are linked to money laundering.[5] Russians are not alone in using shell companies and tax havens, of course, but the country's oligarchs and political leaders have come to rely heavily on such schemes. They need offshores and shell companies to conceal illegal dealings and, no less important, to hide their assets from the grabbing hands of other oligarchic clans in Russia. Offshores are so embedded in Russian corporate life that it is hard to imagine business without them.

The oligarchs and political elites who govern Russia are, in the words of one Russian commentator, an "offshore aristocracy."[6]

You might suspect that such a system would deter investment by making honest business more difficult. The combined risks of corruption and expropriation, which are far worse in Russia than, say, in Poland, do indeed reduce investment and slow growth. Yet here, too, the past two decades present a story that is more complicated than it at first appears. Continued corruption has coincided with tremendous economic growth. Even as oligarchs milked state-owned firms for personal use, parts of the private sector have thrived. During almost every year since the Soviet collapse, more capital has left Russia than has arrived. But new private sector capital formation has also been an important driver of Russian GDP growth, which surged ahead in the first decade of the 2000s.[7] Productivity, too, has improved, especially in the services sector. Despite the state sector's continued inefficiency, many privately held Russian firms have charged ahead. The unexpected reality is that, especially during the decade before the 2008 financial crisis, but continuing in some sectors today, Russia's continued rule by an "offshore aristocracy" has coincided with a business boom.

One explanation for the boom is luck. The most obvious area of luck was oil prices, which more than tripled in real terms between 2000 and 2008. At the height of the global financial crisis, oil briefly crashed, but it then recouped its losses and surged to a new peak in 2011. The billions of petrodollars that flowed into Russia each year transformed the economy. The government used bulging tax revenues to boost pensions and state salaries, while firms that supplied the energy sector, from pipeline producers to manufacturers of railroad cars that transport Russian oil, made higher profits.[8] The booming economy meant pay hikes—and Russians used their newfound affluence to fund a growing consumer economy. No matter how you slice the numbers, the effect of high oil prices was enormous. Subtracting the full cost of production, Russia received twice as much money from oil and gas sales in 2005 as in 2000, a sum reaching nearly $200 billion annually by the mid-2000s.[9]

A second explanation was ruble devaluation. The ruble crashed against foreign currencies during the 1998 crisis.[10] This made Russian consumers poorer as imports became far more expensive. But a cheaper ruble was good news for export-oriented firms, because their goods were more competitively priced. Devaluation reduced the price of Russian labor, land, and domestically produced inputs relative to those of other countries. This provided a one-off boost to exports that spurred business expansion in the early 2000s.

However, the gains from devaluation were felt primarily in the immediate post-crisis years. Most evidence suggests that the devaluation boost ended in the early 2000s.[11] And though the high oil price helped, it was not the whole story. Not all oil exporters managed to improve productivity so rapidly. By most estimates, total factor productivity, a measure of the overall efficiency of an economy, grew more rapidly during the 2000s in Russia than in many Central European countries.[12] Labor productivity increased by nearly 50 percent in the decade after 1998.[13] From 1998 to 2014, the efficiency with which labor was used grew more rapidly than in the Czech Republic and was only slightly slower than in Poland or Slovakia.[14] Russia also outperformed other oil and gas producers, from Saudi Arabia to Algeria to Venezuela.[15] Foreign investment boomed, too. According to the World Bank, $500 billion in foreign direct investment flowed into Russia in net terms between 1999 and 2015.[16]

Research on the causes of Russia's GDP growth has pointed to various factors, but most studies suggest that both productivity growth and capital investment were key drivers.[17] One explanation for productivity growth and capital investment is that businesses and entrepreneurs, both foreign and domestic, were willing to invest. One reason was Russia's rich natural resources. A second was that the oligarchs and Putin pals who constituted the "offshore aristocracy" found the investment climate sufficiently attractive to keep at least a portion of their wealth in the country rather than moving all of it to Swiss bank accounts.

Despite the expropriation and imprisonment of Yukos-owner Mikhail Khodorkovsky, many other oligarchs concluded that their optimal strategy was to continue investing in their businesses in Russia. Most of Russia's richest men could have sold their assets in Russia and retired in the French Riviera. Some chose this strategy. For example, Dmitri Rybolovlev, a Russian potash magnate, sold his 53 percent share in Uralkali for several billion dollars and used the proceeds to buy Monaco's soccer club, a slew of famous paintings, and luxury properties in New York, Palm Beach, Geneva, the Greek Islands, and, of course, Monaco.

What is surprising, however, is how few of Russia's leading oligarchs cashed out. Most, of course, bought property in Europe's elite beach towns and ski resorts. But they also kept billions of dollars of assets in Russia—even after Gusinsky and Berezovsky were stripped of their assets, even after Khodorkovsky was thrown in jail. Why did the oligarchs stay in Russia? Why not trade uncertain property rights in Russia for a seaside estate abroad? There were three main reasons. First, unloading assets rapidly, especially without government approval, required selling at a below-market price. Second, the government in the early and mid-2000s promised to improve the business environment, and many oligarchs believed it would do so. Third, the Kremlin gave strong implicit guarantees of the oligarchs' right to continue holding their property. Putin stated repeatedly in public that he believed in private property.[18] He delivered the same message to Russia's leading business owners in private. These implicit property rights were not fully trustworthy, as Khodorkovsky's fate proved, and as several other oligarchs would later discover. But the Kremlin's reassurances about the stability of ownership rights were evidently credible enough to convince most oligarchs that their optimal strategy was to continue investing in their firms, reasonably confident that they would reap the rewards.

Not only did most oligarchs choose a strategy of continued investment, some of them proved to be competent managers. A study by economists Sergei Guriev and Andrei Rachinsky, for example, found that of all types of owners except foreigners, oligarchs were the most adept at improving productivity. This is surprising, the study found, because oligarchs were under the same political pressure as other domestic owners, which prevented mass layoffs of unneeded personnel. Because of this, oligarchs had to make their firms more productive not by cutting costs, but by increasing output and sales. On average, they succeeded.[19] This isn't to say that Russia's private sector oligarchs were optimal business owners. But, at least in the private sector, they were evidently not the worst type, either—especially in comparison to continued mismanagement at Russia's state-owned firms.

Economist Philip Hanson has written that Russia has a "dual economy," with different rules and different outcomes in each sector.[20] In the spheres dominated by state-owned firms and crony capitalists, business remained corrupt and productivity gains were limited. In other sectors, though, particularly those that were more isolated from Kremlin politics and the grabbing hands of Putin's cronies, Russian firms rapidly modernized. The continued backwardness of the first sphere coupled with rapid productivity growth in the second sphere helps explain why Russia experienced strong growth alongside corruption and expropriation.

## Russia's State-Run Firms

Given that Vladimir Yakunin, the former boss of Russian Railways, said that he was paid around $70,000 per year, one might have expected allegations of his family's immense fortune to have come as a surprise.[21] But the corporate titans who run Russia's state-owned companies are known neither for their transparency nor their honesty, and Yakunin's reputation was no different. While publicly claiming only a modest salary, he pointedly refused to publish his income or property holdings.[22] Yet the biggest cost to the public was not the salaries of state-company CEOs, but state-owned firms' inefficiency and incompetence. With only several exceptions, Russia's state-owned firms wasted and stole money on a vast scale, seizing market share from private sector firms that did not benefit from cheap loans and other benefits of state-ownership.

Nonetheless, it was the large but mysterious salaries of CEOs of state-owned firms that made the news (though rarely Russia's state-controlled TV news). Media reports alleged that Yakunin's actual salary was $15 million per year, though no one is certain.[23] Anticorruption campaigners say that Yakunin's family assembled an array of properties and companies—a lifestyle that would be difficult to fund even with a $15 million salary, let alone $70,000 per year.[24] Amid the haze of Cypriot shell companies and offshore bank accounts, many details are vague. What is clear, however, is that during the decade that Yakunin ran Russian Railways, from 2005 to 2015, the firm was emblematic of the inefficiency of the state-owned portion of Russia's economy. In theory, the government-controlled monopolies were the property of the government and, ultimately, the public. In reality, many state-owned companies functioned as the private property of the oligarchs who controlled them. At Russian Railways, Yakunin was an ineffective manager even as allegations swirled about his family's wealth.[25]

Despite the controversy over whether Yakunin, as head of a state-owned firm, should declare his assets and reveal his salary, few Russians were surprised to hear allegations that the boss of a state-owned firm was exorbitantly wealthy. Yakunin was no simple railroad boss: he was a railroad boss with a decades-long friendship with Vladimir Putin. Widely rumored to be a KGB veteran, in the 1990s, he was a member of the Ozero dacha cooperative, a group of vacation homes outside of St. Petersburg whose owners included several key members of Russia's elite, including Putin, billionaire businessman Yuri Kovalchuk, and the father of Putin's son-in-law, Nikolai Shamalov.[26] Yakunin's career followed Putin's for over two decades. When Putin began work at the Presidential Property Management Department, Yakunin was named the head of its office in the Northwest Region. When Putin became president, Yakunin was appointed deputy minister of transport and given control over the nation's seaports.[27] Later he was made chief of Russian Railways.

Yakunin is also, paradoxically, one of Russia's leading opponents of globalization, a concept he (wrongly) credits Karl Marx with having invented.

Globalization—which Yakunin, in one article, defined as "millions of young-sters sitting around screens" with "earphones on their heads"—was a process outside forces use to degrade governments such as Russia's. Globalization threatens the very basis of Russian statehood, and, left unchecked, could cause governmental collapse and social chaos. Yakunin expresses little doubt which outside force is driving globalization. Historically, he has argued, waves of globalization were driven by great empire-builders: Alexander the Great, Augustus, Tamerlane, and Genghis Khan. Today, Yakunin writes, "it is more than clear: globalization is the hegemony of the United States, victorious in the Cold War."[28]

With views like these, Yakunin has been a leader among Russian con-servatives who are skeptical of the West. A foundation linked to Yakunin is alleged to have funded a series of conferences called "Dialogue of Civiliza-tions," which brought together a motley array of activists each year for discus-sions about combating the influence of the United States and the European Union.[29] He has published antiglobalization manifestos alleging that "corpo-rate borrowing in foreign currencies . . . can be used as a lever for significant economic influence and profit extraction."[30] Russian anticorruption cam-paigners, however, allege that whatever Yakunin's ideological proclamations, his children have taken advantage of globalization by living in luxury homes in European capitals.[31]

Many Russians might have ignored the corruption allegations if Russian Railways had been well managed. Yet the firm was a case study in pathologies of Russia's state-owned companies. Yakunin and other top managers faced few personal incentives to make the railroads efficient. But Russian Railways managers would bear great political cost for any changes that threatened entrenched interests, whether the more than 800,000 Russians who worked for the firm, or the companies and municipalities that benefited from rail service at below-market prices.[32]

In every country, the regulation of natural monopolies—industries such as railroads and electricity grids, where high fixed costs make unified large organizations more efficient than multiple smaller ones—creates difficult trade-offs.[33] When monopolies are run by the government, they face few incentives to keep costs low or service quality high. In the hands of a single private firm, however, monopolies raise prices and gouge consumers. Even countries with little corruption and well-developed legal systems struggle to manage these trade-offs.

In theory, Russian Railways is moving toward a system that includes greater private ownership, which, if properly designed, could boost competition and performance.[34] The firm was separated from the Ministry of Railways in 2003, though it remained state-owned. A key question for introducing competition in any country's railway monopoly is to determine whether multiple firms will share the same track or whether firms will own separate tracks. Russian Railways, the government, and other industry stakeholders have been debating this for over a decade, yet no resolution is in sight.

Though some competition has been introduced in both the freight and passenger sectors, movement is slow. Oligarchs such as Gennady Timchenko and Vladimir Lisin have invested in the railcar business and now are alleged to lobby for favorable regulation.[35] The government has increased subsidies to the industry. Some amount of government subsidy is present in nearly every rail industry, but it is far from clear that higher Russian spending is correlated with higher performance. The lack of regulatory clarity and the prominence of oligarchic interests suggest the opposite. It remains politically impossible to reduce rail subsidies, and one attempt to do so in early 2016 sparked protests after firms reduced passenger rail services. Yet no one has proposed other politically feasible methods of making the sector more efficient.[36] The industry remains on the wrong track.

Despite this, corruption allegations continued to swirl around former CEO Yakunin. Alexei Navalny, the anticorruption campaigner, made Yakunin a key target of his investigations, alleging that the railroad boss owned a palatial residence in the Moscow suburbs and family homes in Switzerland and London, funded by a long series of questionable business transactions. The Moscow "palace," as Navalny termed it, allegedly included among other features, "its own forest, a fenced river, a few artificial ponds, [a] 2,000 square meter bathhouse, [a] room for prayer," and, most notoriously, a special facility for storing fur coats. On top of that, Navalny alleged, Yakunin had illegally seized part of the land his palace was built on. Navalny's team took aerial photos of the alleged mansion that proved it was vast and gaudy.[37] The luxurious London manor that Navalny alleged to be property of the Yakunin family was estimated to be worth $7.2 million, while an alleged Swiss residence sits on the shores of Lake Geneva.[38] Navalny claims that Yakunin's elder son, Andrei, owns stakes in seventeen hotels built next to railway stations. Younger son Viktor Yakunin is allegedly involved in similar property schemes.[39]

Indeed, many large state-owned companies, especially but not only in the energy sector, have been managed in ways that benefit the small clique that controls them, at the expense of their ostensible owners, the Russian public. Gazprom, Russia's largest energy firm, is a prime example. It buys gas pipelines from two companies, Stroitransgaz and Stroigazmontazh. The first is owned by Gennady Timchenko, the latter by the brothers Arkady and Boris Rotenberg, judo buddies of Putin's. Regulating any industry with only two main suppliers presents a challenge given the suppliers' market power. This is especially true when the two suppliers are longtime friends of the president.[40] There is no reliable data on the two firms' profits, but economist Sergey Aleksashenko has estimated that the firms made $16 billion since 2008.[41]

## Kaluga Attracts Foreign Investment

Yet even as some oligarchs were milking millions of rubles from government-owned firms, other political leaders were setting a better example. Anatoly Artamonov, the sixty-two-year-old former collective farm boss, is perhaps an improbable exemplar of good governance. Yet Artamonov, a graduate of the Moscow Institute of Agriculture Production Engineers and former Communist Party member, knows better than any other Russian governor how to attract foreign investment.[42] He has governed the Kaluga region since 2000, in part because of his vigorous and effective campaign against corruption, which won him not only praise but also heaps of foreign investment. When Russian leaders decide to tackle corruption, Artamonov's example shows, the business climate can improve rapidly. But a system in which businesses must hope to get lucky with their provincial governor is not one likely to provide a strong investment climate across the country.

Artamonov's tenure as Kaluga governor shows both the possibilities and the limits of good leadership in Russia's fight against corruption. The governor has done nothing to alter the region's political structures. He is fully loyal to the Kremlin. What he has done is improved the business climate and made foreign firms comfortable investing. The province has good infrastructure, for example. But many firms report that what makes Kaluga stand out is its low level of corruption. The province can do nothing, of course, about the high-level theft that occurs in state-owned firms. That is a task for the Kremlin. But corruption occurs at several levels of government, and Kaluga has managed to cut corruption at the regional level—and it has reaped the benefits of higher investment.

The lowest level of corruption is small-scale bribery—think of police asking for a "small fee" to ignore a speeding violation, or driving test administrators requesting cash in exchange for a passing grade. This type of corruption infuriates citizens, but its economic effect is limited by the minor sums involved. It is unlikely that many fewer Russians receive driver's licenses in regions where it requires a bribe, grumble though they might. A far larger issue is when corruption begins to affect businesses. Many regions in Russia have suffered from "raider attacks," in which one business group bribes law enforcement authorities to falsify claims or legal proceedings against a firm and transfer ownership to a rival group. This type of activity involves larger sums than bribery related to speeding tickets. And it discourages investment, since entrepreneurs are less likely to invest if there is a risk their business might be stolen.[43]

Corruption at the highest level, in which top political leaders enrich their allies, is more varied. Politicians are expected to provide benefits to the groups that put them in power. When politicians hike pensions to reward the older voters who elected them, we do not consider that corruption. When political leaders funnel subsidies to a specific industry, such as U.S. Democrats subsidizing solar power or Republicans cutting taxes on the oil sector, we may view that more skeptically but do not consider it corruption in the traditional sense. Only when political leaders or their friends are personally enriched have they crossed a line. In economic terms, however, the effects of this type of high-level corruption depend on how it is extracted. If, hypothetically, a leader were to take 1 percent of tax revenue out of the budget and place it in his or her pocket, the economic costs would be relatively limited, since the corruption scheme would function like a tax. In Russia, however, high-level corruption must be at least slightly veiled from public view, which forces elite groups to construct elaborate schemes for stealing money.

How has Russia dealt with these three levels of corruption? At the high level, as leaks such as the Panama Papers demonstrate, corruption continues unabated, in ways that waste money and deter growth. By contrast, many areas have reported decreases in low-level corruption. In Moscow, for example, anecdotal evidence suggests people pay fewer bribes than two decades ago to the traffic police or to obtain a driver's license.[44]

At the midlevel, however, there is significant variation between regions.[45] This is where officials such as Kaluga's governor, Anatoly Artamonov, stand out. There were not many reasons to expect that Kaluga would become a hub for foreign investment. During the Soviet period, defense industries made up 60 percent of the region's industrial output, and most went bankrupt when the USSR collapsed.[46] About half of the region's workforce was employed in the military-industrial complex.[47] Other than its location—not far from Moscow—the region had little to recommend it. Electricity costs, for example, are higher than in other regions, and the proximity to Moscow means that the province struggles to retain talented workers, who prefer to live in the capital.[48]

Governor Artamonov has responded by seeking out foreign investment and creating the conditions big firms desire. On many regulatory questions, governors can—if they wish—significantly improve the business climate. One study, for example, found that the time it took to receive a construction permit was 40 days in the quickest province, compared to 530 days in the slowest.[49] Artamonov has targeted issues such as this to attract foreign investors, putting money into infrastructure, ensuring taxes are reasonable, and—above all—eliminating the type of corruption that deters businesses, especially foreign businesses that can face penalties at home for corrupt practices abroad.[50]

Survey data suggest that Kaluga has succeeded in tackling midlevel corruption of the type that chases away investment. KPMG, an audit firm, found that 86 percent of foreign investors in Kaluga reported no significant bribery, while the 14 percent who did report bribery all said it occurred only on a small scale.[51] By many measures, the region has the best investment climate of any province in Russia.[52] Studies have found, not surprisingly, a significant positive correlation between a region's governance quality and the quantity of foreign investment it receives.[53] Kaluga has received more foreign investment than any region besides Moscow, St. Petersburg, and gas-rich Sakhalin.[54] Some of the world's largest firms have invested in the province. Foreign investment began in the automotive sector, including car plants built by Volkswagen, Peugeot, and Mitsubishi, as well as a Volvo truck factory and a variety of car parts firms. By 2015, the province had produced over a million cars, and the industry made up 42 percent of provincial output.[55]

Where automobile makers built factories, other corporate titans soon followed, from Samsung's TV arm to L'Oréal cosmetics, from AstraZeneca pharmaceuticals to Lafarge cement.[56] When the economy entered recession in late 2014—and particularly after the ruble collapsed around the same time—close links with foreign firms began to cause some problems. When car sales across Russia fell 36 percent in 2015, the province's auto industry was hard hit, with many firms laying off workers or suspending production.[57] Others, though, continued to bet on Kaluga. Volkswagen opened a new plant in Kaluga in 2015, despite the crisis.[58] Artamonov banned use of the word *crisis* to describe the economy.[59] He sought new investment from Asia. And unlike many Russians who speak about ties with Asia with little to show for it, Kaluga is already attracting some. A Chinese firm set up an automotive glass plant in the province in 2015.[60] A Thai food company invested in the region. Artamonov visited Vietnam in 2016 to drum up further investment.[61]

The governor's supporters—and there are many among the country's business elites—praise him as a good manager. The concept of a *khozyain,* a Russian word that describes a mix between a manager and a boss, is a common theme in Russian politics. Many people believe that a good khozyain can fix the problems of Russian governance, fighting corruption and red tape. Artamonov shows the possibilities and the limits of this approach. Midlevel corruption has declined. But Kaluga is still subject to the same trends that affect all Russian business—both external shocks and nationwide problems with the business climate.

Kaluga is not the only province to perform reasonably well on business climate indicators. Voronezh, a poor agricultural region, has encouraged local elites to invest far more than their counterparts in other regions do, thanks in large part to better-than-average governance.[62] If Vladimir Yakunin's mismanagement of Russian Railways demonstrates the downsides of state-capitalism in the Putin era, Artamonov's Kaluga demonstrates why many Russians think that the system's faults are reformable—so long as the right people are in place. In 2000, few would have guessed that backward Kaluga would become a manufacturing powerhouse, or that the region, long dependent on subsidies, could be a net contributor to the federal budget.[63] But Artamonov transformed the province's government and its economy. In a country with notoriously stubborn bureaucrats, Artamonov gives foreign investors his personal cell phone number. "We take care of our investors," he explained to one journalist, "like parents look after their children."[64]

### Supermarket Superpower

The differences between Artamonov's management of Kaluga and Vladimir Yakunin's governance of Russian Railways explain much about Russia's two-speed economy.[65] Where oligarchs and government cronies ran monopolies or built businesses dependent on state procurement contracts, business was inefficient and corrupt. In other sectors, however, business developed along a different track, marked by efficiency gains and productivity growth. One variable that explained whether an industry was dominated by crony capitalism or governed by market principles is the ease with which new entrants to the market could be controlled. Seizing oil firms was relatively easy, at least in the short run, because you could keep pumping existing wells. Expropriating a retail chain was harder, because unless the chain was well managed, other chains would take market share and the value of seized assets would decline.

Because of this, Russia's retail industry, to give one example, operated on very different principles than the crony-capitalist energy sector. To anyone familiar with shopping in the Soviet Union, it comes as no surprise that Russia's retail industry during the 1990s was a mess. Even though Russia had abandoned communism, the process of buying food was still difficult and inefficient. The cancellation of price controls in 1992 guaranteed that, unlike throughout much of the Soviet period, a wide variety of food products was finally available, though at higher prices than consumers were used to. The process of shopping, however, was poorly designed, wasting resources and shoppers' time. In the Soviet period, much food was purchased in stores called *gastronoms*. In size, gastronoms were usually equivalent to what Americans might call a mom-and-pop shop, smaller than a supermarket. The food quality at gastronoms was varied, though employees were not generally known for the care with which they treated your tomatoes. Nor were they known for friendliness.

The biggest problem with gastronoms, however, was the system of selecting and paying for food, which often required interacting with at least three separate employees to select, purchase, and verify food, giving each worker a chance to bruise your bananas. Their inefficiency drove up costs, increasing the number of workers by about one-third compared with other grocery formats, without leading to higher sales or better customer service.[66] The service provided by Soviet gastronoms was so bad that after Russia liberalized and privatized the food retail sector, nearly half of Russian food sales shifted to small outdoor kiosks and agricultural markets. Shockingly, outdoor markets were more efficient at delivering and selling food than Soviet-style stores. It was as if shopping was moving backward in time. Gastronoms' market share fell from 90 percent in 1992 to 40 percent by 1997, with kiosks and outdoor markets gaining market share.[67] Russia's key problem, however, was a lack of supermarkets of the type that dominate food sales in advanced economies. Only 1 percent of Russian food sales in 1997 took place in modern supermarkets, compared to 70 percent in the United States.[68] This was a major reason that the sector's labor productivity was only 23 percent of U.S. levels.[69] For an industry that employed 2.8 million Russians and consumed a major share of Russian household spending, this inefficiency represented a huge waste—and a huge opportunity.[70]

Whoever could unlock the secret to making Russian shopping more efficient had a market ready for disruption. The solution was not complicated. Shifting most of Russian shopping into modern-style supermarkets could nearly triple the industry's productivity levels, one study estimated.[71] Red tape, corruption, and unfair business practices—the average supermarket faced 83 inspections per year in 1997—all presented serious roadblocks to selling food efficiently.[72] But the range of possible improvements was so vast that surely someone would succeed.

The person who played the largest role in remaking Russian shopping chose the most inauspicious year to begin. Sergey Galitsky opened his first grocery store in the southern city of Krasnodar in November 1998, three months after Russia's economy had crashed into a deep recession, as the ruble plummeted and the government defaulted on its debt.[73] Galitsky was not a typical businessman, and Krasnodar was not a typical place to found what would grow to a billion-dollar firm. Galitsky was born in 1967 on the shores of the Black Sea to a family of ethnic Armenians. When he married, he dropped the Armenian-sounding surname of Arutyunyan for that of his ethnic-Russian wife.[74] He studied economics in the Soviet period, but after the end of communism he became what newly capitalist Russia called a *biznesmen*. After borrowing $25,000 and obtaining a license to sell Procter & Gamble products in Russia, Galitsky soon established a thriving retail business. Turning toward groceries was an obvious next step.[75]

Unlike many of Russia's billionaires, Galitsky has no significant political or mafia connections that explain his rapid rise. His business was not the result of Soviet-era connections in the Communist Party, or the result of gangland battles for control of factories or mines. (Though one gang was reported to have fired a rocket at his office in the 1990s.)[76] Nor did business success encourage Galitsky to get involved in politics. He continues to live in provincial Krasnodar, which marks him as eccentric among Russia's Moscow-centric business elite. And he steadfastly refuses to comment on political questions, telling one journalist that "when it comes to politics, I sit down on a sofa and grab some popcorn—or sometimes I crouch down in order not to get shot."[77] The industry he chose is well suited for avoiding politics. Owning a supermarket is an unlikely platform for political success. At the same time, supermarkets are complicated to expropriate, because they take managerial skill to run. Galitsky has stayed out of politics, and politicians have stayed away from him.

Rather than political connections or mafia methods, the core of Galitsky's success is a clever business model, executed with ruthless efficiency. Russian consumers, Galitsky realized, wanted inexpensive groceries and efficient shopping, which the existing mix of stores did not provide. After setting up his first grocery store in 1998, Galitsky expanded his chain, called Magnit (magnet), rapidly, opening his 1,500th store just seven years later. His trick was to standardize and to cut costs; not for nothing is Galitsky compared to Walmart founder Sam Walton.[78] Magnit prospered by focusing not on relatively wealthy consumers in Moscow and St. Petersburg but on typical Russians in cities such as Galitsky's hometown of Krasnodar. Two-thirds of its stores are in cities of less than 500,000 people.[79] Indeed, for a long time, Magnit had no stores in Moscow at all. Having identified a market opening, Galitsky obsessively ensured that Magnit had the most efficient processes and the lowest prices. The firm is known for its well-organized logistics, its effective IT systems, and strong financial control mechanisms.[80] Galitsky enforces these principles personally, forcing executives to take polygraph tests to prove their loyalty.[81]

The results have been tremendous. Galitsky is now a multibillionaire, complete with a private jet and a yacht more than 300 feet long, though he still lives in provincial Krasnodar.[82] His main interest is FC Krasnodar, the local soccer club, which he founded in 2008 and has turned into an unexpected powerhouse.[83] He retains a dominant stake in Magnit, though it has listed shares in London and is part-owned by some of the world's largest investment funds. Magnit was not the only firm to see the opening for supermarkets in Russia's retail sector. X5, a retail firm owned by Russian oligarch Mikhail Fridman, has also grown quickly. Foreign chains such as France's Auchan have also moved into Russia. By 2007, a decade after Galitsky founded Magnit, the food retail sector had become an industry with $230 billion in annual sales, with productivity levels beginning to catch up to international standards—though still with plenty of room for improvement.[84]

The main driver of higher productivity was the shift away from old-style stores to modern supermarkets. Magnit alone opened hundreds of new supermarkets per year throughout the mid-2000s from Murmansk to Vladivostok. Across the Russian food retail sector, modern formats, which constituted just several percent of the market in 1997, made up half of the market by 2010.[85] Thanks to cost-cutting prowess, Magnit and firms like it continue to transform shopping in Russia. What began as a small-town grocer is now one of the world's largest retailers.

## Reforging Stalin's Steel Industry

Besides its name, the steel mill Magnitogorsk has little obvious in common with Magnit, the supermarket chain. The steel business is capital-intensive, dependent on advanced technology, and oriented toward export markets. Yet steel producers such as Magnitogorsk show that it was not only low-tech retailers that boosted productivity in the 2000s. The vast steel industry created by Stalin learned to target export markets and cut costs, achieving rapid profit growth. As in supermarkets, steel was a story of Russian business taking advantage of the newly stable macroeconomic climate while avoiding the worst crony-capitalist influence of the Kremlin. Compared to oil, Russia's steel firms were smaller—so Russia's politicians tended to leave them alone rather than trying to expropriate their assets.

Located in the southern Ural Mountains, not far from the Kazakhstan border, the vast steel mill of Magnitogorsk Metallurgy Kombinat was considered a triumph of Soviet industrialization. The firm was built on the edges of Magnitaya Mountain, so named because it contained a half billion tons of iron ore, enough to move a compass. Small-scale mining began as early as the 1700s, but the city boomed under Stalin, who turned it into a test case of his program of shock industrialization. By 1932, the city's first blast furnace was running, converting the mountain's iron ore into steel that could be shipped across the Soviet Union. During World War II, the company's steel mill made a third of artillery shells and half the tank armor.[86] It is nearly impossible to imagine the Soviet Union without Magnitogorsk, and without Magnitogorsk, it is unlikely that the USSR would have survived the war.

The Magnitogorsk mill was central to the Soviet Union's identity and industrial economy, but it was also exemplary of the problems that Soviet steel—and all heavy industries—faced. On the one hand, output levels were impressive. Steel production kept growing throughout the Soviet period, with production peaking at 163 million metric tons in 1988. That made the USSR the world's largest producer of crude steel.[87] On the other hand, other metrics were far less impressive. Some estimates suggested that half of Soviet steel output was wasted because of poor quality control. When the planned economy was unwound, and the Soviet Union's steel industry lost its guaranteed customers, production plummeted. In the first three years after 1991, Russian steel output fell by over 25 percent, as a significant chunk of the domestic market evaporated.[88] Some Russian steel consumers found they could purchase better quality products abroad, while others, especially in the old enterprises that dominated Soviet heavy industry, found their own output reduced as well.

Even as the steel market was shrinking, tumultuous privatization was upending the industry. By 1993, most of Russia's steel mills were in private hands, though often these were the hands of the Red Directors—the class of Soviet managers who used ostensibly prolabor privatization provisions to grab legal control over the companies they already effectively dominated. Yet the Red Directors did not survive long. Traders, banks, and mafias—often all working together—soon muscled into many of the largest steel conglomerates, using subterfuge and fraud to seize control from previous owners. By the end of the 1990s, most Russian steel mills were run by a new class of owners.[89]

One reason for this struggle for corporate control was that property rights were difficult to protect during the 1990s, given the role of mafia groups and the dissolution of state authority. A second reason, perhaps more important, was the increasingly clear reality that some of Russia's steel mills could quickly become highly profitable if they were managed competently. The key was exports. The Soviet Union exported relatively little steel, but the volume of Russian exports of semifinished and finished steel almost quadrupled between 1992 and 1995.[90] At a time when other industries faced shrinking sales and a collapsing ruble, Russia's steel firms found that they could ship steel abroad and earn dollars in return.

That is not to say that all was well in the Russian steel sector. Some technology lagged the world's best performers. Many mills used open-hearth furnaces that were only a fraction as efficient as international benchmarks.[91] Smaller mills struggled to break even. Russia's larger firms, however, began optimizing their processes and targeting foreign customers. Magnitogorsk was not the best performer on the efficiency front—that accolade goes to Severstal—but the transformation of the Soviet steel behemoth into a capitalist commodities giant exemplifies the changes the entire industry has experienced. In 2006, Magnitogorsk closed its last inefficient open-hearth furnace, transitioning to newer models.[92] It produces the same amount of crude steel today as a decade ago—roughly 12 million tons per year—but with nearly 25 percent fewer employees.[93] In 1999, according to KPMG, its auditor, the firm declared its first profit, making $133 million.[94]

The firm also began investing again. It issued a 100 million euro bond in 2002.[95] And it used increasingly plentiful financing to shift from cost cutting to investing. Between 1997 and 2006, total investments were $2.6 billion. By 2008, the firm invested $2 billion in a single year. Sales boomed, not only to the profitable export market but also to the construction and manufacturing sectors at home. A third of Magnitogorsk's steel was consumed less than 500 kilometers from its factories.[96] Russia's big steel firms performed well in large part because of their cost structure. Raw materials, electricity, and labor are three of the most expensive inputs into steel, and Russia has inexpensive and conveniently located sources of each. Russian steel sector wages are lower than most peers, especially those in advanced economies such as Japan or the United States.[97]

# Understanding Russian Business

In 2005, Vladimir Putin visited New York's Guggenheim Museum, where a Kalashnikov rifle made of glass—and filled with vodka—was on display. It is hard to think of an item that better fits Western stereotypes of modern Russia: showy, violent, and drunk. It apparently attracted Putin's attention, too. According to one journalist, Putin nodded to his bodyguard, who picked up the glass Kalashnikov and walked away with it, to the astonishment of his hosts.[98] One might read this incident, as some journalists have, as evidence of the president's greed, and interpret it as a metaphor for Putin's Russia.[99] There has indeed been greed and theft aplenty in modern Russia, as the gaudy palaces and missile-armed yachts show. Much of this has been related to the president's friends, who have used corrupt contracts with state-owned firms to accumulate fortunes worth billions of dollars. The cost of this corruption is not only the money diverted from better uses, but also the investments that did not occur because potential entrepreneurs feared for the safety of their firms.

But the development of Russian business over the past two decades has followed a logic more complicated than Putin's alleged seizure of the glass Kalashnikov suggests. Here, too, the priorities of Putinomics have determined which industries have succeeded, and why. Government-owned firms are managed with political goals in mind. Most government firms are important sources of revenue or of political patronage. Their bosses know that their key performance metric is not return on equity but political utility. Yet in sectors with less relevance to the political process, market mechanisms have been far more relevant. The retail sector demonstrates that serious productivity improvements have been possible in sectors where growth rather than political control is a priority. At the local and provincial level, as the Kaluga region shows, some governments have found ways to support economic growth without overturning the political consensus, though anticorruption steps at the national level remain impossible, because such moves would limit the tools the Kremlin uses to maintain power.

Magnitogorsk, the steel company, provides a good example of the mixed demands placed on Russian businesses. The steel industry had little relevance to high politics—the sums of money involved, for example, were only a fraction of those available in the energy industry—but steel firms nonetheless had to place social and political stability before profit. Magnitogorsk's ability to improve productivity was limited by implicit prohibitions on firing excess workers. Russian steel firms remained far from optimal productivity, employing too many administrative workers, for example.[100] As late as 2007, Russian steel firms had three times as many employees per ton of steel produced than did American companies.[101] Reaching optimal efficiency levels that year, according to one estimate, would have required firing 140,000 workers.[102]

Mass layoffs were never a realistic option, given social and political pressure to retain high employment levels. Instead, firms reduced headcount by not replacing workers who leave or retire.[103] So long as steel company managers continued to employ excess workers and did not obstruct social stability, they were otherwise left largely free to pursue profit. This is the hierarchy of Putinomics: first, political control; second, social stability; third, efficiency and profit. For the steel industry, low costs and strong world and domestic steel demand created several world-class steel firms. By the mid-2000s, Russia was the fourth-largest net exporter in the world, behind only China, Japan, and Ukraine.[104] In 2007, shares of Magnitogorsk Iron & Steel Works were listed on Moscow's stock exchange. Now any capitalist can buy into the icon of Soviet industry.

# CHAPTER 6

## Wages and Welfare

"Oleg Vladimirovich, did you sign this?" Vladimir Putin asked Oleg Deripaska, once the richest man in Russia, as the television cameras rolled. "I don't see your signature."[1] Deripaska was a quintessential oligarch, married into the family of President Boris Yeltsin, and a survivor of the mafia wars of the 1990s. When Putin demanded a meeting in the summer of 2009, many people thought that Deripaska was about to suffer the same fate as the other oligarchs Putin toppled as he consolidated power. Unlike the other elite businessmen Putin jailed or exiled, Deripaska had not engaged in dissident activities. It was his business—and his labor management practices—that attracted the Kremlin's ire.

Deripaska was the ninth-richest person in the world in 2008, but by the time of his meeting with Putin, the global financial crisis had pummeled his businesses. *Forbes* estimated that the oligarch lost $25 billion between 2008 and 2009, as aluminum prices tanked and the former nuclear physicist struggled to refinance his debts.[2] Many Russian businesses were trying to survive the crisis by slashing costs and cutting output. Three factories in the struggling rust-belt town of Pikalevo, population 22,000, were among the victims.

Pikalevo's three factories—one for cement, one for potash, and the third for alumina—were built in the Soviet era. Each depended on the others for business. Once the first factory closed, the others were doomed. Together, these three plants provided the bulk of the town's jobs, making Pikalevo a *monogorod*, a Russian word for a city precariously dependent on a single Soviet-era industrial cluster. Almost all monogorods dated from the Soviet era, and many teetered on the brink of bankruptcy. When Pikalevo's factories shut down, 4,500 employees—one-fifth of the city's population—were laid off or put on unpaid leave. The three factories owed employees at least 41 million rubles in unpaid wages.[3] As the factories shut, the town spiraled toward crisis. It soon ran up a $4.5 million debt to Gazprom after not paying its gas bill. The town's heating plant was shut down, leaving Pikalevo's residents without hot water.[4]

With no other option, the town's residents took to the streets, blocking a major highway and creating a 250-mile traffic jam.[5] The Kremlin feared that industrial unrest might spread. Putin arranged a visit to Pikalevo to show Russia's working class that he had their struggles in mind. The president compared the businessmen who owned the city's factories to "cockroaches." "Why has your factory been so neglected?" Putin inquired of Deripaska. "They've turned it into a rubbish dump."[6] Putin forced Deripaska to pay the outstanding wages.[7]

As the crisis subsided, Deripaska retained his business empire, avoiding the fate of other oligarchs. But he had tested the limits of Russia's implicit social contract and highlighted the contradictory rules of Russia's labor market. Those rules are opaque, but hugely significant. They structure the relationship not only between employers and employees but also between citizens and the government. Broad-based improvement in living standards was a key source of Putin's legitimacy. It remains the metric by which many Russians judge their government today.

Higher living standards were provided by surprising and contradictory mechanisms. On the one hand, many workers were stuck in dead-end jobs, often in isolated cities. They could form unions, but union bosses were coopted by the government, strikes were relatively rare, and there was little evidence that unions raised wages or improved working conditions. Faced with the threat of accident or unemployment, Russians had only a limited safety net. The quality of public services such as health and education was low. Given demographic and budgetary challenges, there is no guarantee that the hefty social security taxes that workers pay today will guarantee the generous pensions that most Russians expect. If the Soviet Union's promise of a workers' paradise had been a pipe dream, postcommunist Russia did not, from this perspective, look much better.

On the other hand, two powerful forces sustained Russia's social contract through the stresses of the 2008 financial crisis and the 2014–15 oil price slump. The first was low unemployment. Even at the height of the post-Soviet recession, when every company faced pressure to cut headcounts, Russia's unemployment rate was far lower than one might have expected. It decreased further during the boom of the 2000s and has stayed low since. The government has taken special care to avoid unemployment in monogorods such as Pikalevo, where laid-off workers have few options other than protest.

The second factor sustaining Russia's social contract is rapid wage growth. In inflation-adjusted terms, wages have grown in every year but two since Putin took power in 1999. In some years, wages grew by double digits, a level of increase seen only in other booming emerging markets such as China. Higher incomes represented, to most Russians, an end to the chaos and depression of the 1990s. Improving living standards were widely seen as the fruits of a government that guaranteed stability. And this newfound prosperity underwrote a new consumer culture, especially in Moscow and St. Petersburg but in the provinces too, visible in Russians' new taste for sushi and for beach holidays in Sharm el-Sheikh.

The boom in wages, pensions, and living standards undergirded one of Putinomics' three pillars. Higher pay and pensions kept the population satisfied, building up a deep reserve of legitimacy combined with a fear that, if the current government were to leave power, the economic gains over which it presided might be reversed. The drive for higher living standards was not absolute, of course, and there were many instances in which demand for more social spending or greater worker protections were rejected—especially when these aims conflicted with the need to maintain political control. The oligarchs who continued to play a large role in Russia's economy, however, understood the importance of this social contract to the country's leaders. The Kremlin did not hesitate to place pressure on oligarchs when their actions threatened social peace, as did Deripaska's in Pikalevo. But for most of the 2000s, this was an easy balancing act, as rapid economic growth meant that the challenge of politics was distributing a rapidly growing pie.

### Russia's Labor Market Puzzle

Low unemployment undergirded the government's popularity, but the policy had skeptics in high places. Perhaps the most surprising opponent of low unemployment was Prime Minister Dmitry Medvedev. Unlike his peers in other countries—whose fate depends on ensuring everyone has a job—Medvedev repeatedly argued in favor of higher unemployment in Russia. "We have to avoid the policy of retaining population employment at all costs," he urged in 2013. "It is obvious that someone—and this may include a considerable number of citizens—maybe have to change their jobs, and even their profession and place of residence, but it has to be done. This is the way we are going to develop."[8]

Medvedev was right about the need for more labor mobility. Even today, Russia suffers from the distortions of the Soviet period, with hundreds of thousands of people stuck in towns that offer no real hope of economic sustainability.[9] Low unemployment in monogorods permits people to stay in jobs that serve no useful purpose, and in cities that offer no hope of growth. This is expensive for the economy—because resources and workers are used inefficiently—and costly, because the government must pay for subsidies. From the perspective of economic growth, it would be better to encourage people out of monogorods and inefficient jobs and toward new cities and new work. But if such a policy moves too rapidly, it becomes socially disruptive and politically untenable—as the protests in Pikalevo showed.

Because of this, Russia developed a system for managing industrial decline based on keeping unemployment low. Unexpectedly low unemployment has been a puzzle since the early days of post-Soviet Russia. Between 1991 and 1998, for example, official measures of GDP showed production falling by around 40 percent, but employment declined by less than 15 percent.[10] Russia's share of the population with a job has been consistently above most other postsocialist countries.[11] Nearly everywhere else in the postsocialist world, industrial restructuring was accompanied by mass layoffs. Why did Russia not experience the same?

Several explanations can be ruled out. Labor unions did not play a key role in deterring layoffs. In many Western European countries, for example, unions block job cuts. As the Soviet Union collapsed, several big strikes, including by coal miners, led some analysts to predict a larger role for labor in post-Soviet Russia, but this did not materialize. Russian workers had many reasons to complain, especially during the 1990s. But they did not do so in an organized fashion. The number of strikes in Russia is lower than in comparable countries. One reason is labor legislation, which places tough limits on who can strike, and under what circumstances.[12] Because of this, many strike activities take place outside of what is legally allowed, such as the Pikalevo workers' decisions to block a highway.[13] A second reason, some analysts argue, is that the main Russian labor union, the Federation of Independent Trade Unions of Russia (FNPR), is close to the government and is intended "to manage workers rather than represent them."[14] A third reason that unions did not play a larger role during the 2000s is that rapid wage growth made unions seem irrelevant to many workers.[15]

Nor is it the case that Russia's labor markets are so efficient that market forces keep employment high. It is true that Russia lacks some measures that many economists think restrict employment in other countries. For example, some evidence suggests that high minimum wages may reduce employment by preventing companies from offering sufficiently low wages to low-skilled workers. Russia's minimum wage, however, has been so low that it rarely factors into businesses' hiring decisions. For most of the 2000s, for example, the legal minimum wage was less than 10 percent of the average wage.[16] Similarly, many economists think that generous unemployment benefits can discourage workers from finding jobs.[17] In Russia, however, unemployment payouts have been low, less than 15 percent of the average wage for most of the 2000s.[18] This, too, means that people are unlikely to be dissuaded from working by the availability of benefits.

Yet by other measures, Russia's labor market is far less flexible than it seems. Though workers move between jobs with reasonable frequency, they move between regions far less often.[19] There are several reasons why. A poorly developed mortgage market coupled with high levels of homeownership makes moving expensive. Administrative barriers to moving add further cost.[20] Whatever the cause, the result of low regional labor mobility is that too many workers remain stuck in regions with far lower labor productivity than the best performing parts of Russia. That means that workers earn lower wages than they might, and the government must bear the burden of subsidizing some of the difference.

As economies change over time, nearly every country faces the challenge of moving people from areas with low productivity to regions where they are more likely to thrive. In the United States, for example, the population of some rust belt cities has declined for decades as manufacturers use less labor. Workers have moved to faster-growing regions such as the South and West, in search of plentiful work. In the United States, such movements took place over decades, though they were still highly disruptive, especially in rust belt cities such as Detroit, which suffered a tremendous exodus. Russia's challenge is greater, because Soviet rigidity meant that there was almost no adjustment until 1991.

The monogorods—cities like Pikalevo, which depend on one industry—were the greatest problem. Firms in such towns generate less revenue per employee, are less profitable, and are more indebted than Russian companies as a whole.[21] Firms in monogorods employ more people than is economically efficient, because their owners face pressure to avoid layoffs, even for employees who play no productive role.[22] *Vedomosti*, the leading Russian business newspaper, has argued that government pressure "encourages the preservation of excess employment under the guise of 'social responsibility.'" The result of this, *Vedomosti* argues, is that "employment problems are solved with a stroke of the prime minister's pen or a phone call from a governor," a policy that "enables the state to maintain a surplus labor force and support social stability at the expense of business."[23] There is little doubt that businesses face such pressure, as Oleg Deripaska's experience in Pikalevo showed. The benefit is low unemployment. The cost is to keep people in dead-end Siberian jobs, with little hope of wage growth.

How has Russian business reacted to social and political demands for high employment and no layoffs? There are three main tactics. First, when the economy slows and businesses face pressure to trim budgets, businesses reduce labor costs not by laying off employees but by delaying wage payments. This strategy was common during the late 1990s and during the 2008–9 crisis, when the number of workers whose wages were delayed jumped from fewer than 1 million to more than 2 million.[24] This tactic is becoming less popular over time, however. The 2009 peak of wage arrears was significantly lower than the peak of the late 1990s.

Instead, businesses now rely on other tools to keep work arrangements flexible and to reduce labor costs when the economy slows. One common tactic is to rely on Russia's inflation rate to degrade the real value of pay. For example, during 2015, when the devaluation of the ruble caused inflation to hit 12.9 percent, businesses let higher prices cut wages for them. Employers kept wages roughly static in nominal terms, causing a 9.5 percent decline in wages after adjusting for the reduced purchasing power of the ruble.

A second technique use to keep labor costs flexible is to compensate employees using variable pay. Often workers are involuntarily shifted to three- or four-day workweeks during downturns, which provide only partial paychecks. Even when employees are working full time, pay is often surprisingly variable. Unlike in advanced economies, where most workers' bonuses or performance pay constitutes a small share of overall salary, many Russians make half of their income in supplementary payments. In 2005, for example, such variable payments constituted 58 percent of compensation in the oil and gas sector and 52 percent in the metallurgy industry. The high proportion of variable pay makes sense in businesses dependent on volatile commodity prices. But variable pay was also important in the food industry (36 percent of pay) and even the health care sector (35 percent).[25] Variable payments such as these provided flexibility for businesses, which could trim costs by a third without layoffs or having to renegotiate contracts. Because of this, the rise in unemployment in 2008 and 2015 was less than what it might have been.

## Reforming the Soviet Safety Net

Russia did not inherit from the Soviet Union what we would call a "welfare state." The system of retirement security, subsidized health care, education, antipoverty programs, and disability benefits that governments in advanced economies provide to their citizens was only partially developed in the USSR. Rather than the government providing such social programs, the Soviet state relied on enterprises—from car factories to food processing facilities—to ensure that their employees were well provided for. In a system in which enterprises were fully owned by the government, the distinction between state provision and company provision might seem irrelevant. In the post-communist period, however, companies' role in welfare provision shaped the development of Russia's social programs. Unlike under communism, independent Russia encouraged loss-making firms to declare bankruptcy and shut down. This was a sensible policy in terms of shifting resources away from wasteful uses—of which there were many in the Soviet period—toward productive purposes. The ability to allocate resources efficiently was one of the main reasons Russia adopted a market economy.

In addition to decreasing waste, however, bankruptcies threatened the social contract that had underpinned Soviet labor. Individual firms provided services from kindergartens to subsidized food. When firms shut down, so too did the kindergartens, which lacked resources to survive on their own. Governments were unprepared to fill the gap—and the persistent budget deficits of the 1990s left little money to fund new social programs.

Russia also inherited from the Soviet Union a wide array of in-kind benefits to various groups. Most of these in-kind benefits were structured as discounts on services, from cheaper electricity for veterans to free train tickets for police. These benefits did not appear as a cost on the government budget, though the price in terms of lost revenue was real. In the early 2000s, as Russia's improving financial position let government officials think about restructuring the social support system, replacing these in-kind benefits with a safety net of the type that most advanced economies used was high on the to-do list.

The idea of scrapping in-kind benefits was sensible. The benefits were targeted toward three main groups: the disadvantaged ("orphans, the disabled and the elderly without pensions"); certain types of workers (veterans, laborers in dangerous industries); and government employees. Most governments provide benefits to the first group, and to a certain extent to the second. For the third group—government employees—in-kind benefits functioned as a disguised pay raise.[26]

Within these three broad categories of recipient, however, were dozens of variations. Over 230 categories of people were eligible for at least one benefit, and over 150 types of benefits were offered.[27] Half of households included a member with at least one such privilege.[28] A study by the World Bank estimated that the total cost of these discounts and benefits constituted 4.2 percent of GDP, about what Russia's government spends on education.[29] The system was vast but wasteful. For one thing, it was ineffective at helping the poor. Many well-off families received benefits, but many who were poor did not. In the early 2000s, 90 percent of social spending was not targeted based on income.[30] Poverty alone was not a guarantee of many benefits, which depended on falling into the right category. Because of this, one study found, "only 8% of this spending reaches the poorest 20% of the population."[31]

The system had other biases. It benefited urban citizens at the expense of rural ones. Some beneficiaries received public transport discounts that were irrelevant because they lived in small towns without subways or bus systems. Those who were not healthy enough to access services found that the "benefits" they received were useless. Up to 40 percent of people in certain categories of recipient did not use the benefits to which they were entitled.[32] Those who used too much of a service gained the most benefit. Subsidized energy, for example, benefited the wasteful the most.

Despite these inequalities within the system, surely there were good reasons behind the 230 categories and 150 benefits on offer? Hardly. World War II veterans received discounts on their telephone fees but had to pay for phone installation. Victims of communist-era political repression, by contrast, were granted free telephone installation but had to pay full monthly service fees. The reason why veterans and communist repression victims were receiving discounted telephones rather than, say, discounted tomatoes was not clear. The desire to help those who had suffered was noble, but the system made no sense.[33]

Many Russian leaders—including the president—had long advocated scrapping benefits and raising salaries, pensions, and other cash payouts in response. "Wouldn't it be better to raise the salaries?" Putin asked. "If you gave them just a little bit more money, they could pay their own fares and wouldn't be put in such a humiliating position. . . . I'm sure the leftist opposition will jump on me, saying that people are losing their benefits and that this is a blow against the helpless working people, who already have it so hard. But a government that doesn't fulfill its obligations is not a government. And that's why there's such a lack of trust in the government now."[34]

The optimal solution, the government decided, was a system of cash pay-

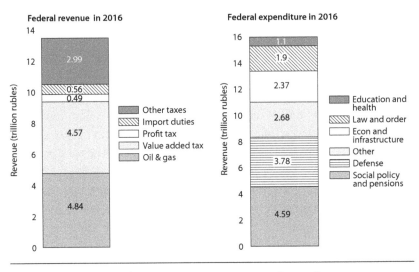

**FIGURE 8** Russian government revenue and expenditure, 2016 (trillion rubles). Ministry of Finance.

ments to the needy that could replace the web of cheap train tickets and discounted telephone installation. The proposal—known as the "monetization of benefits," since it replaced in-kind benefits with a money payment—was intended as an important step in the creation of a modern system of social support. Implementation, however, provided further evidence of the difficulty of modernizing the Russian state. The initial round of reform split benefits between the federal and regional levels. At the federal level, some changes were mandatory, while citizens could opt in to others. Much of the responsibility, however, was turned over to regional governments.

Regional leaders, however, were far from prepared for the new responsibility. They had no systematic register of who was eligible, so the conversion to cash benefits was chaotic.[35] This made it difficult to target payments to the poor. At the same time, regional governments had little incentive to innovate. President Putin had recently canceled elections for regional leaders, so they were now responsible not to their citizens but to the Kremlin. Yet the federal government had a long history of legislating new benefits and forcing the regions to fund them—so regional leaders were skeptical of new federal initiatives.[36]

As soon as the changes began, perhaps hundreds of thousands of Russians took to the streets in a grassroots protest—the first significant protest of Putin's presidency.[37] The unhappiness was understandable. Both the federal and regional governments failed to explain the changes underway. Polls in early 2005 showed that at least 44 percent of people were unaware of the compensation they should receive in lieu of in-kind benefits. The reforms also occurred simultaneously with unrelated hikes of utility tariffs—which many people angrily presumed were connected.[38] Some of the protesters' concerns were legitimate, especially as regional governments used the reform not only to shift payment from in-kind benefits to cash but also to cut the total cost.[39] Many regional governments opted to slow down the change. But the federal government was not deterred, pushing through the changes it wanted, remaking the Soviet system of social support into something more efficient—even if that was not what many vocal citizens appeared to want.[40] Yet the Kremlin also learned a lesson: benefit cuts, like tax hikes, risked bringing average Russians into the streets. This encouraged the Kremlin to take a cautious approach to future benefit changes, most notably by declining to cut pensions.

### Pensions and Politics

In the West, Vladimir Putin is widely known for his Soviet nostalgia. The collapse of the Soviet Union, he famously declared, was the "greatest geopolitical catastrophe" of the twentieth century."[41] Wars in Ukraine and Georgia and military bases in Moldova, Tajikistan, and Armenia demonstrate the government's desire to retain what it can of the USSR's regional predominance. Russia brought back the music of the Soviet national anthem in 2000.[42] And a plurality of Russians now believe that Stalin's rule brought more good than bad, according to polls.[43]

In 2012, however, Putin argued that the greatest achievement of the Soviet state was neither its military preeminence nor its geopolitical stature. It was something more mundane, but no less complicated: old-age pensions. "Pension guarantees are probably the biggest achievement and the biggest problem for our country," President Putin mused that year.[44] Few issues have caused such debate—and such indecision—in Russian government circles. The reason is that few policies have been so crucial in forging Putin's political coalition. The rationale behind Putin's claim that pensions were the greatest achievement of the Soviet Union is straightforward. Government-provided pensions are the main source of income for most older Russians. One recent survey found that 93 percent of retirees say that they currently live off their pension. Only 5 percent reported having income from assets to support them in retirement, while 14 percent reported some work income.[45]

Also straightforward is why pensions represent, in the president's view, the "biggest problem for our country." Like nearly every country in Europe, Russia faces a wave of retirements, as the current generation leaves the workforce and is replaced by a generation of much smaller size. Experts debate the extent of Russia's demographic challenge, but there is little doubt that Russia faces a shrinking workforce, in which many retirees are not replaced.[46] Much of Russia's population growth comes from regions such as the North Caucasus, where education and skill levels are lower. Immigration from Central Asia and the countries of the South Caucasus will also counteract some of the aging of Russian society, but these immigrants are also generally low-skilled and poorly educated. The result, as in many other countries, is that Russia's pension bill will grow even as the number of workers contributing to the pension fund decreases.[47]

In one sense, aging is a relatively good problem for the Russian pension system to have. Only fifteen years ago, its challenges were far more severe. During the 1990s the pension system struggled to collect pension contributions due to the collapse of the tax system. In 1998, which was probably the worst year, the country's pension fund at one point was spending 16 billion rubles per month while collecting only 11.5 billion in contributions.[48] With a financial position like this, the fund often failed to pay pensions on time—or at all. In October 1998, total pension arrears were estimated at 30.5 billion rubles.[49]

For retired Russians, the near-collapse of the pension system was a disaster. No surprise, then, that they voted in droves for the Communist Party.[50] Many blamed Yeltsin (unfairly) for causing the pension problem or (legitimately) for lacking a strategy to resolve it. Many more people associated the Communists with high and stable pensions, since they introduced pensions when their party ran the Soviet state. Older voters' support for the Communists represented a persistent problem for Yeltsin—and a challenge for his successor.

When Putin took power in 1999, the previous year's financial crash had helped the government pay pensions, but between the mid-1998 and 1999, inflation reduced the real value of pensions by nearly half.[51] This made it easier to convince firms to hand over the contributions they owed, helping the fund reach a stable financial position. Putin, too, took a more active interest in the fund's operation, ordering it to pay all the money it owed the country's long-suffering pensioners—something that was easier now that the real value of pension payouts was, thanks to inflation, much reduced.[52]

Putin likely believes that Russia has a financial obligation to the country's elderly. He also clearly understands that pensions are crucial to his legitimacy—and to his political survival. Before parliamentary elections in late 1999, he decreed a 15 percent pension hike, and his party performed better than expected. In February 2000, a month before the presidential election, he raised pensions by an additional 20 percent and won more votes from pensioners than did the Communist Party's candidate, Gennady Zyuganov.[53] Since then, pensioners have played a pivotal role in the political coalitions underpinning Putin's rule. The relative importance in these coalitions of the middle class and industrial working classes has shifted over time. Pensioners have remained Putin loyalists.

From the beginning of his presidency, however, Putin's reliance on pensioner support has created a dilemma. The government's tax collection abilities have improved since the 1990s, but the demographic challenges to the pension system remained daunting. Some important voices in government economic circles advocated drastic changes. Chile's pension reform, which replaced government-administered pensions with private retirement accounts, was cited as a model. The proposal made some sense, as Chile was also a middle-income country that depended on copper exports much as Russia did on oil. Andrei Illarionov, the free-market economist who was then Putin's personal economic adviser, invited José Piñera, the architect of Chile's pension system, to visit Moscow in April 2000. Piñera urged the Russian government to "follow the principles applied in Chile: workers should be allowed to place their retirement savings in their own accounts to be privately managed by competing firms, which would invest that money in capital markets over the working lifetimes of their clients." Such a system, he predicted, would be "wildly popular" in Russia.[54]

Most postcommunist countries decided to include private investment as part of their reformed pensions systems.[55] When Russia's government began consultations about reforming its pension system, it naturally considered the experience of its neighbors. When the new pension plan was launched in 2001, it included three parts: a minimum payment for all Russians, an additional payment based on the amount paid in, and a third portion allotted for personal investments.[56]

The plan was intended—at least by some of its supporters—to be more fiscally sustainable than the Soviet-style system that independent Russia inherited. Yet though the new system looked different, the political forces driving pension decision making were unchanged. Key to securing passage of the 2001 pension reform was an increase in the minimum pension, as well as the pension hikes of 1999 and 2000.[57] The population associated the 2001 pension reform not with personal control or fiscal sustainability but with

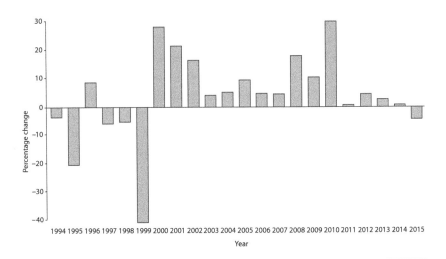

**FIGURE 9**  Russian government pensions, percentage change
per year, inflation-adjusted, 1994–2015. Rosstat.

higher payouts. And in the same year that the Duma passed the 2001 pension reform, it also passed a variety of pension hikes for individual groups, such as residents of the Far North—the exact type of pension handout that the new reform sought to avoid.[58]

Most significant, the power to determine how much to adjust pensions to account for each year's inflation rate remained in the hands of the government. It was a powerful political tool, which the government did not hesitate to use when it felt its popularity slipping. Yet the temptation to increase pensions above inflation without gathering additional revenue added to the risk that the post-2001 pension system might be no more fiscally stable than the old one. Indeed, pension payouts grew steadily throughout the 2000s. After adjusting for inflation, the average pension more than doubled between 2000 and 2009.[59]

The 2008–9 economic crisis sparked a new round of pension debates. For one thing, the demographics were only slightly better than some of the worst-case predictions from a decade earlier. One report found that the number of pensioners would equal the number of workers around 2030.[60] At the same time, many of the individually controlled pensions, which were expected to provide higher returns, performed poorly. VEB, the bank where 84 percent of people kept their pension accounts, averaged a 5.7 percent return on pension investments between 2002 and 2010, compared with an inflation rate that hovered around 10 percent. By 2012, the pension fund had a deficit of nearly

2 percent of GDP, which had to be filled by tax revenue.[61] Since the government's tax take struggled to reach 20 percent of GDP during good years, this represented a significant burden on the budget.

There were two competing proposals for filling the pension gap. The "social bloc" of the government—the bureaucrats responsible for ensuring social stability—advocated scrapping the personal investment accounts and using the funds to pay today's pensions. Such an approach meant spending Russia's savings today, since the government would be responsible for paying pensions upon retirement to people who had personal accounts. The alternative approach, backed by Finance Minister Alexei Kudrin, was to cut benefits and raise the retirement age, balancing the pension system by reducing payouts.[62]

The politics of pensions made the winner of this debate obvious. Beginning in 2013, the government chose to confiscate the individual accounts and to apply these funds to current pension spending. That widened the long-run deficit but made it possible to pay today's pensions without cutting benefits or raising taxes. Retirement age hikes are still likely in the medium term, but the government will postpone them as long as possible. In theory, the decision to use individual pension accounts to fund current payouts is a temporary decision, but it looks unlikely to be reversed. Already the government spends several trillion rubles per year filling the gap between the pension fund's income and revenue.[63]

No one knows how to fund the pensions that people who previously had individual accounts still expect will be paid out when they retire. "Nobody is going to refund that money, because it went to Crimea, to anti-crisis measures," Finance Minister Anton Siluanov fumed in 2014. The revenue ostensibly allotted for funding the individual accounts "will, in all probability, go toward socioeconomic development programs in Crimea and Sevastopol."[64] Russia has continued to allocate the funds that were supposed to be devoted to long-term individual pension savings to immediate spending instead.[65] This adds to Russia's long-term pension deficit but resolves the immediate demand of Russia's political system: do not alienate the pensioners.

### The Social Contract

Thanks to a booming economy and relatively tight labor markets the first fifteen years of the twenty-first century produced the best economy Russians have ever known. Russia's wealth distribution remained extraordinarily unequal, but the improvement in living standards of the early 2000s was

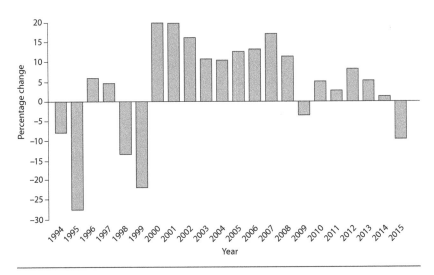

**FIGURE 10**  Russian wage growth, percentage change per
year, inflation-adjusted, 1994–2015. Rosstat.

broad-based. A rising tide combined with huge pension hikes lifted all boats. Russians remained unhappy with the role that personal connections played in business, and by the huge profits earned by corporate titans whose firms grew thanks to corruption rather than innovation. But whatever their complaints, very few people of any income level would have traded the Russia of 2007 for the Russia of 1997.

The economic growth of the early 2000s let Putin's government forge a new social contract that has proven surprisingly durable—persisting through economic crashes, recessions, and protest movements. What was this social contract based on? Did it change over time? And how durable was it? The foundation of the social contract in Putin's Russia was rapidly growing real wages coupled with aggressive pension hikes. Beyond establishing a stable economic framework—no small feat given the deficits and inflation of the 1990s—Russia's government was not itself responsible for the large increase in real wages. Economic expansion sparked by rising commodity prices and improving productivity underwrote wage growth. Higher economic growth also provided the resources with which to fund higher pensions, ensuring that the fruits of growth were shared relatively broadly.

For the first decade of the new century, this social contract—high wages coupled with high pensions—was a recipe for political stability. So long as nearly everyone was getting wealthier at rapid rates, most people were willing to ignore the government's other shortcomings. The brouhaha over the mon-

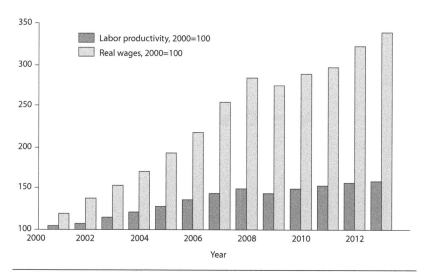

FIGURE 11 Russian wage growth vs. labor productivity growth, 2000–2012 (rebased so that 2000=100). Rosstat.

etization of welfare benefits, for example, was quickly forgotten as pension payouts continued to increase. Corruption in the government was unfortunate but excusable, many Russians concluded, so long as wages were rising so rapidly. And the Kremlin's moves to degrade the country's democratic institutions were ignored.

Two dilemmas hung over this new social contract. One question was whether all constituents would continue to support it. The second was whether the economic boom that underlay it would persist—and if not, what the political ramifications would be. It was no secret, for example, that high commodity prices explained a significant portion of the boom. Real wages rose significantly faster than labor productivity, underwritten by unexpectedly high oil prices.

There was no guarantee that commodity prices would stay high. The oil-price decline of the mid-1980s had contributed to the Soviet collapse. Even if commodity prices fell, however, higher productivity levels meant that Russia would remain far wealthier than during the 1990s. And there was no reason to think that Russia could not continue to improve productivity simply by importing technology and production practices from more developed countries, behind which it continued to lag. But a shift from high to low oil prices would bring unexpected consequences, threatening the political coalition that Putin's social and economic policies had brought together.

# CHAPTER 7

## From Crisis to Crisis

Russia never had a period with as benign an external environment as the early years of the twenty-first century. Commodity prices grew steadily. Foreigners lent large sums to Russian firms. The country felt sufficiently secure to let its military decline. Its neighbors sought to integrate rather than isolate Russia. Much of this external environment was of Russia's making. Moscow's generally friendly relations with neighbors in the early 2000s—especially in comparison with its relations in most of the twentieth century—were the fruits of Gorbachev's and Yeltsin's desire to improve ties with the countries of Eastern Europe. The post–Cold War "peace dividend," much discussed in the United States, was far more important to Russia. Foreign investment flowed in, thanks in part to responsible policy making, including better governance compared with the 1990s.

The year 2008 marked the end of this honeymoon. In both politics and economics, Russia's foreign links became much more complicated, deterring rather than promoting growth. As foreign policy became tenser, the first principle of Putinomics—preserving state power and authority—began to obstruct the pursuit of economic growth. The double shock of war and recession transformed Putinomics, as the government shifted toward more cautious, conservative policy making. This agenda that saw the country through the 2008 crash preserved Putin's political system and rebuilt Russian military power. These were the priorities, and Putinomics achieved them. The cost, however, was to ignore other, less immediate priorities. Efficiency was sacrificed, the private sector was squeezed, and investments were deferred. Putinomics saw Russia through the crisis, but it failed to lay the groundwork for a return to growth.

## Foreign Tensions Rise

When Vladimir Putin traveled to Beijing in August 2008 to celebrate China's first Olympic Games, it is unlikely that he had war on his mind. The Beijing Olympics were widely seen as a coming-out party for China, evidence that the Western powers could no longer write the rules of global order alone. Now the BRICS—Brazil, Russia, India, China, and South Africa—were rising. America, the global hegemon, was mired in Middle Eastern wars and was slipping toward a financial crisis. The U.S. investment bank Bear Stearns had gone bust in March 2008, and Lehman Brothers, whose collapse in September would freeze U.S. financial markets and push the country and the world into recession, was just weeks away. A country as integrated into the global financial system as Russia was not immune to such shocks. Visiting Beijing, however, Putin had reason to think that history was on his side.

If the collapse of the Soviet Union had proven that economic decline makes geopolitical retrenchment inevitable, Putin intended to show that the reverse was also true. Russia's rising wealth should, he believed, be reflected in the country's geopolitical standing. During the early years of Putin's presidency, the main security question was Chechnya, where a violent insurgency and brutal counterinsurgency had destroyed the province and facilitated the rise of jihadist terrorists. The U.S. War on Terror after the 2001 attacks in New York and Washington, D.C., therefore corresponded with the Kremlin's own foreign policy goals.

By the mid-2000s, however, Russian leaders had come to see increasing contradictions between their aims and the policies of their Western neighbors. The West supported prodemocracy and anticorruption efforts in countries such as Georgia and Ukraine (as well as in Russia), countries that the Kremlin considered part of its sphere of influence. At times, the West supported groups who took to the streets to pressure their governments, funding investigative journalists, for example, and training civil society activists. In 2003, an American-educated lawyer, Mikheil Saakashvili, led protests that toppled Georgia's decrepit president Eduard Shevardnadze, who had governed Georgia since the Soviet period. The following year, Western-backed protests against a fraudulent presidential election forced Ukraine's authorities to allow a new, fairer vote, which brought to power Viktor Yushchenko, a Western-leaning politician with an American wife.

These protest movements were cheered in the West but were primarily driven by locals fed up with corruption and stagnation. In the Kremlin, however, Georgia's 2003 Rose Revolution and Ukraine's 2004 Orange Revolution

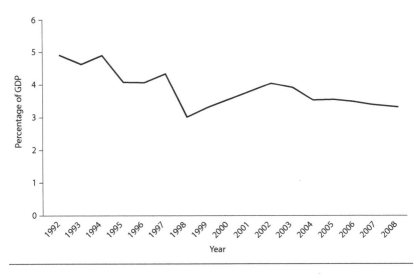

**FIGURE 12**  Russian military spending as percentage of GDP,
1992–2008. SIPRI Military Spending Database.

were seen as CIA plots to install pro-Western regimes on Russia's doorstep. In the mid-2000s, the Kremlin began mobilizing to prevent "color revolutions"—popular, antiregime street protests—from spreading to Moscow, funding a variety of progovernment and reactionary groups and investing in the military.[1]

Though Putin saw restoring Russia's geopolitical stature as a key goal, this was not initially envisioned as a primarily military task. Russian military spending as a share of GDP fell for most of his first two terms as president.[2] Of course, given the rapid rise in Russia's GDP during those years, defense spending was growing at a decent clip. But it was evidently not a priority. One reason is that the military phase of Putin's effort to pacify Chechnya was mostly complete by 2000. Russia's armed forces accomplished the goals Putin set in Chechnya, effectively if not necessarily efficiently, and after 2000 the counterinsurgency was mostly outsourced to police, intelligence, and—most important—pro-Kremlin Chechen forces loyal to the Kadyrov family, which rules the province as a personal fiefdom to this day. In the Kremlin's view, the military did its job in Chechnya with existing resources. So why give it more?

An additional factor limiting military spending during the 2000s was widespread agreement that the defense sector was a swamp of corruption and inefficiency. In every country, defense contractors are more wasteful, and military procurement deals more fraudulent, than the other sectors of the economy, for two reasons. First, there is little real competition, because most countries only buy enough submarines to support a single submarine shipyard. Second, because security is at stake, governments rarely cancel projects, even if they are accompanied by wild cost overruns. The current U.S. F-35 fighter, for example, will cost 50 percent more than initial expectations, but Washington has concluded it has little choice but to buy the planes, pricey though they may be.[3] Given the cost overruns in American defense contracting, where firms must at least issue financial information to shareholders and where contracts can be audited, one can imagine the scale of waste in Russia's defense industry.[4] Seeing defense reform as hopeless, the Kremlin focused elsewhere.

That changed in 2008. As Putin joined other world leaders in Beijing to watch the opening of the Olympics, a conflict was brewing on Russia's southern border. Russian forces had been stationed in South Ossetia—a small territory in northern Georgia—since a civil war in the early 1990s between the Georgian government and the province's ethnic Ossetians. The Kremlin described its forces in the territory as peacekeepers, and they did indeed enforce a tenuous peace. They also ensured that Russia retained a powerful tool with which to shape Georgian politics. When Georgia's 2003 Rose Revolution brought to power Mikheil Saakashvili, a harsh critic of Russia, tensions grew. Georgian and Russian forces clashed as world leaders watched the Olympic opening ceremonies in Beijing. Soon, Russian planes were bombing Tbilisi, Georgia's capital, while Russian troops occupied several key Georgian cities. A week later, satisfied that it had taught Saakashvili a lesson, the Kremlin called off its assault. The war looked like a dramatic Russian victory. Saakashvili remained in power, but the Kremlin proved it could oust him if it wanted. True, the United States and other Western powers criticized Russia's actions—but many European leaders criticized Saakashvili, too, for helping to provoke the conflict. And the West did nothing to stop Russia.[5]

In Moscow, however, the war was interpreted rather differently. Yes, it represented a strategic success for the Kremlin. But the conflict also highlighted huge problems in the Russian military. Georgia—a country with 4 million people, compared to Russia's 143 million—had put up a spirited defense. Russia's army moved too slowly, its air force was poorly coordinated with ground troops, and the navy barely contributed at all, despite Georgia's location on the shores of the Black Sea.[6] Decades of low investment and mismanagement had created a military incapable of modern warfighting.

After the war ended, Putin sprang into action. Anatoly Serdyukov, Russia's recently appointed minister of defense, launched a military reform. He fired 160,000 officers to streamline the force structure, cut the length of obligatory military service, and demanded efficiency from defense contractors.[7]

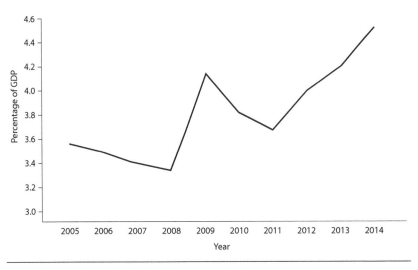

**FIGURE 13** Russian military spending as percentage of GDP, 2005–2014. SIPRI Military Spending Database.

In exchange, the government's armament program promised sizeable spending hikes. Military procurement doubled as a share of GDP, from around 1 percent of GDP in 2012 to 2 percent of GDP by 2014.[8] Over the decade to 2020, the government announced, it would spend 20 trillion rubles—over $300 billion dollars—to modernize 70 percent of Russia's weapons.[9] Overall military spending as a share of GDP increased from 3.1 percent in 2012 to 4.3 percent by 2015.[10]

## From Riches to Ruins

The war with Georgia shocked Russia's neighbors, though Western leaders declined to cut off economic ties with Russia in response. Yet the problems brewing in Western financial markets would soon cause Russia more pain than any sanctions. As 2008 began, however, Russia moved from strength to strength. In the final quarter of 2007, the Russian economy posted its fastest level of GDP growth—9.5 percent—in nearly a decade.[11] The boom was driven by oil prices, which surged ever higher, seemingly without limit. At the global level, some analysts worried about the future, especially given troubling news from the U.S. mortgage market. But many investors concluded that America's financial market wobbles were good news for commodity prices, since this would push the U.S. Federal Reserve to lower interest rates. The U.S. federal funds rate was decreased from 5.25 percent in August 2007 to only 2 percent in April 2008. This helped push commodity prices higher by bolstering demand.[12]

Combined with strong Asian oil consumption and worries about stability in the oil-rich Middle East, the price of oil marched ever higher. Oil started the year around $100 per barrel before surging to $120 by May and peaking above $140 in July. Russia's government was one of the greatest beneficiaries, as its export tax on oil was linked to world prices. Russia's export duty thus increased from $275.40 to $333.80 per ton of oil, a new record.[13] Russia's treasury received an additional 220 billion rubles in the first quarter of the year—nearly $100 billion.[14] Russia's leading business newspaper, *Vedomosti*, reported that oil prices would end the year with a higher average price than in 2007, barring a sharp fall in price. But this was "unlikely," *Vedomosti* predicted, because "demand will not fall sharply, and production will not noticeably increase."[15]

Thanks to high commodity prices, other parts of the Russian economy were booming, too. Russian car companies sold 38,500 more cars than the previous year, an increase of 6.3 percent.[16] Industrial production was growing at a rate of 6.4 percent per year.[17] One research institute even predicted that Russia was on the cusp of a new wave of import substitution, as the increasing efficiency of domestic production in spheres such as food processing and transportation infrastructure meant that firms producing in Russia were edging out foreign rivals.[18]

Positive economic data meant that, despite worrisome news from New York, Russian firms continued to find foreigners willing to lend at low interest rates. Indeed, problems in U.S. credit markets initially supported Russian external borrowing in the early months of 2008, because the Federal Reserve responded by pushing down interest rates, making Russian assets relatively more attractive. Capital continued gushing into Russia. By the beginning of 2008, Russian banks and nonfinancial corporations had borrowed a total of $317 billion from abroad. Banks alone accounted for $102 billion—nearly double the figure just two years earlier.[19] Indeed, Russia's central bank worried that the inflow of capital was driving up inflation, which reached 2.31 percent in monthly terms in January 2008.[20] The central bank and the Finance Ministry blamed state-owned companies for excessive borrowing, which drove up inflation.[21] There was no way, the bank feared, to keep inflation under control given the economy's seemingly unstoppable growth.[22]

From the beginning of the year, some analysts feared that the problems brewing in U.S. financial markets might spread to Russia. The combination of financial chaos in the world's largest economy and booming oil prices did not make sense. Given the risk of a U.S. recession, oil prices should have

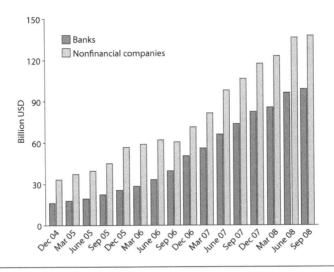

**FIGURE 14** External (foreign) lending to Russian banks and corporations, 2004–2008 (billion U.S. dollars). Bank of Russia.

been falling, not rising. Indeed, investors in Russia's financial markets seemed unsure how to interpret these signals. The country's MICEX stock index hit a peak in late 2007, then slumped by over 10 percent in January 2008, before regaining its high after a feverish 10 percent jump in May.[23]

The stock market, as jittery as ever, staggered around its May peak for two months. In July, it fell off a cliff, dragged down by oil prices, which in July began descending as rapidly as they had risen in the first half of the year. The oil market swung wildly, ending July nearly $20 below its peak. This marked the beginning of a long plunge into an abyss. In August, oil lost around $10. In September, it dropped nearly $15 more. October, the worst month, saw oil fall by over $30. November, it was down over $10 more. Finally, in the depths of the Russian winter, oil prices hit bottom, at under $35, a quarter of the price five months earlier.[24]

The oil price collapse dragged everything down with it. By December, the Moscow stock market was at a third of its peak. The economy was contracting faster than at any point since 1998. Retail sales crashed in late 2008 and early 2009. Industrial production soon began plummeting, too.[25] The credit markets that had funded the voracious expansion of Russian banks and nonfinancial corporations were beginning to freeze. The collapse of Lehman Brothers, a U.S. investment bank, caused a flight from risk—and oil-fueled emerging markets suddenly seemed risky indeed.

## Stabilizing the Financial System

By late 2008, Russia was in a painful recession. Yet it was far from clear that the economy had hit bottom. The crisis spread from one sector of the economy to others. First, foreigners began demanding ever-higher interest rates to lend to Russia, to the point that all but the most creditworthy Russian firms were closed out of international debt markets. Second, the combination of higher funding costs and falling asset prices threatened Russian banks, which struggled to raise money even as they discovered that assets they held were now worth much less than expected. Third, the recession caused the ruble to crash, as both Russians and foreigners dumped rubles and bought dollars and euros. The central bank tried to defend the ruble's value by buying rubles and selling dollars, a policy that caused its foreign currency reserves to plummet. The combination of these factors led Russian nonfinancial corporations to halt investments and consumers to cut back on spending, decisions that sent aggregate demand spiraling downward. Pain that began in the energy sector quickly spread to every corner of the Russian economy.

The government mobilized to tackle each of these issues. First was the problem of external debt. Russia's banks and its nonfinancial corporations—firms ranging from steel companies to supermarkets—relied on external funding. There were sensible reasons for this. Before the crisis, foreign investors, impressed by Russia's tremendous economic growth in the mid-2000s, began to see the country less as a basket case and more as a growth market. As the perception of Russia's risk declined, foreigners grew willing to lend to Russian firms at lower interest rates. Indeed, so long as returns on Russian assets were higher than returns in the United States or Europe, fund managers found Russia attractive. At the same time, large Russian firms discovered they could borrow funds abroad more inexpensively than at home.

In terms of volume and percentage, Russian firms' external borrowing boomed. By the end of 2004, Russian banks had borrowed $32 billion abroad, while nonfinancial corporations had borrowed $65 billion. A year later, bank borrowing was up by 50 percent—reaching $50 billion—while nonfinancial corporations' loans from abroad had nearly doubled, to $112 billion. As the crisis approached, foreign borrowing grew at breakneck speed, buoyed by Russia's high growth and increasing investor confidence. Russian banks' borrowing doubled in 2006. It kept growing it 2007. The growth rate slowed slightly in the first half of 2008, restrained only by worries about U.S. financial markets. By September 2008, borrowing by banks reached $197 billion, while

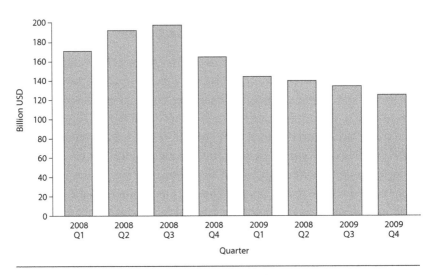

**FIGURE 15**  External lending to Russian banks, 2008–2009
(billion U.S. dollars). Bank of Russia.

nonfinancial corporations borrowed an additional $275 billion more. Then lending fell off a cliff.

As oil prices tumbled downward in late 2008, the investment thesis that had underpinned foreigners' willingness to lend to Russia began to look shaky. If oil prices remained below $50 per barrel, what would drive Russian growth, investors asked? Could the ruble retain its current level, or would it fall sharply against the dollar? If the ruble collapsed, could firms pay back funds they borrowed from foreigners, most of which were denominated in dollars or in euros? If the Russian economy stopped growing at such a rapid rate, were the valuations placed on Russian firms still realistic?

The answer, most investors concluded, was a resounding no. External lending to Russian firms all but froze in the fourth quarter of 2008. Banks' foreign borrowing fell by 16 percent in the final three months of 2008, while nonfinancial corporations reduced their borrowing by nearly $25 billion dollars. By the end of 2009, external lending to Russia's banking sector had fallen by 36 percent since the peak. A third of foreign financing for Russia's banks in 2008 was in short-term loans. By the end of 2009, such short-term lending had fallen by more than half. Nonfinancial corporations fared slightly better, in part because most lending to nonfinancial firms was of longer duration, so lending volumes could not change so rapidly. Yet nonfinancial corporations nonetheless experienced a sharp decrease in foreign funding.[26]

The most immediate victim of the freeze in foreign financing was the banking sector. Russia's banks were already reeling from the crisis. The sector held 230 billion rubles' worth of Russian equities and 1.4 trillion rubles in debt securities. The market value of these holdings plummeted, imperiling banks' financial position.[27] Economist Sergey Aleksashenko has estimated that losses on such securities during the third quarter of 2008 amounted to 200 billion rubles—"approximately 7–8 percent of total banking system capital."[28] Fears of bank runs spread. Russia had painful experience with financial crises during the late Soviet period and from the 1998 crash, and many Russians prepared for a repeat.

The best measure of this fear—and its effect in freezing Moscow's financial system—was the interest rate at which banks lent to each other for short periods. Banks use short-term loans, often with a term of only a single day, to ensure they have the liquidity needed to meet customers' demands. In January, before pressure began building, the overnight interbank rate was 2.8 percent. It increased slightly by the middle of the year to 4.4 percent in July. In November, with the oil price tumbling and global credit markets tightening, the Moscow interbank rate spiked to 9.5 percent.[29] Russia's banks were afraid to lend to their peers. Russian bankers knew the entire financial system was fragile, as asset prices plunged and credit froze.

There are no absolute lessons from economic history, but one rule comes close: do not let your banking system collapse. Economies can recover from all range of bankruptcies and failures. But a banking system—a means of allocating credit between savers and borrowers—is the lifeblood of any economy. If it freezes, the entire economy seizes up. Across the world in 2008, banks and credit markets looked on the verge of collapse. Indeed, whole markets, such as those for securitized mortgages in the United States, all but ceased to exist. Governments in every major country took steps to shore up their banks, ensuring that the recession would not cause bank runs. Every major central bank took steps to counteract the contraction in lending by cutting interest rates or bolstering bank balance sheets.

Russia was no different. In the fall of 2008, as Moscow's stock market swooned, Russia's government stepped in with a bank bailout. The Ministry of Finance offered 505 billion rubles of capital injections to a range of banks, including 45 billion rubles to Rosselkhozbank, 180 billion to VTB, and 175 billion to VEB, over the course of 2008 and 2009. The central bank and VEB, meanwhile, announced 1.7 trillion rubles of financial support to Russia's banks.[30] VEB, in addition, offered credit to a wide array of Russian nonfinancial corporations, from steel maker Evraz to Rusal, then the world's largest aluminum firm.[31]

## Containing the Crisis

Like countries across the world in 2008 and 2009, Russia's response to the credit crunch focused above all on stabilizing the financial system. Like other G20 countries, Russia pumped funds into its banks in a desperate attempt to stave off collapse. In hindsight, economists debate the extent to which bailouts unfairly benefited bank owners at public expense. By establishing a track record of government bailouts in times of crisis, the Kremlin's decision to back its banks to the hilt created a dangerous precedent. Bigger banks now knew they would be bailed out in times of crisis, so they faced fewer negative consequences for riskier lending, a phenomenon economists call moral hazard. Some Russian officials wish in hindsight that the government had taken a tougher line on the banks. Indeed, the scandalous bailout of the Bank of Moscow, which was taken over by VTB with the help of government funding, is a case where better regulation could have prevented a bailout.[32] But letting the Bank of Moscow collapse during the crisis was not an appealing option—Lehman Brothers' bankruptcy had proven that. As in many other countries that faced banking busts in 2008, the Kremlin erred on the side of caution—which meant bailing out the banks. In the end, only two banks were allowed to fail.[33]

The government took several steps to ensure that the country's banking system would survive. First, the central bank rejigged regulation, loosening the rules meant to ensure that banks had sufficient capital. This let banks keep lending even as they took losses on their loan portfolios. The central bank reduced the requirement that banks set aside reserves to cover problematic loans, even as such nonperforming loans were increasing in number.[34] This prevented banks from having to raise new capital at a time when markets were unlikely to be forthcoming. At the same time, Russia's banks were suffering a drain of deposits, as depositors feared that banks would go bust, leaving them with no money. To protect the banking system from an exodus of deposits, the government expanded its deposit insurance program, which unlike in most developed countries had previously been limited.[35]

The similarity between Russia's bank bailouts and programs of bank nationalizations in the United Kingdom or the TARP program in the United States was not the only way that Russia's crisis response mirrored that of other countries. The Kremlin focused its energies on monetary rather than fiscal policy, devoting vast sums to stabilizing the monetary and financial system, but a relatively smaller amount of resources to boosting the real economy. To be sure, the government ran a large deficit in 2009, using its ability to continue spending and borrowing to offset private sector deleveraging.[36] In 2009, the government used cash from its Reserve Fund to fill the budget deficit, taking advantage of the money that Finance Minister Kudrin had saved in good times to use when oil revenues were low.[37] The Reserve Fund fell from 7.4 percent of GDP at its peak in early 2008 to 1.3 percent of GDP at the end of 2011.[38]

The Kremlin adopted several other measures to ease fiscal policy and support spending. Taxes were cut by 345 billion rubles in 2009.[39] Scheduled labor tax hikes were postponed to encourage employment.[40] As in other countries, stimulus programs sparked controversy. The government's expanding role worried free-market advocates, who feared a reversal of recent liberal trends. Aleksandr Shokhin, head of one of the country's largest business lobby groups, issued a document titled *An Appeal to the Country's Leadership* in October 2008, criticizing bailout plans for aiding individual firms rather than the economy as a whole.[41] President Putin himself echoed these concerns. Speaking at the World Economic Forum at Davos in 2009, Putin argued that "during a crisis there is a powerful temptation to grasp at simplistic and populist solutions.... One such error would be for the state to intervene in the economy, to display a blind faith in its omnipotence."[42] Under his management, of course, the government was intervening in the economy, expanding the role of state-owned banks. Putin drew parallels with the communist era to emphasize what he believed Russia should avoid. "During the Soviet period," Putin argued, "the state acquired absolute hegemony. The end-result was an economy that was completely lacking in competitiveness and we have paid a heavy price for this."[43]

Yet Russia's crisis response did increase the state's role in the economy, and in worrisome ways. The financial sector bailout was probably necessary, though the boost it gave to state-owned banks—which in Russia have a poor record of managing money—has yet to be reversed. According to calculations by three leading Russian economists, 42 percent of anticrisis funds went to financial sector firms.[44] That high share was understandable, given the sector's critical role. Yet the second-largest recipient of funds, according to this estimate, was the oil sector, which received roughly one-quarter of bailout funds.[45]

Special aid for the energy sector represented a victory of politics over policy. Thanks to the strength of the oil lobby, for example, Russian oil firms received a 140 billion ruble cut in export tariffs, providing an immediate boost to profits.[46] Few means of boosting the economy would have been less effective. In a time of crisis, the effect of a stimulus measure is determined by the likelihood that the funds get spent. Unlike hard-pressed consumers, oil firms were unlikely to use their new funds to boost spending. With oil prices low, new investment in energy infrastructure made little sense. And, despite the industry's requests for more government subsidies, it had made bumper profits in the run-up to 2008 thanks to high oil prices. To be sure, Russian oil firms' stock prices had slumped. But even as the government was cutting oil export tariffs to help the "struggling" sector, several of the country's oil firms were paying out billion-dollar dividends.[47]

Russia was not, of course, unique in the extent to which the 2008 crisis response was shaped by political factors, or diverged from what economic theory might have advised. Indeed, in its failure to use fiscal policy effectively, Russia was sadly similar to many Western countries that also relied excessively on monetary policy and bank bailouts. Where Russia differed from many advanced economies was the role of currency policy. The ruble had been kept at around twenty-five per dollar. This policy had served Russia reasonably well, limiting currency risk, which helped importers and exporters set long-term plans. The relatively fixed exchange rate was easy to enforce when oil prices were high. Large commodity-funded inflows increased demand for rubles, pushing the price upward. In response, the Bank of Russia sold rubles and bought foreign currency, above all dollars. As the Bank of Russia sold rubles, the quantity of rubles in the market increased, reducing the ruble's value relative to other currencies. This maneuver counteracted the upward pressure on the ruble from high demand. As a result, the central bank's foreign exchange reserves grew and grew, reaching nearly $600 billion on the brink of the crisis. The main downside was inflation, as the increased supply of rubles in Russia caused domestic prices to increase.

When oil prices began to fall, however, the risks of a fixed exchange rate increased. Money rushed out of Russia as foreigners and Russians sold rubles and bought dollars and euros. This put downward pressure on the ruble, presenting the central bank with a challenge it had not faced since the 1998 crash. To keep the ruble at around 25 to the dollar, the central bank was forced to spend ever more of its reserves, exchanging the dollars and euros it had stocked away in exchange for rubles. By decreasing the supply of rubles on the market, the bank helped support the ruble's price. But this was a game the central bank could play for only so long as its foreign currency reserves lasted. The pressure on the ruble, however, caused reserves to fall sharply in the second half of 2008.

The bank faced a choice. It could keep spending reserves to defend the ruble, though this policy risked running down the bank's reserves and forc-

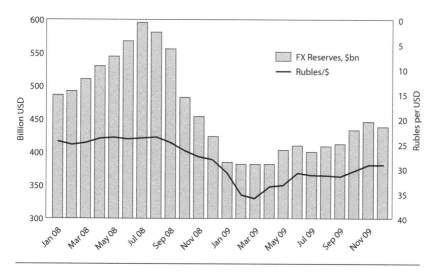

**FIGURE 16** Russian foreign exchange reserves and exchange rates, 2008–2009. Bank of Russia.

ing a disorganized currency crash. The alternative was scarcely more appealing. By ending its fixed exchange rate policy, the central bank could let the currency float—though during a crisis, everyone knew the ruble would sink. Each policy offered costs and benefits to different groups. Exporters, especially those in commodity industries, advocated depreciation, because a cheaper ruble would decrease the relative value of their domestic costs, which were priced in rubles, while export revenue, priced in dollars, would be unchanged. Importers—and the country's beleaguered consumers—faced very different incentives. A devaluation of the currency meant that imported goods—priced in dollars—would cost more in ruble terms. Consumers would find that higher prices ate into the real value of what their wages would buy.

For months, the Bank of Russia tried to hold the currency steady. It poured billions of dollars into foreign exchange markets, buying up rubles in a futile attempt to convince currency traders that the ruble would not fall against the dollar. But as the central bank's reserves sank, worries grew about a repeat of 1998, when the government ran out of money and had no choice but to devalue. No one in Russia wanted to return to 1998. This required devaluing now rather than later. The central bank began letting the ruble slip in late 2008. In January 2009 the rate of decline accelerated, prompting fears that the currency would fall faster than the Bank of Russia expected. But by March, the ruble had stabilized, even regaining some of its value. Devaluation had worked—and was not catastrophic. But the decision to wait several months before devaluing had cost nearly $200 billion in foreign exchange reserves.

## Medvedev the Modernizer

Russia's greatest tsars are known by the epithets that accompany their names—think Peter the Great, or Ivan the Terrible. Dmitry Medvedev, Putin's long-time deputy and Russia's president from 2008 to 2012, is never likely to be considered one of Russia's great leaders. But if he had an epithet that described his rule, it would be Medvedev the Modernizer. Medvedev believed that he could bring a new, modern style to Russia's government, introducing more transparency, more competition, and more room for dissenting voices. And he promised to reinvigorate Russia's economy by reducing its reliance on raw materials exports and investing instead in technology.

After the oil price crash of 2008, few of Russia's leaders doubted the wisdom of diversifying away from Russia's reliance on volatile commodity prices, especially oil. Even the spectacular return of oil prices to precrisis levels by 2009 did not dent support for the idea of diversifying Russia's economy. The notion that dependence on uncontrollable oil prices was a cause of the Soviet Union's demise was widespread among Russia's elite. Medvedev believed he had a solution. And most of Russia's leadership publicly backed his plans.

Indeed, Putin's choice of Medvedev as president signaled that Russia's paramount leader recognized that Russia's economy needed to change. Russia's constitution limited Putin to two consecutive terms in office, so Putin had to choose a "successor" as president, while he assumed the role of prime minister, without, of course, surrendering his status at the top of Russia's political hierarchy. Putin had several potential presidential candidates that he could have put forth in 2008. Sergei Ivanov, former KGB agent and longtime minister of defense, represented continuity and could be trusted to maintain control and represent the interests of the *siloviki*, Russia's securocrats. Viktor Zubkov, an associate of Putin's since his earliest days in the St. Petersburg government, was a capable administrator and lacked a personal power base that could threaten Putin's own authority. Most observers discounted the prospects of First Deputy Prime Minister Medvedev because he was too liberal and lacked the profile needed to be president. But polls suggested he was most Russians' preferred choice.[48] And unlike other possible candidates, Medvedev offered a new strategy for modernizing Russia's economy.

After Putin nominated Medvedev, the new president was elected in a vote emblematic of the many shortcomings of Russia's ostensibly democratic institutions. There were no viable opposition parties, the government dominated the media, and political competition was a vehicle for clan rivalries rather than policy alternatives. Yet despite being placed in office through such methods, Medvedev believed that the system needed to change. He drew this conclusion not only because he feared that Russians would tolerate tutelary rule for only so long, but also because he thought that a more open and competitive political system was a prerequisite for a modern economy. Medvedev was no saint—some of his allies were as corrupt as any in Russia—but the political coalition he tried to assemble was different from Putin's core supporters. Medvedev may have been naive in thinking that other Russian elites, especially the securocrats, or Putin himself, would tolerate such changes. But he bet that if his reforms sparked greater economic growth in the noncommodity sector, it would provide the legitimacy needed to reform Russian politics and marginalize some of the more retrograde political forces. For Medvedev the Modernizer, political openness and economic diversification went hand in hand.

But what did modernization mean in practice? How could a government foster diversification? Medvedev laid out his plan in an article published in September 2009, titled "Go Forward, Russia!"[49] He began by criticizing Russia's economy for overreliance on resources. "Should a primitive economy based on raw materials and endemic corruption accompany us into the future?" he asked. "Twenty years of tumultuous change [since the collapse of the USSR] has not spared our country from its humiliating dependence on raw materials. . . . Achieving leadership by relying on oil and gas markets is impossible."

The challenge Russia faced, Medvedev argued, was nearly existential: how to overcome "backwardness" and "make our country both modern and viable." To do so required casting off dependence on oil and on Soviet-style industries. "Finished products produced in Russia are largely plagued by extremely low competitiveness," Medvedev argued, explaining why the country's economy "declined much more than in other economies during the crisis" of 2008. "We did not do all we should have done in previous years," he concluded. "And far from all things were done correctly."

To modernize its economy, Medvedev argued that Russia needed to streamline bureaucracy and cut corruption, so that businesses and entrepreneurs found it profitable to invest. He argued that modernization could not rely on methods employed by previous Russian leaders such as Stalin or Peter the Great, whose heavy-handed methods achieved some economic results but at "too high" a price to Russian well-being. Medvedev's modernization would be driven by "intellect, honest self-assessment, strength, dignity and enterprise . . . not by coercion, but by persuasion. Not through suppression, but rather the development of the creative potential of every individual. Not through intimidation, but through interest."

Some of this, of course, was language you might expect from a politician. What political leader doesn't promise "strength, dignity, and enterprise"? Yet the contrast with the rhetoric that had marked Russian politics during Putin's first two presidential terms was striking. Where Putin promised stability, Medvedev offered growth. And he had concrete ideas about how it could be achieved. Medvedev proposed investing in specific sectors where Russia, he believed, had a comparative advantage: energy efficiency and new fuels, nuclear power, information technology, space and satellite equipment, and medical devices. And, he added, "Russia will be well-armed," promising additional funding for the military-industrial complex, which had suffered since the Soviet collapse but which remained an important source of exports.

Medvedev poured money into his modernization initiatives. The flagship enterprise of the Medvedev era, the Skolkovo Innovation Center, aimed to create a Russian "Silicon Valley" in a Moscow suburb. Endowed with ample government funding, backed by several key oligarchs, and boasting support from Western tech firms, including a $100 million investment from Cisco, the project was intended to foster start-ups and spark innovation.[50] Medvedev personally backed the project—aides claimed it was the president's own idea—and he embraced the image of a high-tech president, opening a Twitter account and snapping selfies.[51] Some of Medvedev's enemies suggested that Skolkovo was solely a corruption scheme, designed to help Medvedev's friends pocket millions in kickbacks and bribes.[52] That is unfair. But critics who argued that an incubator such as Skolkovo did not address the root causes of Russia's undiversified economy had a point.[53] It has not lived up to expectations.

How realistic were hopes that Russia could diversify its economy? Could Russia have developed new, noncommodity export sectors that grow more rapidly than oil and gas revenues?[54] Diversification is a popular political slogan. If it means cutting waste, reducing corruption, investing in education, or improving business conditions, it is hard to disagree with. But it is not clear that any of these steps would have led to a substantive increase in noncommodity exports. Russia's most promising exporters, such as the steel industry, were already performing well. The country had a relatively large manufacturing sector, but much of it could not compete internationally. Manufacturing exporters, such as the long-suffering aerospace sector, struggled to survive without state preferences and subsidies. Russia's defense sector was competitive abroad, but it made up only a small share of exports by value. Tech and outsourcing companies had begun setting up shop in Russia, but the value of their sales was marginal.

What sectors, then, could have realistically driven the diversification of Russia's exports? In a historical perspective, diversification away from oil is difficult if not impossible. It is hard to find countries as rich in resources as Russia that have managed to reduce reliance on oil by rapidly growing exports of services or manufacturing. Malaysia—rich in oil, tin, and other resources—might be one example, though its low wages when industrialization began limits the utility of Malaysia's lessons for Russia. There are few other examples to learn from. The other challenge that the diversification hypothesis faced was the major inefficiencies in the country's energy sector. Optimal energy policy—including cutting waste at Gazprom and Rosneft—would have increased oil and gas profits, benefiting the country but contradicting the goal of reducing dependence on oil and gas.

### Putin's Return

As Medvedev's first term reached its final year, one question dominated Russian politics: who would be the next president? It was not an open question. There would be no real electoral competition. But seven months before the presidential vote scheduled in March 2012, no one knew whether Dmitry Medvedev would serve a second term or whether Putin would return to the presidency. For a political system as carefully managed as Russia's, this counted as extraordinary drama.

Medvedev wanted to run again, but in September 2011, Putin decided to reclaim power. Declaring his candidacy in front of the annual conference of the United Russia party, Putin proposed Medvedev as his new prime minister. Medvedev claimed that the decision was "deeply thought out . . . we actually discussed this variant of events while we were first forming our comradely alliance." Most observers, however, thought Medvedev was surprised and disappointed.[55] "The most important thing," Medvedev told the party congress, "is that the choice always remains with you, with the whole people."[56]

Putin may have hoped that his return to power would stabilize Russia's political system after uncertainty about the succession. Instead, it sparked a crisis. Leading figures openly dissented from the plan to swap roles. Arkady Dvorkovich, Medvedev's economic adviser, tweeted that "there is no reason to celebrate." More dangerously, Finance Minister Alexei Kudrin announced,

"I don't see myself in the new government," under prime minister-to-be Medvedev. "Nobody has offered me a position, but I think that the disagreements I have will not allow me to be part of the new government," Kudrin declared a day after the United Russia party congress.[57] Medvedev promptly sacked Kudrin for insubordination. Kudrin's comments were "improper," Medvedev lectured him during a televised meeting. "If you disagree with the course of the president, there is only one course of action and you know it: to resign."[58] Kudrin promptly did.

The clash with Medvedev was prompted in part by rival ambitions, as Kudrin had hoped to be named prime minister under soon-to-be president Putin.[59] Yet the dispute pointed to a broader debate, not only about personnel but also about policy. Kudrin believed, with significant justification, that his cautious policies had shepherded Russia through the greatest crisis of the decade with surprisingly limited pain. After the 2008 crash, the country's industrial output shrank and pressure on its currency grew. Yet thanks in part to the funds Russia had saved during Kudrin's tenure as finance minister, chaos and collapse along the lines of the 1998 crisis were averted. The 2008–9 crisis proved, in Kudrin's view, that for an oil-rich emerging market, conservative fiscal policies, spending caps, and reserve funds were crucial to managing the ups and downs of commodity prices and the global economy.

Yet even as Kudrin felt that his policies were being vindicated in practice, Medvedev was discarding them. Spending limits were broken. Money flowed into the defense sector after the Russian-Georgian War. The budget began to presume sky-high oil prices. Modernization and diversification required investment, Kudrin admitted, but Medvedev's spending plans threatened the stable currency and macroeconomic environment that made private-sector investment possible. Kudrin's message may have been prudent, but it was not popular. Medvedev's investment promises won powerful allies, all of whom stood to lose if Kudrin succeeded in implementing a restrictive budgetary policy. Medvedev pushed Kudrin aside.

After he was fired, Kudrin made public his complaints about Medvedev's economic policies. "For several months, despite my objections . . . decisions were taken in the sphere of budget policy that without any doubt increased risks for meeting the budget," Kudrin complained. "And these risks, connected most of all with increased spending in the military and social spheres, would inevitably spread to the entire national economy."[60]

Had the course of Russian politics continued as nearly everyone expected—with new Duma elections in December 2011 returning a majority to the ruling United Russia party, followed by an uneventful presidential election in March 2012 ratifying Putin's continued rule—perhaps Kudrin would have succeeded in winning back influence in the new Putin administration. But a new force intervened in Russian politics with a power and immediacy that almost no one expected. The government's response, hiking spending for pensioners and others in its core group of supporters, pushed budget policy in an even less cautious direction.

Few Russians expected the Duma elections in December 2011 to be competitive. Everyone knew that the Kremlin would mobilize what Russians euphemistically call "administrative resources"—the power of the state bureaucracy, government-run media, and related assets—to support the governing United Russia party. Yet three factors made administrative resources less effective in 2011 than in the past. For one thing, Medvedev's promises of political transparency implied that elections would be fairer, raising popular expectations. Second, the middle classes in Russia's big cities, especially Moscow, felt that Putin's refusal to let Medvedev serve a second term contradicted their aspirations for cleaner, more liberal government. Third, Russia now had a new generation of middle class–oriented opposition leaders who were not seen as tainted by the chaos of the 1990s.

The Kremlin, by contrast, offered Russians the same stale choices: the corrupt and ideology-free United Russia party; the party of far-right buffoon Vladimir Zhirinovsky; the tired old Communists, who promised a return to the Brezhnev era; and Just Russia, a party created by the Kremlin to attract votes from citizens who knew only that they did not like the other three options. By 2011, however, at the end of the Medvedev presidency, Russians increasingly believed they should have a real choice.

When the results of the Duma elections were announced in December 2011, United Russia had lost 77 seats but retained its majority. The three pseudo-opposition parties won seats. No other party made it past the threshold needed to win representation in the Duma. The result was not surprising. But the way that United Russia "won" the election was galling. In Chechnya, the formerly secessionist region now run as a personal fiefdom by a former militiaman, Ramzan Kadyrov, the United Russia party was reported to have won 99.48 percent of the vote, on 98.6 percent turnout—in a province that the Russian military had all but burned to the ground over the course of a decade-long counterinsurgency. Chechnya did not report a single complaint of voting irregularities.[61]

The only conceivable interpretation of these data was vote-rigging on a massive scale. Other provinces in the troubled North Caucasus region reported similarly high turnouts—and similar levels of support for United Russia. In the days after the vote, Muscovites took to the streets to protest and found that they were far more powerful than they had realized. On December 10, thousands assembled on Bolotnaya Square, across the river from the Kremlin.[62] On December 24, many thousands more gathered on the street in central Moscow named after Andrei Sakharov, the Soviet dissident—a not too subtle message that, like the regime whose protests Sakharov helped to topple, Putin's government was weaker than it appeared.

Russia's president-to-be heard the message clearly—and began devising a response. There was no way, he decided, to accommodate the protesters' demands. Yes, he could sack the election commissioner or promise a cleaner vote in the future. But that would signal weakness. There were too many protesters chanting *doloi Putina*—down with Putin!—to compromise. Instead, he mobilized against the protesters, disparaging them as U.S.-backed hooligans.[63] At the same time, Putin moved ahead with the March presidential election, again mobilizing administrative resources to win a first-round majority, protesters be damned.

Yet Putin realized repression alone might not be enough. Even before assuming the presidency again, he announced a new economic program designed to shore up his hold on power. Unlike Medvedev, who promised growth and entrepreneurialism designed to attract the middle class, Putin's new program doled out benefits to core supporters: state employees, pensioners, and the security services. In a lengthy article in the newspaper *Komsomolskaya Pravda* published a month before his inauguration, Putin declared that "Russia's government is a social government." He praised Russia for having "far higher social guarantees" than countries at a similar level of development. And he promised that the "construction of justice" would be the main goal of social policy in his third term as president.[64]

On his first day in office, May 7, 2012, Putin signed a dozen decrees putting his new program into practice. One decree offered bonuses of 1,000 to 5,000 rubles to veterans of World War II, as the elderly constituted a key support group. Other decrees promised to grow real wages by 40 percent by 2018, increase life expectancy to seventy-four years, provide more mortgages, build more housing, and reform the education and health systems. And, for good measure, he also decreed that by the end of his term, the government should receive satisfactory ratings from no less than 90 percent of the population.[65]

Putin was far from the first leader who, after a decade in power, thought he could decree his way to popularity. Yet his strategy worked brilliantly, driving a wedge between the urban upper middle class, who wanted a more liberal government, and his coalition of industrial workers, rural residents,

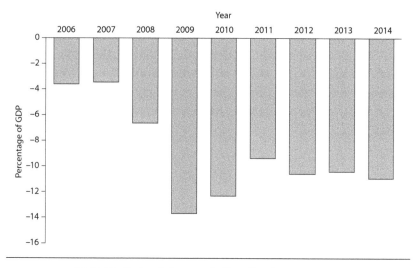

**FIGURE 17** Budget balance excluding oil and gas revenue as
percentage of GDP, 2006–2014. Ministry of Finance.

and—above all—government employees.[66] The Kremlin turned to conservative social policy to demonstrate the cultural chasm between the Moscow intelligentsia and the typical Putin voter. After an anti-Putin stunt in a Moscow cathedral, the Kremlin imprisoned the radical punk rock group Pussy Riot in 2012, but only after parading them on TV as evidence of a threat to traditional Russian values. The following year, the Duma passed legislation outlawing "gay propaganda," again using cultural debates to isolate Russia's besieged liberals.

In economic terms, Putin's strategy of shoring up support was successful, at least in the short run. But it had real costs, which over time were difficult to ignore. Paying for his promises—higher wages for state employees, more spending for favored industries, increased investment in the defense sector— placed a growing burden on the budget. In the 2000s, Russia had prepared for a crisis like the one that came in 2008 and 2009 by saving during the good times. It ran a sizeable budget surplus for much of the decade before 2008. In 2006, the Russian government budget would have broken even with an oil price of $21 at then-current exchange rates.[67]

Putin's new spending commitments cast out such restraint. He hiked outlays without increasing taxes, counting on oil prices to stay high. By 2012, given present exchange rates, the budget's break-even oil price was above $100 per barrel—and it would stay that high for the subsequent two years. Had this burst of spending been accompanied by higher growth, perhaps fiscal conservatives such as Alexei Kudrin would have found it tolerable. But despite the higher government investment levels, growth stayed far below its pre-2008 peak. Real incomes had risen by double digits through the mid-2000s, but growth struggled to hit 5 percent after Putin's return. The government was pressing on the accelerator, but the economy barely lumbered forward. And the gas tank—or, more accurately, the petrodollar tank—would not be full forever.

# CHAPTER 8

## Putinomics under Pressure

In September 2013, notables from across Europe and the world gathered in the Livadia Palace, a vacation retreat built by the last emperor of Tsarist Russia just outside of Yalta, a resort town in the Crimean Peninsula. The Livadia Palace was where Stalin, Churchill, and Roosevelt met in February 1945 to carve up Europe at the end of World War II. The Yalta Conference, and the deal that the "Big Three" signed there, is remembered primarily for separating Europe into two halves, one capitalist and the other communist, laying the ground for a decades-long Cold War.

Most attendees of the 2013 conference in Yalta—including a former German chancellor, CIA director, and World Bank president—did not fully understand the historical irony at play. One person who did understand was Sergey Glazyev, President Putin's leading adviser on Eurasian integration, who represented Russia at the conference. In late 2013, the European Union appeared ready to sign a free-trade deal with Ukraine, a move the Kremlin saw as Western intrusion on its sphere of influence. Speaking at the conference, Glazyev warned the audience that for Ukraine, the long-discussed trade agreement with the European Union would be "suicidal." He urged Kyiv to sign a Russian trade pact instead. Petro Poroshenko, then Ukraine's trade minister and now its president, struck back, telling Glazyev that thanks to punitive Russian trade sanctions on Ukraine, "for the first time in our history more than 50 percent of people support European integration. Thank you very much for that, Mr. Glazyev."[1] The audience, mostly of Western officials and business leaders, applauded.[2]

At the sidelines of the conference, Glazyev spoke with journalists to make sure that his point got through. "Ukrainian authorities make a huge mistake if they think that the Russian reaction will become neutral. . . . This will not happen." To the contrary, he promised that the trade deal with the European

Union would lead to Ukraine's default and an economic crisis. He predicted that Ukraine would suffer social division if it signed the trade agreement, hinting that separatist movements in the Russian-speaking eastern and southern provinces of Ukraine might be one result. "We don't want to use any kind of blackmail," Glazyev claimed. "This is a question for the Ukrainian people. But legally, signing this agreement about association with [the] EU, the Ukrainian government violates the treaty on strategic partnership and friendship with Russia." The risk—or threat—was clear. "Signing this treaty will lead to political and social unrest," Glazyev insisted. "There will be chaos."[3]

On that score, Glazyev was right. Less than six months later, Russia seized Crimea and fomented a rebellion in eastern Ukraine, prompting international financial sanctions and sending investors fleeing. At around the same time, the price of oil crashed, from over $100 per barrel in early 2014 to half that price by the middle of the year. Russia's economy was already teetering on the brink of recession before it was hit by the combination of war and an oil shock. The years following 2014 were the most difficult Putinomics had faced. The Kremlin responded by betting that 2014 and 2015 were a repeat of 2008 and 2009, years that also saw recession, low oil prices, and foreign wars. As in 2008 and 2009, Putin's mix of cautious fiscal and monetary policies proved sufficient to steer Russia through the crisis, but failed to restart rapid economic growth.

## No Time for a Crisis

Even before the shocks of 2014, Russia's economy was veering toward recession. Investment and GDP growth were sliding downward. Annual growth of around 4 percent in 2010 and 2011 fell to barely 1 percent by 2013. The causes of the slowdown were varied. Putin's return to the presidency in 2012 had done little to improve things. An atmosphere of stagnation set in, and private investment slumped. During the 2008 crash, money fled the country, as foreigners and wealthy Russians alike moved capital to more secure markets. But though the country had seen strong levels of capital inflows in the years before the crisis, the end of the recession did not see capital return to Russia. Instead, money continued to flow out, not at the devastating rate of 2008, but leaving nonetheless. That meant less capital to fund investments in Russia.

One reason for the investment slowdown was that Putin's cronies were playing an ever-larger role in the economy. In 2012, for example, Rosneft, the state-owned firm run by long-time Putin associate Igor Sechin, announced it was buying TNK-BP, an oil company jointly owned by a group of Russian

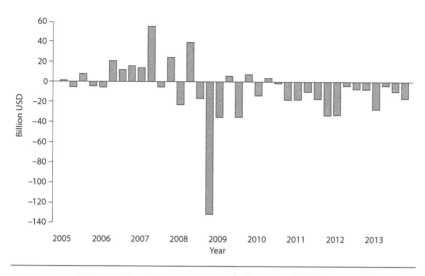

**FIGURE 18** Private capital inflows, 2005–2013 (billion U.S. dollars). Bank of Russia.

businessmen and BP, the British energy giant. It was not only in the energy sector that big, state-owned, crony-controlled firms expanded. By 2013, the three biggest state-owned banks controlled 60 percent of all banking sector assets. Meanwhile, the government failed to significantly improve conditions for private sector firms, with Russia ranking in the bottom half of World Bank metrics on the ease of getting a construction permit or trading across borders.[4]

The government responded to falling private investment by boosting public investment, especially through big prestige projects. The 2014 Sochi Olympics, for example, were not only a sporting event. Nor were they simply a PR project to boost the government's popularity—though, like every Olympics, that was surely part of the government's goal. Sochi was also a massive construction project, designed to revitalize the entire region. In 2012, Vladivostok hosted the Asia-Pacific Economic Cooperation (APEC) summit—and received a $21 billion infrastructure investment in advance to spruce up the city.[5] Kazan got similar funds before a 2013 sporting event.

Russia needs infrastructure investment, especially outside of Moscow and St. Petersburg. Yet projects such as the Sochi Olympics cost far more than they will provide in future growth. Estimates of the total cost of the Olympics vary depending on what types of investments are included in the calculation. What is clear, however, is that a significant share of the funds invested were wasted or stolen. Alexei Navalny's Anti-Corruption Foundation has alleged numerous well-documented instances of corruption related to Sochi construction projects.[6]

The way that Sochi was financed allowed its costs to be hidden from public view, at least at first. Most of the major construction projects in Sochi—from hotels to transport to the Olympic village—were managed either by oligarchs or by state-owned firms. This model was chosen because it gave powerful groups access to large revenue streams, and because it gave the government specific individuals to hold responsible if problems emerged. As a management model, the system was far from optimal, though it was well suited to the oligarchic class that Putin had raised.

The individuals and state-owned firms who received contracts to build Sochi got most of their funding from the state. This came not in terms of cash grants but through "loans" from a "bank"—Vneshekonombank, or VEB, the state development bank. VEB is called a bank, but it does not accept deposits and in practice functions like an investment fund. Its mandate is to lend to projects that boost long-term growth. VEB played a crucial role in funding Sochi, extending credit for hotels, a new airport, a new power plant, and even the Olympic village itself.[7] Most of these transactions, however, were not really loans. When real banks make real loans, they expect them to be repaid. At VEB, by contrast, it is unlikely that managers expected most of their Sochi "loans" to be repaid. From the beginning, it was clear that costs were inflated, that expectations of post-Olympics income were overestimated, and that the oligarchs who received VEB credit had the political clout they needed to wiggle out of whatever repayment commitments they made.

VEB disbursed around 250 billion rubles (over $7 billion) for Olympics-related projects.[8] By labeling handouts as "debt"—as if it would be repaid in the future—Russia's leaders disguised reckless and corrupt spending schemes as "investment," postponing the bill for several years by hiding the true cost on VEB's balance sheet. The final price tag for VEB's bailout will be billions of dollars.[9] Stuffing VEB with corruption-fueled debt was a clever political move. But schemes like this were hardly the type of investment that Russia needed to restart economic growth.

### The Eurasian Economic Union and the Protectionist Turn

The state spending boom of the post-2012 period only had a chance of working if new funds were directed toward projects that would boost long-term growth. Russian leaders realized that trade could play a key role in supporting growth, especially in manufacturing industries. Several policy initiatives sought to encourage trade between Russia and its neighbors. After nearly two decades of debate, for example, Russia finally joined the World Trade Organization in 2012, reducing tariffs and eliminating other trade barriers. Many Russian economists, however, believed the country needed grander integration plans if it was to retain its economic and political weight. When Russian leaders looked at the world, they saw several rising trade blocs. The European Union had integrated the economies of its twenty-eight member states and imposed binding rules on other major trading partners such as Turkey, Switzerland, and Norway. The United States, which already had the North American Free Trade Agreement, had begun negotiating the Trans-Pacific Partnership with some of Asia's largest economies. China's economy was growing by double-digit rates each year and had become the largest trading partner even of faraway nations such as Brazil.

Russia had no such trading blocs—and no interest in being a junior member in Europe's trade zone. If Russian manufacturing were to boom, some economists argued, the country needed supply chains that crossed national boundaries, as did those in China and Southeast Asia. Russia's existing trade infrastructure made this kind of tight integration difficult. The countries on Russia's borders, especially Belarus, Kazakhstan, and Ukraine, the Kremlin concluded, could play a role not unlike the one Mexico plays for the United States, or Poland today plays for Germany—suppliers of quality but lower-priced labor, as well as large markets for consumer goods.

When framed this way, the idea of an economic union with neighbors in the post-Soviet space made sense. Ukraine, Belarus, and Kazakhstan combined had a population 50 percent the size of Russia's. If united, they would drastically expand the potential market for Russian firms. Belarus and Ukraine had industrial bases that despite post-Soviet difficulties were still closely integrated with Russia's. Kazakhstan was in an oil-fueled boom. And all these countries had Russian-speaking elites with personal connections to Russia dating from Soviet and even pre-Soviet days. From this perspective, an economic union between Russia and Ukraine might have made even more sense than one between the United States and Mexico.[10]

Yet Russia was ambivalent about trade deals. During Putin's first term as president, the government appeared to be moving quickly toward joining the WTO, spurred on by China's successful membership application in 2001. Domestic opposition, however, soon gathered strength. The basic impediment to WTO membership was Russia's trade profile. Countries generally choose to sign trade deals to gain access to export markets. Russia, however, did not have an export industry that was pushing for trade deals. The country's biggest export products were oil and gas, followed by industrial and precious metals. Commodities face far fewer trade barriers than do manufactured goods, because countries that don't have their own supplies of oil or diamonds have no choice to buy them on the world market.[11] Import substitution is impossible.

The existence of relatively open markets in commodity trade was good news for Russia's powerful commodity producers, but it meant that these firms had no reason to advocate for trade deals. Russia had many firms, however, that sold manufactured goods to the domestic market and feared competition from cheaper Asian firms or higher-quality European ones. Oligarchs such as Oleg Deripaska, whose companies produced cars and airplanes, mobilized their political machines against WTO accession. Agricultural interests pointed out that WTO rules would restrict farm subsidies. Retail and service businesses feared competition from efficient foreign chains. What sounded to the government in the early 2000s like a good idea quickly became a political quagmire.[12]

As market reforms stalled in the mid-2000s, so too did WTO accession. The president lost interest, apparently deciding the economic benefit from greater trade was outweighed by the political cost. Only when Dmitry Medvedev became president in 2009 did the WTO process restart, driven by liberally inclined advisers who believed more trade would help Russian firms modernize through cross-border integration.[13]

The long delay over WTO membership contrasts with the rapid push for Eurasian integration that began after Putin returned to the presidency. One reason that the Eurasian Economic Union developed more rapidly than Russia's WTO membership is that Russian firms sensed real benefits coupled with limited costs. Yet there was also a strong political rationale to Eurasian integration. Even as some Russian economists pointed to the benefits of greater trade, other Russian leaders saw a contest for political influence—and even for control. Discussions about trade blocs are never politically neutral, of course. Some countries are in, meaning that others are out. Someone writes the rules that others must follow. The European Union, for example, dictates rules to new member states. Belgium, which has been an EU member since the beginning, has had far more influence than Croatia, which joined in 2013. U.S. rhetoric regarding the failed Trans-Pacific Partnership bloc was more openly political, with Barack Obama insisting that "we can't let countries like China write the rules of the global economy," arguing that the United States should establish trade rules itself.[14]

In some sense, then, the Kremlin's view of economic integration in geopolitical terms is not surprising. But compared to other countries, Russia's view of economic integration seemed to preference geopolitics more than the European Union, or other trade blocs it was ostensibly emulating. The European Union, for example, has never had a dominant member. While France has always played a key political role in European integration, the German economy was always the powerhouse. Today Germany is widely viewed as the most financially powerful EU country—but it makes up only a fifth of the union's economy. It is regularly outvoted by coalitions of other member states.[15] Even in instances such as the Greek financial crisis, where Germany was seen as the leader of a push for austerity, it was able to implement such a policy only because a group of other countries agreed with it.

The Kremlin's plans for Eurasian integration, by contrast, always had a clear leader in mind. That does not mean other members were uninterested. Kazakhstan, in particular, has supported economic integration with Russia both for economic reasons and as a means of guaranteeing it is not too dependent on China, its largest trading partner.[16] But it was impossible to deny that a union that included Russia and its neighbors would center on its most populous member in a way the European Union never has. That, to the Kremlin, was the point. As one Russian analyst put it, "Russia will still gain real advantages from creating a trade bloc around itself."[17]

Russia's neighbors Kazakhstan and Belarus reacted positively to the idea of greater economic cooperation, as did Tajikistan, Kyrgyzstan, and Armenia. Ukraine—which has a larger population than these countries combined—did not. Unlike the countries of Central Asia and authoritarian Belarus, Ukraine had far less interest in Russia's integration plans. A significant portion of the country's population was strongly anti-Russian in its political views and wanted to integrate with Europe instead.[18] No less important, most of Ukraine's oligarchs feared that a union with Russia would reduce their political and economic influence. They were more skeptical of a move toward Europe—which would impose new rules on their behavior—but had even less interest in closer ties with Russia.[19]

Russia's attempts to cajole Ukraine into further economic integration came just as Kyiv was preparing to sign what in EU jargon is called a "deep and comprehensive free trade agreement," or DCFTA. Unlike a straightforward deal to reduce tariffs, the European Union's DCFTA offered extensive access to European markets in exchange for Ukraine's adoption of EU regulatory standards. These stipulations conflicted with what Russia was seeking from Ukraine to join its own economic union.[20] Ukraine would have to choose between the two. The Kremlin believed that if Ukraine were to join the EU trade zone, Russian influence in the country would decline sharply. Both the

European Union and the Kremlin angled to convince Ukraine to join their respective trade blocs. The European Union softened its stance on whether Ukraine had to release imprisoned former prime minister Yulia Tymoshenko before signing the DCFTA.[21] Russia offered preferential trade provisions.[22]

Yet in addition to offering carrots to Ukraine, Russia also brandished sticks. The Kremlin threatened huge tariff increases on Ukrainian-Russian trade if Kyiv signed the DCFTA.[23] Yet Ukraine still leaned toward the EU. Europe's economy was far larger than Russia's, and more developed. Ukraine itself was divided, though most of the country's oligarchs, and the middle classes of its capital city, Kyiv, believed the EU option was better for economic and political reasons. Russia responded by restricting Ukrainian exports beginning in the summer of 2013, imposing painful losses on Ukraine.[24]

Ukraine's president, Viktor Yanukovych, faced a dilemma. He had alienated the country's oligarchs and Kyiv's middle class with his family's rapacious corruption.[25] The country's economy was in a tailspin, caused in part by Russian trade sanctions. The European Union was pressuring him to release his main political opponent from jail, where she sat on trumped-up charges.[26] The government was also running out of money, and Yanukovych knew the IMF would demand politically unpopular fiscal changes if he were to seek a bailout. When Russia swooped in to offer $15 billion plus discounted gas sales in exchange for his rejecting the EU trade deal and promising to join Russia's own trade bloc, it was an appealing proposition.[27]

### War in Ukraine

Appealing, that is, to Ukraine's president. Kyiv's middle classes were rather less impressed with a deal that tied their corrupt dictator to a more powerful neighboring one and closed off the prospect of using closer ties with the European Union as a lever for democratizing their own country. Urged on by Mustafa Nayyem, a crusading journalist, Kyiv took to the streets and demanded that Yanukovych sign the deal with Europe. Ukraine's class of oligarchs was no less fed up with Yanukovych, though for far less noble reasons than Ukraine's citizen protesters. The middle class and the oligarchs turned up the pressure on Yanukovych. After violence broke out on the Maidan—Kyiv's central square—the president fled to Russia, and a new government, which backed the trade deal with Europe, took power.

Russia interpreted the new government in Kyiv as a threat. The Kremlin resented the loss of influence in Ukraine. It feared for the security of its naval base in Crimea and its gas deals. It resented what many Russians saw as a U.S.-led strategy of regime change in Kyiv. It was terrified of the spread of "chaos" and "disorder"—the terms Russian leaders most frequently used to describe the Maidan protests.[28]

In response to what it saw as an "illegal coup," Russia annexed Crimea and fomented a rebellion in eastern Ukraine. It is hard to imagine a worse time for a war for Russia. Whatever positive impressions the Sochi Olympics had created in world public opinion were immediately erased. The West united against Russia, ejecting it from the G8. A patriotic fervor swept over Russia. It quickly became clear that the Kremlin lacked a plan for how to integrate Crimea into Russia given Ukraine's hostility. Crimea lacked direct transport links to Russia, necessitating the construction of a multibillion-dollar bridge to the peninsula. Similarly, Russia began drawing up hasty plans to create new electricity links and to hike Crimean pensions as a means of solidifying support. The adventure in Ukraine was turning out to be an expensive proposition.[29] "The Ministry of Finance was not asked in advance about the possible price of the decision on the accession of Crimea," Deputy Finance Minister Tatyana Nesterenko explained after the fact.[30] It would struggle to deal with the consequences.

## Sanctions and Countersanctions

The most immediate cost to Russia came from the economic sanctions that Western countries slapped on Russia's economy. After Russia's annexation of Crimea, the West levied relatively light economic sanctions on Russia, prohibiting investment in Crimea and punishing individuals involved with the annexation decision. The more economically significant sanctions were imposed beginning in July 2014, after the United States prohibited energy firms such as Novatek and Rosneft and state-owned banks Gazprombank and VTB from accessing U.S. capital markets.[31] The European Union soon followed with its own financial sanctions. As Russia's intervention into Ukraine expanded, so too did U.S. and EU sanctions, hitting a larger number of firms in different sectors.[32]

By the end of 2015, Western powers had prevented most of Russia's largest banks and energy firms from raising capital or refinancing debt in Western markets. They also prevented the export of high-tech oil extraction equipment to Russia and imposed sanctions on Russia's defense industry.[33] U.S. and EU sanctions were implicitly or explicitly followed by Norway, Switzerland, Japan, Australia, Canada, and several countries in the Balkans.[34] No less significantly, firms in many Asian and Middle Eastern countries have declined to expand lending to Russian entities, fearing retribution from American regulators.

The Ukraine war was not the first time economic sanctions have played a significant role in Russian foreign policy. In the Soviet period, for example, Western countries imposed extensive restrictions on trade with the USSR, though over time many were removed. Still, countries such as the United States sought to link trade with Soviet behavior. For example, the Jackson-Vanik Amendment, passed by the U.S. Congress in 1974, limited trade with the USSR unless Moscow let Jews emigrate and unless it respected other human rights standards. The Jackson-Vanik Amendment was only formally repealed in 2012, though its provisions had long been waived. However, it was replaced by the Magnitsky Act, a bill that freezes the assets of Russians implicated in the death of Sergei Magnitsky, a lawyer who died after being beaten in a Russian jail, where he was imprisoned for uncovering government corruption. The Magnitsky sanctions had a negligible economic effect, but they enraged the Kremlin.

Yet it is Russia, not the West, that has most enthusiastically embraced the use of economic sanctions in Eastern Europe.[35] Over the past decade and a half, the Kremlin has repeatedly imposed politically motivated trade sanctions on nearly all its neighbors. Georgia, for example, suffered heavily from Russian trade sanctions during the 2000s. In 2003 the Rose Revolution brought to power a government that criticized Russia, tried to reestablish control over separatist regions backed by Moscow, and sought to integrate rapidly with the West. In response the Kremlin imposed a series of economic sanctions on Tbilisi. The conflict began with a steep hike in gas prices, followed by a complete cutoff, which forced Georgia to turn to its neighbor Azerbaijan for supplies. Then Russian health inspectors declared Georgian wine—a major export product—unsafe for consumption. A health ban on mineral water, another important export, quickly followed. Trade volumes plummeted. In 2005, before the sanctions, Georgia exported over $150 million to Russia each year, but that fell to only $20 million by 2009.

Moldova's experience has been similar. In 2013, as Moldova prepared to sign an Association Agreement with the European Union, Russian health inspectors claimed that they found traces of plastic in Moldovan wine and announced a ban on imports. This was not the first time Russia had prohibited Moldovan wine—in 2006, it was also banned for a year. Russia hoped that the economic pressure would "persuade" Moldova that joining the Russian-led Customs Union was a better idea than moving closer to the European

Union.[36] Central Asian countries have also suffered from Russian economic pressure, for example, when Russian leaders threaten to deport migrant workers.[37]

It was ironic, then, that Russian leaders so loudly criticized Western sanctions amid the war in Ukraine. The West's sanctions hurt, especially the decision to prohibit many large Russian firms from accessing Western capital markets. They forced a significant deleveraging of the Russian financial system, as the country's biggest banks paid back dollar- and euro-denominated loans and were unable to find new ones.[38] Sanctions pushed down the value of the ruble, and probably knocked at least 0.5 percent off Russian GDP growth in 2015.[39]

The most significant cost of Western sanctions, however, was political. So long as the sanctions persist, Russia faces the stigma of Western condemnation. It makes sense, then, that the Kremlin's main response to Western sanctions was also fundamentally political. The "countersanctions" that the Kremlin implemented beginning in August 2014 banned the import of food products from countries that levied sanctions on Russia.

One rationale behind the "countersanctions" was simple retribution. The West punished Russia, so Russia had to strike back. Most estimates of the financial losses caused by sanctions, however, indicate that their cost to Europe was limited and declined over time. (Only 1 percent of U.S. agricultural exports were sent to Russia, so sanctions had an even less significant effect on America.)[40] European producers found new markets for most produce that previously went to Russia. Some sectors, notably dairy, fruits, and vegetables, saw export declines that were linked to Russian sanctions.[41] But economists who have researched the issue have found that a year or two after Russia imposed its ban on European food imports, most European producers had found new export clients willing to pay similar prices.[42]

The ability of European farmers and food producers to adjust undermined the Kremlin's second goal of countersanctions: convincing Europe to abandon sanctions against Russia. One rationale for punishing Europe's farmers is that they are politically powerful and well-organized. If they turned against sanctions on Russia, one might surmise, support for sanctions in Europe would decline. This has happened to a certain extent, but the utility of agricultural lobbies as an antisanctions force was not as significant as Russia apparently hoped.[43]

The inability of Russian countersanctions either to impose a large cost on Europe or to change EU policy led some Russians to conclude that the

Kremlin had a third aim in mind: benefiting domestic producers by cutting off foreign competition. Indeed, after the countersanctions were imposed, the Kremlin itself began talking about the benefits of "import substitution," the process of replacing less expensive imports with more expensive but domestically produced goods.[44]

Some import substitution would have happened anyway in 2014 thanks to the ruble's devaluation, which drastically increased the price of imported goods. Prohibitions on imports sped this process along. Certain business groups and some Russian officials promised that import substitution would boost domestic production and encourage long-term growth.[45] Russian journalists, however, noted that less high-minded motives also played a role in the continuation of the food import ban. Some top officials, including Agriculture Minister Aleksandr Tkachev, owned large agribusinesses themselves and thus benefited from Russian prohibitions on agricultural imports.[46]

## The Oil Crash

Even as Russia struggled to jump-start its economy and work around Western sanctions, a new threat emerged over which the government had far less control. America's energy industry was causing Russia far more pain than any sanctions Washington could impose. Thanks to the technology-driven tight-oil boom, U.S. oil production nearly doubled between 2007 and 2015.[47] In mid-2014, oil traders, who had not expected such a rapid increase from the United States, suddenly realized that the world faced a glut of oil. As new American supply rushed onto world markets, the price of oil crashed. Oil traded above $100 per barrel in early 2014, but by the end of the year it hovered around $50. The price bounced slightly higher toward the middle of 2015, only to dive even deeper in early 2016.

To Russia, 2014 felt like 2008 in repeat. The country was as dependent as ever on oil export revenue, having only recently dragged its economy out of the previous recession. To the Russian government, however, the analogy with 2008 was reassuring. They had survived that crisis, many reasoned, so they could survive this one, too. The 2008 crash provided lessons, the government believed, that could shape its policy response. The Kremlin was determined not to make the same mistakes twice. In the 2008 crisis, Russia's central bank held the value of the ruble roughly constant against the dollar, even as oil plunged. Doing so required spending billions of dollars from the central bank's currency reserves. Yet facing the risk of running out of dollars, the bank had to let the ruble fall against the dollar. Between July 2008 and

July 2009 the ruble fell from twenty-three per dollar to thirty-five per dollar, where it stayed for the next several years.

After the 2008 crisis, however, Russia's leaders concluded that their monetary policy response made little sense. The Bank of Russia had spent over one-third of the country's currency reserves defending the ruble—over $200 billion—only to let the ruble fall in the end.[48] The next time, they concluded, it would be far better to let the ruble adjust more rapidly, preserving the reserves. A speedier devaluation might also bring positive economic effects, since a cheaper ruble would benefit exporters, making their products more competitive abroad.

Devaluation was also key to preserving a stable government budget. In 2009, because of the delayed devaluation, the budget swung into a huge deficit, reaching over 7 percent of GDP.[49] Russia's budget depended heavily on the ruble/dollar exchange rate. The reason is oil. A significant share of Russia's government revenue is collected through taxes on oil production and export. (The share of oil in total government revenue varies, of course, based on oil's price.) Oil is priced in dollars. Almost all of Russia's government spending, however, is priced in rubles, from pensions to road building to officials' salaries. If the ruble falls against the dollar, each dollar of oil taxation brings in more rubles. Devaluation, therefore, is a tool to balance the budget.

Russia's central bank chief, Elvira Nabiullina, prefers to describe its policy since the 2014 oil price crash as "inflation targeting," referring to a strategy of monetary policy making in which a central bank tries to hit a certain level of inflation—4 percent in Russia's case—rather than keeping the currency at a specific level. Even before the 2014 crisis, the Bank of Russia had announced plans to move toward an inflation-targeting regime, though it only did so in late 2014, when the sliding oil price forced its hand.[50]

Yet it would be naive to think that inflation is the only concern of monetary policy makers. In theory, the Bank of Russia is independent from political meddling. Russia's weak legal institutions mean the country's central bank is far more susceptible to political influence than peers in advanced countries. Off the record, policy makers speak relatively openly about ramifications of the exchange rate for the federal budget, something that "independent" central banks in theory should not do.[51] Most foreign exchange investors realize that the person who ultimately decides monetary policy is the president. It is no surprise that Putin's public statements often cause the ruble's value to fluctuate.[52]

With the president's support, the Bank of Russia let the ruble's value

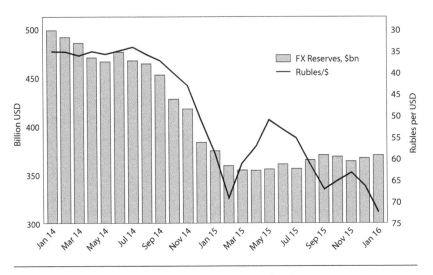

**FIGURE 19** Foreign exchange reserves and exchange rates,
January 2014–January 2016. Bank of Russia.

collapse in 2014.[53] Dragged down by the sinking price of oil, the ruble fell
from thirty-five per dollar in mid-2014 to nearly sixty by the end of the year.
Newspaper headlines often screamed that the ruble was falling out of control,
but devaluation was a deliberate strategy. Letting the ruble sink saved the
government budget by increasing the number of rubles the government collected from taxing oil exports. The downside of devaluation, however, was
inflation. Many Russian consumer goods—from food to clothes to cars—are
imported and priced in dollars. Devaluation increased the number of rubles
needed to buy these goods. This caused inflation to hit 11.4 percent in 2014
and 12.9 percent in 2015. For only the second time since Putin took power, the
inflation-adjusted value of wages fell in 2015, by a whopping 9.5 percent. For
the first time, inflation-adjusted pension payouts fell, too. The central bank's
decision to let the ruble slump functioned like a tax on household incomes.
Devaluation saved the budget, but it did so by shifting the costs of the crisis
onto the population. This also fit the preferences of Putinomics: wage growth
was a goal, but preserving budgetary stability—and thus the Kremlin's room
for maneuver—was more important.

## Credit Where Credit Is Due

The family budgets of the Russian population thus were not the first worry
of economic policy makers as the ruble fell. Many Russians, especially the

poor, suffered a painful decline in living standards as inflation increased. But after fifteen years of rapid wage increases, everyone knew how to survive an economic crisis—especially given that even after real wages fell in 2015, they decreased only to 2012 levels, still double the level of the early 2000s.[54] The memory of recent economic hardship, combined with a widespread belief that the crisis was caused primarily by oil price swings and aggressive foreign sanctions, meant that there was little popular pressure on the government.[55]

The immediate threat of devaluation was to the country's banks. If there was one lesson from the 2008 global financial crisis, it was the risk of letting big banks fail. The collapse of Lehman Brothers in September 2008 froze U.S. financial markets and pushed the country into a devastating recession. In that same crisis, Russia acted aggressively to bail out its own banks, hoping to avoid similar contagion. In 2014, the risk to Russia's banking sector was not nonperforming loans but Russian banks' funding model. Russian banks made most of their profits—from banking services to car loans—in rubles. In the decade up to 2014, however, they had borrowed huge sums in dollars and euros. This made business sense: Russia's biggest banks could borrow dollars and euros from Western financial markets at low interest rates, lend in rubles to Russians at higher interest rates, and pocket the difference.

It was a good model so long as the exchange rate was stable. When the ruble slumped, however, foreign currency debt was transformed from the cornerstone of Russian banks' business model to the greatest threat to their survival. Imagine a bank that had to repay a $1 billion loan at the end of 2014. At the beginning of the year, the ruble traded around thirty-five to the dollar—roughly the same rate as the previous five years. The hypothetical bank would have allotted around 35 billion rubles to repay its dollar debt. Yet when the end of 2014 arrived, thanks to the devaluation it now took nearly sixty rubles to buy one dollar. Yet bank revenues—denominated mostly in rubles—were no larger. In fact, because devaluation stressed household budgets, bank profits declined as consumers were increasingly unable to repay their loans. Banks that looked healthy in mid-2014 teetered on the brink of bankruptcy by the end of the year.

Russia's private sector—banks plus nonfinancial corporations—had borrowed $659 billion by mid-2014 from external sources.[56] A third of this was borrowed by Russia's banks. State-owned corporations, especially those in the energy sector, were a second driver of external borrowing. Most of Gazprom's debt, for example, is denominated in foreign currencies, and by 2016 the firm had over $20 billion in outstanding foreign currency bonds.[57]

Rosneft, the oil giant, was even more indebted, entering the crisis having just spent $55 billion buying the oil company TNK-BP.[58]

Rosneft in particular faced worries over debt repayments. According to Moody's, the credit rating agency, Rosneft had to repay or refinance $26.2 billion between mid-2014 and the end of 2015. It had traditionally relied on Western investors to finance its expansion, and so long as oil prices were high, investors were happy to lend at low rates. But sanctions shut out Rosneft from Western financial markets, and Rosneft struggled to find other financing options. In the end, it refinanced only with help from Russia's central bank, which agreed to accept newly issued Rosneft bonds as collateral, allowing domestic Russian banks to buy the bonds and promptly exchange them at the central bank. That maneuver took pressure off Rosneft, though the lack of transparency spooked markets and drove down the ruble.

Energy companies were hard hit by the crisis, but they had one advantage over other firms: commodities are priced in dollars, so their revenue was not reduced by the devaluation. Instead, they benefited from the cheaper ruble, which reduced the relative value of their production costs. Russia's banks faced the opposite challenge. Many struggled to refinance foreign currency loans. On top of that, some of the biggest banks, including Sberbank, VTB, VEB, and Gazprombank, were placed under Western economic sanctions, freezing them out of dollar and euro capital markets.

Russia's leaders knew that devaluation posed stark threats to the country's banks—and that if any of the biggest banks were to fail, Russia's entire financial system could freeze. The central bank was tasked with saving the banking system. First, it loosened regulations, giving banks the option of using the old exchange rate when calculating their capital.[59] This let banks avoid raising additional funds to compensate for the ruble's sharp decline against the dollar. Second, in November 2014, the central bank introduced a new program of extending yearlong dollar loans to Russia's banks, using the country's foreign exchange reserves to fill the gap that Western capital markets played before sanctions.

Not all the steps that Russia's government took to deal with the liquidity crisis were helpful. The 2014 decision to let Russian banks buy bonds from Rosneft and exchange them for cash at the central bank stands out as particularly poorly designed, though the central bank was likely under political pressure. Overall, though, the central bank has taken steps to limit the potential downside of its liquidity provision efforts. The main risk to this type of program is that the central bank is left holding obligations from banks that go bust. Bank of Russia governor Elvira Nabiullina, however, has coupled

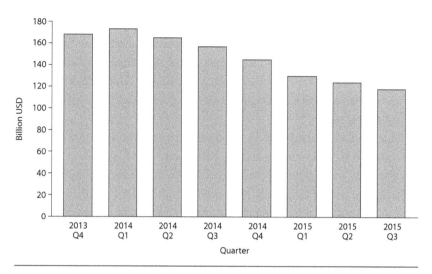

**FIGURE 20** Financial sector external (foreign) debt, 2013–2015 (billion U.S. dollars). Bank of Russia.

expanded liquidity with an aggressive campaign to close poorly run banks, limiting the chance that Russian taxpayers will be on the hook for bad debts. Thanks to Nabiullina's campaign against mismanaged banks, a quarter of the banks that were operating as recently as 2014 had been shut by mid-2016.[60]

Sensible policies by Russia's central bank ensured that devaluation did not spark a banking crisis. Russia's banks decreased external borrowing by 38 percent between 2014 and mid-2016, down to $129 billion. External debt owed by nonfinancial firms fell by over $100 billion, a decrease of nearly 20 percent. In general, of course, declining external debt is not good news. Before the crisis, inflows of foreign capital were evidence that investors expected growth. Today, reduced lending is a sign that both Russians and foreigners lack confidence in Russia's economic prospects. Nonetheless, the rapid but relatively painless decrease in Russia's external debt burden is an unsung success story, especially for Russia's central bank. Rarely do countries deleverage so rapidly with so little financial chaos.

## The Bill Comes Due

Prime Minister Medvedev's visit to Crimea in May 2016 should have been an opportunity to celebrate one of the government's few recent success stories. The annexation of Crimea was still popular in Russia, and though the decision to seize the peninsula from Ukraine was primarily associated with

Putin rather than Medvedev, surely the prime minister expected at least to bask in the annexation's afterglow. Yet while shaking hands with citizens, the reaction he received was rather different. Rather than accolades, an old woman demanded that Medvedev raise pensions to offset high inflation. "It's not possible to live in Crimea—prices are crazy high! They didn't raise [pensions] enough!"[61]

Though Russia's response to the oil slump was orderly, it was not painless. How could it have been? In 2013, Russia exported $350 billion in oil and gas products. In 2015, it exported only $216 billion.[62] That money could not be easily replaced. The population paid the price of the crisis through inflation, and like the Crimean pensioner nearly all Russians felt it acutely. The government's response was to blame outside forces—the global oil market and Western sanctions—while promising a return to growth soon. To some, this sounded like an attempt to evade responsibility. Medvedev's response to the Crimean pensioner, for example, inspired derision. The government hadn't decided to index pensions for inflation, Medvedev told the pensioner, annoyed that she was badgering him. "There simply isn't any money now. If we find money, we'll index them. Hang in there. All the best!" Then the prime minister promptly left.[63]

Medvedev's answer was daft politics, but it also recognized budgetary realities. If oil prices stayed at their 2015 level indefinitely, Russia would have to transform its public finances. Like any government whose spending plans exceeded tax revenue, the Kremlin faced three basic options: slash spending, hike taxes, or take on debt. Running up government debt was perceived as dangerous at a time when the West had levied sanctions on Russia, demonstrating it could cut the country off from international capital markets. The Kremlin began spending down its reserves, but with oil prices at $50 per barrel or lower, the reserves would not last long. At the same time, tax hikes and spending cuts were politically controversial especially given the 2016 parliamentary elections and the government's preparation for Putin's presumed reelection in 2018. Given the Kremlin's wariness about expanding its debt burden, some amount of spending cuts or tax increases were unavoidable. But the biggest spending items—on pensions, for example—were also politically crucial, limiting the government's room for maneuver.

### Whose Bill Was It?

What Russia's government failed to recognize during 2015–16, however, was the extent to which the crisis was self-inflicted. Take the example of VEB, the state-owned bank that lent money to firms that built infrastructure for the Sochi Olympics. Amid the oil-induced austerity drive, VEB—ostensibly a "development bank"—requested a $20 billion government bailout.[64] In addition to having to write down most of its Olympics-related lending within the first three years after the Sochi games, VEB admitted that it also lent $8 billion to metals firms in Eastern Ukraine, in deals that may be linked to Moscow's foreign policy aims in that country.[65] If any of those loans had initial value, they have been devastated by the war in the Donbas. VEB's new management admits it lost at least 1.5 trillion rubles on its loan book, though full losses may well be higher.[66] According to Russian media, at least 40 percent of VEB debts are not being paid on time.[67]

Nearly all VEB's problems were caused by mismanagement or corruption. The Sochi Olympics could have been funded in a transparent and noncorrupt way. VEB management could have implemented sensible risk management procedures. Russia's government could have kept a closer eye on the bank, rather than using it to fund pet projects. The government could have chosen not to invade Ukraine, provoking Western financial sanctions, which targeted VEB and prevented the firm from rolling over its dollar-denominated bonds.

Even without the need to bail out failed development banks such as VEB, the government was still in no fiscal position to deal with a sustained period of low oil prices. The combination of low federal tax receipts—around 15 percent of GDP in 2013, before the oil crash—and the new spending programs Putin launched upon returning to the presidency had caused Russia's non–oil and gas budget deficit to zoom higher.[68] The estimate of the budget deficit if Russia received no oil revenues was always negative, reflecting the reality that Russia could rely on at least some energy taxes. Yet the size of the nonoil deficit ballooned after the 2008–9 crisis and was never reduced. The nonoil deficit, not adjusted for inflation, was around 1 trillion rubles before the 2008 crisis, but never fell below 5 billion rubles after it.[69] At the same time, Russia had stopped setting aside money in its reserve funds at the same rapid rate.

When oil prices plummeted, therefore, Russia's budget deficit spiked, hitting nearly 2 trillion rubles ($25 billion) in 2015, or roughly 2.6 percent of GDP.[70] The deficit would have been much larger were it not for large spending cuts. In inflation-adjusted terms, revenue fell by around 16 percent compared with 2014 figures. Given the political unwillingness to increase indebtedness or hike taxes, this forced a 7 percent reduction in inflation-adjusted spending. Unless oil prices increase, Russia faces a painful choice between hiking taxes, further slashing spending, or increasing its borrowing and thereby placing at risk the macroeconomic stability that has provided the foundation for economic growth since the 1998 crisis. Medvedev's advice to the Crimean pensioner—"Hang in there!"—was more apt than many realized. Russia's rulers, not only its pensioners, face tough choices ahead.

# Postscript
## CAN PUTINOMICS SURVIVE?

In 2000, political scientist Timothy Frye surveyed 500 businesses in Russia, including firms large and small, in several regions. He asked them about the main obstacles to business development. Their responses explain much about the Russian government's economic strategy since then (see table 1). Corruption was on the list of obstacles to business, but Russia's corporate leaders said it was only the sixth-most-pressing problem. Far more worrisome, they believed, was Russia's high tax burden, followed by legal instability, access to credit, and a lack of qualified managers.[1] Since 2000, taxes were cut and interest rates lowered. A new class of corporate managers, educated abroad, now runs most of Russia's large firms. The government provided macroeconomic stability, keeping inflation reasonably low and growth reasonably high.

From the perspective of the late 2000s, therefore, the Russian government had addressed many of business's main complaints from the beginning of the decade. True, corruption was at best marginally reduced, with new oligarchs replacing old ones. The jailing of oil baron Mikhail Khodorkovsky deterred investment by reminding business owners that their property could be seized at government whim. Despite this, Russian and foreign firms continued to invest, deeming the businesses climate adequate and the opportunities substantial. After a decade of capital export in the 1990s, money began flowing into Russia in the mid-2000s, a sign of investor confidence.

Yet the years after the 2008–9 crisis were a period of drift. The problem was not the financial crisis per se. Russia recovered relatively quickly, thanks to a decent economic policy response and the rapid recovery of commodity prices. The problem was politics. Putin and the coalition he assembled backed policies that resolved some of the most pressing problems of the 1990s, above all the persistent budget deficit, which fueled inflation and financial instability. By the beginning of the 2010s, however, Russia faced a different

**TABLE 1** Reported obstacles to Russian business, 2000

| Obstacle | Scale of problem (1 = small, 5 = large) |
|---|---|
| High taxes | 4.29 |
| Legal instability | 3.46 |
| Strong competition | 2.90 |
| Difficulty finding credit | 2.74 |
| Lack of managers | 2.51 |
| Government corruption | 2.43 |
| Weak infrastructure | 2.17 |
| Government intervention | 1.98 |
| The "racket" | 1.43 |

Source: Frye, "Capture or Exchange."

set of challenges. Surveys suggested that the biggest issues facing business were different from before: now reducing bureaucracy, improving the rule of law, and increasing regulatory transparency topped the list.[2]

Putin has struggled to retool. The Medvedev era—when Putin's modernizing deputy promised to diversify the economy away from commodities and make government more transparent—offered, some analysts believed, the chance to adapt to new times. Yet Medvedev was kept on a short leash during his four years as president and was not permitted to run for a second term. Reforms were discussed but rarely implemented. The bosses of state-owned enterprises gathered more power, and a small circle of long-time Putin friends, now oligarchs, accumulated a growing array of assets. Though Russia returned to growth after the 2009 slump, the rate was far below the boom years of the mid-2000s. Influential Russian entrepreneurs began investing their fortunes abroad, sensing better possibilities outside of Russia.[3]

## Austerity Begins to Bite

This was the environment Russia's economy faced when it was smashed by the oil price crash, the annexation of Crimea, and Western financial sanctions. A status quo that in early 2014 looked stable but stagnant quickly worsened. The ruble slumped, production froze, and the government budget was driven deep into the red. Russia's political class has slowly come to terms with the painful choice between large spending cuts, tax increases, or a risky bet that

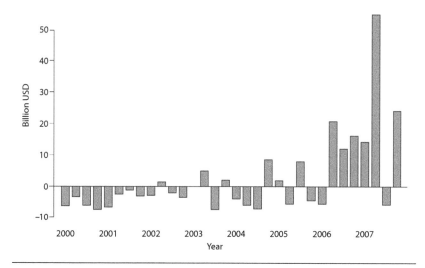

**FIGURE 21** Quarterly private capital inflows, 2000–2007 (billion U.S. dollars). Bank of Russia.

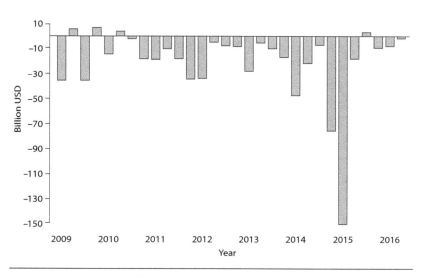

**FIGURE 22** Quarterly private capital inflows, 2009–2016 (billion U.S. dollars). Bank of Russia.

the oil price will quickly improve. The response emphasized spending cuts—but because spending on state salaries and the military had to be protected, long-term investments in health and education were hit hardest. For the first time since Putin took power, the political class has had to impose austerity in a time of recession.[4]

The need for austerity could not have come at a worse time on the Kremlin's political calendar, with a new presidential election looming in 2018. Poorly designed budget cuts and tax hikes risk inflaming popular sentiment. It is easy—and not wholly inaccurate—to blame the recession on uncontrollable foreign factors, above all the oil price. But when the government increases taxes or cuts spending, voters know who to blame. The Kremlin's fear of debt makes belt-tightening inevitable. Political realities—including the fact that many individuals and inefficient state-owned companies are perceived to be untouchable—mean that most of this belt-tightening falls on average Russians. It proved manageable, though harder than some had hoped.

Take tax increases. In 2015, the government introduced a new highway tax system, called Platon, to fund road construction. Collection of the tax was privatized and given to a company owned by Arkady Rotenberg, a billionaire businessman and former judo partner of Putin's. The tax raised only minor amounts of revenue, but it created a huge political storm. Truckers, who were hit hardest by the tax, revolted. They stopped their trucks in the middle of highways, obstructing traffic and creating miles of clogged roads. Many other Russians supported them. Some alleged that the collection mechanism—through a firm owned by the president's friend—was evidence of high-level corruption.[5] Despite Russia's relatively low tax burden, the new tax was seen as illegitimate, and the government partially backed down.

If tax increases are out, spending cuts are the other option for keeping the budget balanced. Yet spending cuts are no less controversial. The problem is not only the elderly, whose pensions impose a significant burden on government finances. Other groups that once loyally supported the government have raised questions about austerity. Industrial workers are one potential source of political uncertainty. If you look at unemployment figures, which only barely increased during the 2014–16 recession, the labor market looks healthy. But low unemployment has been maintained because firms held nominal wages constant and let inflation cut the real value of their wage bill. Many firms face pressure to cut more sharply, either by furloughing workers or by laying them off.

Uralvagonzavod, a firm that makes train cars and tanks, highlights the risk that spending cuts will spark industrial unrest. The company, whose factories are based in Nizhnii Tagil in the Ural region, has seen demand for train cars plummet because of the recession and cut working hours in response. The industrial workers of the Urals were once a bastion of support for Putin, but now some are protesting wage cuts—and blaming the government for their plight. Government proposals to reduce defense spending by 5 percent put new pressure on Uralvagonzavod's tank production. Yet any move to furlough tank workers risks inciting protests and further eroding government support. In one ailing industrial region in 2016, local TV showed videos of riot police training to deal with labor protests.[6] Not for nothing did the government announce in 2016 plans to hire an additional 65,000 employees in the Interior Ministry, even as austerity was forcing spending cuts in other spheres.[7]

Political calculus prevented significant tax hikes before the 2018 election. Putin's approval rating may have been above 80 percent, but the Kremlin was wary of being seen to impose economic pain.[8] The government had already cut administrative expenses, but it was wary of touching defense, state wages, or pension spending. These represented the biggest burdens on the government budget, but they were crucial for retaining key bastions of political support. So the Kremlin chose instead to cut less politically significant areas such as schools and hospitals.

### Can Russia Restart Growth?

As in 2008–9, a strategy of hunkering down worked in 2015–16. The Kremlin avoided a budget crisis like Russia had suffered in 1991 or 1998. Stability was maintained. The political costs, most notably a sharp decline in real wages in 2015, proved manageable, in large part because Russia blamed its economic problems on external factors and foreign enemies. Given the scale of the crisis, reestablishing macroeconomic stability and exiting recession represents a clear success. Stability is something that Putinomics has repeatedly proven capable of providing.

Yet stability does not guarantee growth. The big question of Russian economic policy over the next several years is whether Russia's economy will limp along at growth rates of 1–2 percent per year or whether it can return to the higher rates of the 2000s. The IMF predicts GDP growth no more rapid than 1.5 percent per year through 2021.[9] If oil prices increase to triple-digit rates, faster growth would be possible—but the course of future commodity prices is difficult to predict. What hope does Russia have of developing more rapid growth from noncommodity sectors?

Barring further negative shocks, the success stories of Russia's restructuring will continue performing. Supermarkets and steel firms have plenty of room before they reach Western productivity levels, and there is little reason to think they will not continue to converge toward international best practices. But the rate of convergence depends in part on the broader macroeconomic and investment climate. Some of the factors that aided Russia in the 2000s are now trending in the opposite direction. The ratio of nonworkers to workers fell by 11 percentage points between 1995 and 2010, thanks to a falling birthrate. This provided more funds for investment and contributed to perhaps one-third of per capita income growth during the period.[10] Now that factor is reversing under a wave of retirements. From now on, demographics will be a headwind against which the economy will have to contend.

The regulatory and investment climate should be easier to address, but it is a political minefield. Even amid the 2014–16 recession, Russia's government continued expropriating private firms on trumped-up charges. In 2014, billionaire Vladimir Yevtushenkov was arrested on charges of money laundering relating to his company's acquisition of Bashneft, a medium-sized oil producer. The government produced no evidence that Yevtushenkov's sins were worse than any other oligarch's, and he was released from house arrest after surrendering Bashneft to the government. Two years later, Bashneft was "privatized" when the government sold it to Rosneft, the state-owned oil giant. Most analysts believe the money-laundering allegations were part of a Rosneft plot to seize control of Bashneft. Yevtushenkov was the highest-profile recent victim of expropriation, but he is far from alone. So long as the rule of law is regularly violated, many investors will conclude that the risk of owning assets in Russia is too high to justify. Russian equities are traded at valuations lower than in other countries in large part because of this risk. Yet political constraints—above all, the power of Russia's new class of oligarchs and state-owned firm CEOs—makes it impossible to implement protections against these oligarchs' rapacity. They have the power to overwrite any rules. So long as this political coalition persists, the rule of law will be trumped by politics.

Politics also constrains government investment. Russia should spend more on health and education, which would pay dividends through a more capable workforce. But the political coalition that backs Putin—business elites, state employees, and pensioners—dictates that taxes should be low and that pensions should be well-funded. Neither average citizens nor business elites trust the government to provide quality services, so willingness to pay taxes is low. Demand for spending, meanwhile, is high—especially among politically crucial groups such as state employees and pensioners. This combination leaves little money for productive investments. In response to the budget deficit caused by the 2014–16 recession, for example, taxes were barely increased, and pension spending was mostly protected. Education and health faced far sharper cuts. This is what Putin's political coalition demands.

The economic strategy that Putin's governments have implemented—strengthening the state, keeping the populace content with wage and pension hikes, and, where possible, letting private business improve efficiency—looks less and less likely to solve the problems Russia faces. The agenda of the 2000s ensured that Russia did not end up like Venezuela—or like the Russia of the 1990s. Putinomics underwrote a decade of impressive growth. It continues to provide social and political stability. But the issues that constrain Russian growth today are different from a decade ago. Then, the challenge was implementing sound macroeconomic policies: raising tax revenue efficiently, reducing the deficit, and cutting inflation. Russia's ruling class agreed on the need to tackle these problems, and Putin's political coalition supported the necessary policies. Today, the main questions are different: health and education, regulation, anticorruption, antitrust policy, the rule of law. These are issues that Putin's economic strategy cannot address, because Russia's political elite benefits from the status quo, suboptimal though it may be. The type of political movement that could establish the rule of law, meanwhile, has been neutered. Putinomics has downshifted: after an initial decade of rapid economic growth, it provided a second decade of stability coupled with stagnation. Putinomics will continue to accomplish the Kremlin's main aims of retaining power at home and deploying it abroad. For Russia's leaders, achieving these goals is success enough—even if Russian living standards continue to stagnate.

# ACKNOWLEDGMENTS

This book examines taxes and wages, state-owned and private businesses, crises past and present. Debt, however, is where the project began—debts personal rather than financial. The ideas behind this book germinated over the course of two years in Moscow, where I was fortunate to teach at the New Economic School and to learn from students' curiosity and appetite for debate. I wrote this book with the support of fellowships from the Smith Richardson Foundation, the Kennan Institute, the German Marshall Fund, and the Institute for New Economic Thinking. I am grateful to Matt Rojansky, Steve Szabo, and Al Song for their support. Alan Luxenberg and the entire team at the Foreign Policy Research Institute provided an intellectually stimulating home in Philadelphia. Finally, my colleagues and students at Yale's Brady-Johnson Program in Grand Strategy and at International Security Studies provided an excellent atmosphere for reading, thinking, and writing—including tolerating my frequent absences while on research trips from Moscow to Vladivostok.

Several friends and colleagues served as unofficial sounding boards for many of the ideas presented here, though they may not agree with my conclusions. I presented portions of this research to audiences at the Kennan Institute and at the Osrodek Studiow Wschodnich and received much useful feedback. I am grateful in particular to Andrew Matheny and Yuval Weber for many insightful conversations on politics and economics in Moscow and abroad. Alex Nice and Laura Mills were generous enough to read and comment on the entire manuscript. In researching this book, I have been expertly assisted by Nikolai Avhimovich, Maria Gelrud, Lia Liamaiug, and Danila Smirnov. My greatest debt, of course, is to Liya.

# SUGGESTIONS FOR FURTHER READING

This section suggests additional English-language reading, primarily books, grouped by theme. In addition to the literature listed here, the International Monetary Fund, European Bank for Reconstruction and Development, and World Bank produce annual studies of Russia that are exceptionally useful. The Gaidar Institute for Economic Policy in Moscow also publishes many useful reports in English. Full citations of the works listed here can be found in the bibliography.

## Overviews and Surveys

Important recent surveys of Russian political economy include Pekka Sutela, *The Political Economy of Putin's Russia*, and Neil Robinson, ed., *The Political Economy of Russia*. In addition, the collection of essays edited by Michael Alexeev and Shlomo Weber and published as *The Oxford Handbook of the Russian Economy* represents some of the most up-to-date scholarship. The best recent scholarly attempt to integrate politics and economics is Daniel Treisman's *The Return: Russia's Journey from Gorbachev to Medvedev*.

Russia after the Global Economic Crisis, edited by Anders Aslund, Sergei Guriev, and Andrew Kutchins, examines the country's response to the 2008–2009 crash. Aslund's *Russia's Capitalist Revolution: Why Market Reforms Succeeded and Democracy Failed* and Marshall Goldman's *Petrostate: Putin, Power, and the New Russia* tackle post-Khodorkovsky political economy. Finally, David Owen and David Robinson, *Russia Rebounds*, examines the structural and institutional drivers of Russia's post-1998 recovery.

## The Legacy of the Past

As this book has argued, Russia's economy today cannot be understood without reference to its history. The Soviet past constrains economic growth and reform, while the 1990s shape how Russians perceive the present. Key analyses of the Soviet legacy include Fiona Hill and Clifford Gaddy, *Siberian Curse: How Communist Planners Left Russia Out in the Cold*, and Chris Miller, *The Struggle to Save the Soviet Economy*.

Privatization remains one of the most contested themes from the 1990s. Important accounts include Anders Aslund, *How Russia Became a Market Economy*; Joseph Blasi,

Maya Kroumova, and Douglas Kruse, *Kremlin Capitalism: Privatizing the Russian Economy*; Andrew Barnes, *Owning Russia: The Struggle over Factories, Farms, and Power*; and Marshall Goldman, *The Piratization of Russia: Russian Reform Goes Awry*. A key account from advisers to the Russian government on privatization issues is Maxim Boycko, Andrei Shleifer, and Robert Vishny, *Privatizing Russia*. Chrystia Freeland, *Sale of the Century: Russia's Wild Ride from Communism to Capitalism*; and David Hoffman, *The Oligarchs: Wealth and Power in the New Russia*, provide journalistic color on the wild 1990s, but are also notable for illustrating how few analysts predicted the sharp political-economic changes that occurred between 1998 and 2003.

Less frequently examined than the privatization debates, but probably more important, are analyses of Russian public finances. The best source is Andrei Shleifer and David Treisman, *Without a Map: Political Tactics and Economic Reform in Russia*. Juliet Johnson, *A Fistful of Rubles: The Rise and Fall of the Russian Banking System*, describes the financial chaos of the 1990s. David Woodruff, *Money Unmade: Barter and the Fate of Russian Capitalism*, and Barry Ickes and Clifford Gaddy's *Foreign Affairs* article "Russia's Virtual Economy" examine the strange world of barter-capitalism in 1990s Russia, which rapidly fell from view during the crucial 1998–2003 period.

See also Erik Berglof et al., *The New Political Economy of Russia*; Shleifer, *A Normal Country: Russia after Communism*; and Treisman, *After the Deluge: Regional Crises and Political Consolidation in Russia*. Finally, Martin Gilman, *No Precedent, No Plan: Inside Russia's 1998 Default*, provides a useful account of the International Monetary Fund's negotiations with the government as it prepared for default.

## Politics and Ideas

Dozens of books have been written on Russian politics during the period as Putin consolidated power. Key journalistic accounts include Peter Baker and Susan Glasser, *Kremlin Rising: Vladimir Putin's Russia and the End of Revolution*, and Steven Lee Myers, *The New Tsar: The Rise and Reign of Vladimir Putin*. Richard Sakwa has published several useful scholarly analyses of Russian domestic politics; see especially his *Putin: Russia's Choice* and *The Quality of Freedom: Khodorkovsky, Putin and the Yukos Affair*. I also recommend Fiona Hill and Clifford Gaddy, *Mr. Putin: Operative in the Kremlin*. Alena Ledeneva, *How Russia Really Works: The Informal Practices That Shaped Post-Soviet Politics and Business*, provides a useful examination of the roots of some of Russia's political pathologies. Finally, on Russian foreign policy, see Jeffrey Mankoff, *Russian Foreign Policy: The Return of Great Power Politics*.

## Resources and Energy

Of all sectors of the Russian economy, oil and gas have received the most scholarly and popular attention. The best account of the oil industry is Thane Gustafson, *Wheel of Fortune: The Battle for Oil and Power in Russia*. On gas, see James Henderson, *Non-Gazprom Gas Producers in Russia*, and James Henderson and Simon Pirani, *The Russian Gas Matrix: How Markets Are Driving Change*. Jonathan Stern's *The Future of Russian Gas and Gazprom*, now slightly dated, is still useful. On other resource sectors, see Stephen Fortescue, *Russia's Oil Barons and Metal Magnates: Oligarchs and the State in Transition*.

The debate over the "resource curse" and the politics of managing (or, some argue, mismanaging) resource rents has attracted much scholarly and popular attention. Adnan Vatansever, *The Political Economy of Allocation of Natural Resource Rents and Fighting the Resource Curse: The Case of Oil Rents in Putin's Russia*, is a very useful scholarly account. For a counterintuitive argument about the oil curse, see Pauline Luong and Erika Weinthal, *Oil Is Not a Curse: Ownership Structure and Institutions in Soviet Successor States*. Finally, understanding Russia's oil and gas taxation regime is key to making sense of its fiscal and economic consequences. Much of the best literature on this subject is in Russian, but for an introduction, see Michael Alexeev and Robert Conrad, "The Russian Oil Tax Regime: A Comparative Perspective."

## Social and Regional Policies

Topics outside of oil and corruption tend to attract less attention from scholars writing in English, despite the importance of many of these themes. Nonetheless, much of what is written, though limited in quantity, is of high quality. The best recent account of Russian federalism is Elena Chebankova, *Russia's Federal Relations: Putin's Reforms and Management of Regions*. I also recommend the World Bank report by Migara De Silva et al., *Intergovernmental Reforms in the Russian Federation: One Step Forward, Two Steps Back?*

Linda Cook provides a useful examination of social policy in *Postcommunist Welfare States: Reform Politics in Russia and Eastern Europe*, as does the World Bank report *Russian Federation: Promoting Equitable Growth: A Living Standards Assessment*. On the monetization of benefits report, see Susanne Wengle and Michael Rasell, "The Monetisation of L'goty: Changing Patterns of Welfare Politics and Provision in Russia."

On labor markets, see the many papers written by Vladimir Gimpelson, including his summary with Rostislav Kapeliushnikov, "Labor Market Adjustment: Is Russia Different?," included in *The Oxford Handbook of the Russian Economy*. Demographics remains a matter of vigorous debate; for a summary of this debate, see Irina Denisova and Judith Shapiro, "Recent Demographic Developments in the Russian Federation," also in *The Oxford Handbook of the Russian Economy*.

## Finance, Trade, and Other Sectors

Russia's banking sector—and the opaque but important role it plays in politics—has been the subject of much good journalism, mostly in Russian. Key recent scandals include the Bank of Moscow and Vneshekonombank (VEB), which have been well covered in English by the *Financial Times* and *Bloomberg*. For scholarly economic analysis, see Koen Schoors and Ksenia Yudaeva, "Russian Banking as an Active Volcano," in *The Oxford Handbook of the Russian Economy*, and Andrei Vernikov, "Russian Banking: The State Makes a Comeback?"

The military industrial complex—which consumed an enormous share of the Soviet economy but has shrunk drastically since—has attracted far less attention. A good introduction is Roger McDermott, Bertil Nygren, and Carolina Vendil Pallin, *The Russian Armed Forces in Transition: Economic, Geopolitical and Institutional Uncertainties*. Russell Pittman, "Blame the Switchman: Russian Railways Restructuring after Ten Years," provides a good overview of Russian railroad reform efforts. On agriculture, see Stephen Wegren's many books and papers, notably his *Land Reform in Russia: Institutional Design and Behavioral Responses*. On trade policy, see Anders Aslund, "Russia's Accession to the World Trade Organization," as well as research by Natalya Volchkova.

## Comparative Approaches

No attempt to understand Russia is complete without comparing it with neighbors and other similar countries. Some of the most insightful studies include Timothy Frye, *Building States and Markets after Communism: The Perils of Polarized Democracy*; Anders Aslund, *Building Capitalism: The Transformation of the Former Soviet Bloc*; Scott Gehlbach, *Representation through Taxation: Revenue, Politics, and Development in Postcommunist States*; Hilary Appel, *Tax Politics in Eastern Europe: Globalization, Regional Integration, and the Democratic Compromise*; Gerald Easter, *Capital, Coercion, and Postcommunist States*; and Stanislav Markus, *Property, Predation, and Protection*.

# NOTES

## Preface

1 Hill and Gaddy, *Mr. Putin*, 141.
2 Sakwa, *Putin*, 53.
3 Sanders, "Did Vladimir Putin Call the Breakup of the USSR 'the Greatest Geopolitical Tragedy of the 20th Century?'"
4 Weiss, "Five Myths about Vladimir Putin."
5 The most recent account is Dawisha, *Putin's Kleptocracy*.
6 Everett, "McCain: Russia Is a 'Gas Station.'"
7 "The Making of a Neo-KGB State"; Gessen, *The Man without a Face*.
8 Shleifer and Treisman, "A Normal Country."
9 Kaiser, "One Entrepreneur's Adventures Illustrate Hopes, Frustrations."
10 Nichols, "Doubts Riddle Optimism of Young Russians."
11 Reeves, "Russia Is Down but Not Out."
12 This is according to World Bank data. For a discussion of the definition of rent in the Russian context, see Gaddy and Ickes, "Resource Rents and the Russian Economy."
13 Kronick, "Why Only Half of Venezuelans Are in the Streets."
14 According to World Bank data, per capita GDP in 1999, adjusted for purchasing power parity, in current US$, was $10,981 in Venezuela and $5,914 in Russia. Without adjusting for purchasing power parity, GDP per capita was $4,078 in Venezuela and $1,330 in Russia. The most recent World Bank data on GDP per capita adjusting for purchasing power parity, in 2013, has Venezuela at $18,309 and Russia at $24,165.
15 See Moody's online database at www.Moodys.com.
16 Charlton, "What More Does It Need?"

## Chapter 1

1 Bohlen, "Russia Acts to Fix Sinking Finances."
2 Thornill, "Russia's Moment of Truth"; "Chronology of Russian Financial Crisis."
3 For an overview, see Treisman, "Ruble Politics."

4  Hoffman, "Russia Devalues the Ruble to Prop Up Banking System"; Daigle, "Warnings by Soros Send Markets into Panic."

5  Hoffman, "Russia Devalues the Ruble to Prop Up Banking System"; Daigle, "Warnings by Soros Send Markets into Panic."

6  Chiodo and Owyang, "A Case Study of a Currency Crisis."

7  Bohlen, "Rumors and Contradictions Fuel Russia Market Crisis."

8  "Russia's Shrinking Options."

9  Estimates vary widely based on the assumptions made. For an overview, see Noren, "The Controversy over Western Measures of Soviet Defense Expenditures."

10  Nove, "Agriculture."

11  I address this dilemma in Miller, *The Struggle to Save the Soviet Economy*.

12  Hanson, *The Rise and Fall of the Soviet Economy*, 210; Miller, *The Struggle to Save the Soviet Economy*.

13  World Bank, *Russian Economic Reform*, 8.

14  See, e.g., "Otchet Tsentralnogo Banka Rossiiiskii Federatsii za 1992."

15  Granville, "Farewell, Ruble Zone"; Granville, "The IMF and the Ruble Zone."

16  Hill and Gaddy, *Mr. Putin*, 162.

17  Ibid., 143.

18  Whether Putin formally resigned from the KGB is disputed; see Gessen, *The Man without a Face*, 117–18.

19  Hill and Gaddy, *Mr. Putin*, 276; Dawisha, *Putin's Kleptocracy*, 82.

20  Putin et al., *First Person*.

21  Dawisha, *Putin's Kleptocracy*, 81.

22  Ibid., 82. Whether Putin had legal authority to issue such licenses remains a subject of debate; see Hill and Gaddy, *Mr. Putin*, 173.

23  Dawisha, *Putin's Kleptocracy*, 83.

24  Duhamel, *The KGB Campaign against Corruption in Moscow*.

25  Putin et al., *First Person*, 96.

26  Hill and Gaddy, *Mr. Putin*, 179–82.

27  Ibid., 180.

28  Ibid., 177.

29  Ibid., 176–79.

30  Dawisha, *Putin's Kleptocracy*, 175.

31  Ibid., 176; Putin et al., *First Person*, 117; Gessen, *The Man without a Face*, 139.

32  Bunin, *Biznesmeny Rossii*, 5.

33  For these data, see Shleifer, *A Normal Country*, 159.

34  Sakwa, *Putin and the Oligarchs*, 11.

35  Kramer, "Rem Vyakhirev."

36  For details, see Boycko, Shleifer, and Vishny, *Privatizing Russia*, chap. 4.

37  Fortescue, *Russia's Oil Barons and Metal Magnates*, 54–55.

38  Ibid., 42.

39  Freeland, *Sale of the Century*, 195.

40  Shleifer and Treisman, *Without a Map*, 69.

41  "Godfather of the Kremlin?"

42  Putin et al., *First Person*, 127–28.

43  Shleifer and Treisman, *Without a Map*, 41–43, 92; Cook, *Postcommunist Welfare States*, 67.
44  This section draws heavily on Shleifer and Treisman, *Without a Map*.
45  Ibid., 73, 76.
46  Ibid., 43.
47  Ibid., 144.
48  Ibid., 146.
49  Ibid., 147.
50  Ibid., 146–47.
51  Ibid., 147–49.
52  Ibid., 147, 153.
53  "Russia's Quiet Loan"; Freeland, *Sale of the Century*, 265.
54  Freeland, *Sale of the Century*, 297–98.
55  Ibid., 304.
56  Ibid., 308–10.
57  Paterson, Womack, and Vines, "Russia Rebuffs Soros on Call for Devaluation."
58  Freeland, *Sale of the Century*, 323.
59  Chiodo and Owyang, "A Case Study of a Currency Crisis."
60  Gilman, *No Precedent, No Plan*, 192–93.
61  Ibid., 203.
62  Aslund, *Russia's Capitalist Revolution*, 191.
63  Owen and Robinson, *Russia Rebounds*, 36.
64  Odling-Smee, "The IMF and Russia in the 1990s," 171.

### Chapter 2

1   Putin, "Speech to the Federal Assembly." Translation amended.
2   Olson, "Dictatorship, Democracy, and Development"; Olson, *The Rise and Decline of Nations*.
3   Mau, "Economic and Political Results for 2001 and Prospects for Strengthening Economic Growth," 16.
4   Putin et al., *First Person*.
5   Shleifer and Treisman, *Without a Map*, 115.
6   For a full assessment of the pathologies of Russian taxation in the 1990s, see ibid., 6.
7   Putin et al., *First Person*, 129.
8   Gessen, *The Man without a Face*, 181.
9   Petrov, "The Security Dimension of the Federal Reforms," 7–8.
10  Ibid., 7–8.
11  Ibid., 7–8; Elder, "Fradkov Named Foreign Spymaster." See also Soldatov and Borogan, *The New Nobility*.
12  Berglof et al., *The New Political Economy of Russia*, 89.
13  Only under certain conditions; see Chebankova, *Russia's Federal Relations*, 56.
14  Petrov, "The Security Dimension of the Federal Reforms," 8.
15  Ibid., 10.
16  Aslund, *Russia's Capitalist Revolution*, 215.

17 Kochetov, "Moda na malenkie nalogi."
18 Qtd. in Khodorkovsky, "Forum kritikov pravitelstva."
19 Qtd. in Khodorkovsky, "Net—biudzhetu."
20 Delyagin, "Krizis prezidenta."
21 Abalkin, "Nesostoyatelnost programmy Grefa."
22 Qtd. in Zubkov, "Vremennoe okno dlya Rossii mozhet zaklopnutsya."
23 Ibid.
24 Ibid.
25 "Alternativnaia programma Viktora Ishaeva."
26 Qtd. in Zubkov, "Vremennoe okno dlya Rossii mozhet zaklopnutsya."
27 Dallek, *Franklin D. Roosevelt and American Foreign Policy*, 20.
28 On similarities between the two plans, see "Alternativnaia programma Viktora Ishaeva."
29 Bekker, "Gref vo vtorom izdanii."
30 Qtd. in ibid.
31 Smirnov, "Zhizn i smert programma Grefa."
32 Yasin, "Putin's Undercover Liberalism."
33 Romanova, "Bratya po razumu."
34 Dmitriev, "Strategiia—2010."
35 Berglof et al., *The New Political Economy of Russia*, 98.
36 Zhavoronkov et al., "The Deregulation of the Russian Economy," 36.
37 Aslund, *Russia's Capitalist Revolution*, 217.
38 Berglof et al., *The New Political Economy of Russia*, 99.
39 Ibid., 102–3.
40 Aslund, *Russia's Capitalist Revolution*, 217.
41 "Pravitelstvo predlagayet otmenit litsenzirovaniye po 49 vidam deyatelnosti."
42 "Vstupil v silu zakon 'o valyutnom regulirovanii i valyutnom kontrole'"; "Prezident obelil vyvoz kapitala."
43 "Almazy Rossii ukhodyat ot De Beers."
44 Aslund, *Russia's Capitalist Revolution*, 219.
45 Interview with Andrei Illarionov, Washington, D.C., December 8, 2015.
46 Qtd. in Brym and Gimpelson, "The Size, Composition, and Dynamics of the Russian State Bureaucracy in the 1990s," 112.
47 Luong and Weinthal, *Oil Is Not a Curse*, 148. For recent frustration, see "Russia Improves Position in International Corruption Rating."
48 Ivanova, Keen, and Klemm, "The Russian Flat Tax Reform," 404.
49 Ibid.
50 Martinez-Vazquez, Rider, and Wallace, *Tax Reform in Russia*, 42.
51 Shatalov, "Tax Reform in Russia," esp. 7–8, 12, 18.
52 Ivanova, Keen, and Klemm, "The Russian Flat Tax Reform," 411.
53 Aslund, *Russia's Capitalist Revolution*, 194.
54 Germanovich, "Oligarkhov poprosiat ne bespokoitsya."
55 Gustafson, *Wheel of Fortune*, 292 [translation adjusted]; cf. Reynolds, "Putin Reaches Out to Oligarchs."
56 Sakwa, *Putin*, 149.

57 Qtd. in Germanovich, "Trebuetsya novoe slovo."
58 Ibid.
59 "Under Yeltsin, we 'oligarchs' helped stop Russia from reverting to its old, repressive ways," Berezovsky bragged; see Berezovsky, "Our Reverse Revolution."
60 Fortescue, *Russia's Oil Barons and Metal Magnates*, chap. 2.
61 Qtd. in ibid., 145.
62 Qtd. in ibid., 1.

## Chapter 3

1 Gustafson, *Wheel of Fortune*, 151, citing Spears and Associates, *Petroleum Equipment and Service Needs of the CIS*. Thanks to Richard Spears for speaking with me about the report.
2 Gustafson, *Wheel of Fortune*, 186.
3 Data from U.S. Energy Information Agency.
4 Gustafson, *Wheel of Fortune*, 186.
5 Wrongly, as the cases of Yukos, Bashneft, and others show.
6 Gustafson, *Wheel of Fortune*, 194.
7 Qtd. in ibid., 238.
8 Vatansever, *The Political Economy of Allocation of Natural Resource Rents*, 80.
9 Ibid., 83. Disclosure: The Alfa Fellowship Program, which is supported by Mikhail Fridman, funded one of my previous research projects in 2013–14.
10 Gustafson, *Wheel of Fortune*, 187–88.
11 Fortescue, *Russia's Oil Barons and Metal Magnates*, 117.
12 Ibid., 117–18.
13 Ibid., 117–18.
14 Paxton, "Reindeer Herders Battle Alcohol on Russia's Edge."
15 On the development of these special zones, see Miller, *The Struggle to Save the Soviet Economy*, chap. 6; and Samoylenko, *Special Report: Government Policies in Regard to Internal Tax Havens in Russia*.
16 Fortescue, *Russia's Oil Barons and Metal Magnates*, 118–19.
17 Gustafson, *Wheel of Fortune*, 137.
18 Hoffman, *The Oligarchs*, 110.
19 Gustafson, *Wheel of Fortune*, 138.
20 Qtd. in Gessen, "The Wrath of Putin."
21 Baker and Glasser, *Kremlin Rising*, 276; Gustafson, *Wheel of Fortune*, 139.
22 Gustafson, *Wheel of Fortune*, 140.
23 Baker and Glasser, *Kremlin Rising*, 276.
24 Gustafson, *Wheel of Fortune*, 140.
25 Baker and Glasser, *Kremlin Rising*, 276.
26 Gustafson, *Wheel of Fortune*, 295.
27 Fortescue, *Russia's Oil Barons and Metal Magnates*, 119.
28 Ibid., 119.
29 Gustafson, *Wheel of Fortune*, 287–88.
30 Ibid., 290–91.

31 Ibid., 286, 290–92.

32 Qtd. in ibid., 296–97.

33 Qtd. in ibid., 295.

34 Vatansever, *The Political Economy of Allocation of Natural Resource Rents*, 107.

35 Ibid., 109, 111, 114, 120, 123.

36 Putin, "Priamaia liniia."

37 Baker and Glasser, *Kremlin Rising*, 350.

38 Ibid., 352.

39 Ibid., 352.

40 Fortescue, *Russia's Oil Barons and Metal Magnates*, 127.

41 Baker and Glasser, *Kremlin Rising*, 352.

42 Qtd. in Fortescue, *Russia's Oil Barons and Metal Magnates*, 147.

43 Qtd. in ibid., 162.

44 Qtd. in ibid., 146; "Vospitanie chuvstv."

45 Qtd. in Fortescue, *Russia's Oil Barons and Metal Magnates*, 146. Translation adjusted.

46 Qtd. in ibid., 165. Cf. Luong and Weinthal, *Oil Is Not a Curse*, 158.

47 Fortescue, *Russia's Oil Barons and Metal Magnates*, 118–19.

48 Ibid., 146.

49 Qtd. in Baker and Glasser, *Kremlin Rising*, 351.

50 Gustafson, *Wheel of Fortune*, 267.

51 Ibid., 267.

52 Aslund, *Russia's Capitalist Revolution*, 229.

53 Ibid., 229.

54 Gustafson, *Wheel of Fortune*, 267.

55 Ibid., 267.

56 Dawisha, *Putin's Kleptocracy*; Henderson, *Non-Gazprom Gas Producers in Russia*, 56.

57 Goldman, *Petrostate*, 104.

58 Henderson, *Non-Gazprom Gas Producers in Russia*, 59.

59 Ibid., 57.

60 Goldman, *Petrostate*, 142.

61 Gustafson, *Wheel of Fortune*, 268.

62 Treisman, "Putin's Silovarchs," 11.

63 Aslund, *Russia's Capitalist Revolution*, 230.

64 Toporkov, "Kontrakty trekh glavnikh podriadchikov 'Gazproma' v 2016 godu prevysili 0.5 trln rublei," *Vedomosti*, July 31, 2017.

65 Galaktionova and Miazina, "Rotenburg poluchil bez konkursa podriadi Gazproma pochti na 200 mlrd rub"; Yaffa, "Oligarchy 2.0."

66 Burke, "How Russian Energy Giant Lost $300bn."

67 Soldatkin, "How Gazprom's $1 Trillion Dream Has Fallen Apart."

68 Grey et al., "Special Report: Putin's Allies Channeled Billions to Ukraine Oligarch"; Soldatkin, "How Gazprom's $1 Trillion Dream Has Fallen Apart"; Burke, "How Russian Energy Giant Lost $300bn."

69 Henderson, *Non-Gazprom Gas Producers in Russia*, 32–33.

70 Serov, "Gazprom potraril 2.4 trln rublei na nevostrebovannie proekti."

71  BP, "Rosneft and BP Complete TNK-BP Sale and Purchase Transaction"; Neate, "Rosneft Takes Over TNK-BP in $55bn Deal."
72  Qtd. in Henderson and Pirani, *The Russian Gas Matrix*, 34.
73  Henderson, *Non-Gazprom Gas Producers in Russia*, 212.
74  Ibid.; Henderson and Pirani, *The Russian Gas Matrix*, 122.
75  Henderson and Pirani, *The Russian Gas Matrix*, 32.
76  Henderson, *Non-Gazprom Gas Producers in Russia*, 212.
77  Gustafson, *Wheel of Fortune*, 3.
78  Henderson and Pirani, *The Russian Gas Matrix*, 32–33.
79  Mehdi, "How the Kremlin Accidentally Liberalized Russia's Natural Gas Market."
80  Henderson and Pirani, *The Russian Gas Matrix*, 32.
81  Luhn, "Gennady Timchenko Denies Putin Links Made Him One of Russia's Top Oligarchs."
82  Henderson, *Non-Gazprom Gas Producers in Russia*, 44.
83  Qtd. in ibid., 37.
84  Henderson and Pirani, *The Russian Gas Matrix*, 32–33.
85  Ibid., 33, 318.
86  Ibid., 32–33.
87  Henderson, *Non-Gazprom Gas Producers in Russia*, 32, 33, 165.
88  Panin, "Gazprom's Grip on Russian Gas Exports Weakens as Novatek Gets Export License."
89  Russian Legal Information Agency, "Decision to Deny Rosneft Access to Sakhalin-II Pipeline Upheld."
90  "Gazprom teriaet tarifnoe lobbi"; Serov and Papchenkova, "Chinovniki ne budut otbirat u Gazproma trubu."
91  Pressures have been growing since the late 2000s; see, for example, Henderson, *Non-Gazprom Gas Producers in Russia*, 17.
92  Henderson and Pirani, *The Russian Gas Matrix*, 34.
93  Gustafson, *Wheel of Fortune*, 17–18.
94  Ibid., 364.
95  U.S. Energy Information Agency data.
96  For a summary, see Luong and Weinthal, *Oil Is Not a Curse*, 137–44.
97  Kondrashov, "Taxation in the Russian Oil Sector."
98  Bobylev, "Development Trends In Russia's Oil & Gas Sector"; Kondrashov, "Taxation in the Russian Oil Sector"; Gustafson, *Wheel of Fortune*, 365.
99  Bank Rossii, *Russian Federation: Crude Oil Exports, 2000–15*.
100  Soldatkin, "Russian Oil Output Hits Post-Soviet Record High."

### Chapter 4

1  Qtd. in Gustafson, *Wheel of Fortune*, 361.
2  Vatansever, *The Political Economy of Allocation of Natural Resource Rents*, 185; Chebotareva, "The Structure of State Debt in Long-Term Perspective."
3  Kovalyova, "Duma Calls for Loan to Cover Paris Club Debt."

4  Aron, "The Battle over the Debt."

5  Ibid.

6  Vatansever, *The Political Economy of Allocation of Natural Resource Rents*, 184.

7  Iasin and Gavrilenkov, "The Problem of Settling Russia's Foreign Debt."

8  Tompson, "The Russian Economy under Vladimir Putin," 118.

9  Vatansever, *The Political Economy of Allocation of Natural Resource Rents*, 390.

10  Ibid., 389.

11  Ibid., 390.

12  Qtd. in ibid., 391. Translation adjusted.

13  Putin, "Pryamaya liniya."

14  Fedorin, "Mozhem i bez profitsita."

15  Chung and Buckley, "Russia Finalises Paris Club Debt Deal"; Chung, "Russia Pays Part of Paris Club Debt."

16  Weaver, "Debt Sale Seen as Triumph for Moscow."

17  Of course, the United States has far less reason to run budget surpluses given that tax revenue does not rely on volatile commodity prices.

18  Zolotareva et al., "The Prospects for Creating a Stabilization Fund in the Russian Federation," 5–85; Afanasyev, "Instrumentarii stabilizatsionnogo fonda."

19  "Gref prizyvaet borotsya s gollandskoi bolezniu v rossiisskoi ekonomike"; Sanko, "Rossiiskii variant gollandskoi bolezni"; Kats, "Razgovory s Alekseem Kudrinym."

20  Qtd. in Dabrowska and Zweynert, "Economic Ideas and Institutional Change," 13.

21  Qtd. in Vatansever, *The Political Economy of Allocation of Natural Resource Rents*, 332.

22  Putin, "Address to the Federal Assembly."

23  Munter and George, "Russian Fund Highlights Dependence on Oil"; Dabrowska and Zweynert, "Economic Ideas and Institutional Change," 17; Kudrin, "O stabilizatsionnom fonde RF."

24  Vatansever, *The Political Economy of Allocation of Natural Resource Rents*, 187.

25  Kudrin, "O stabilizatsionnom fonde RF."

26  Vatansever, *The Political Economy of Allocation of Natural Resource Rents*, 187.

27  Thanks to Ilya Voiskoboinikov for pointing this out.

28  Wagstyl, "Deripaska Calls for Changes at 'Ridiculous' Central Bank."

29  Fetisov, "Russia's Monetary Policy," 9.

30  Cited in ibid., 12.

31  Ibid., 27.

32  Clover and Weaver, "Central Bank Succession Grips Russia."

33  Glazyev, "Absurdnost denezhnoi politiki v Rossii."

34  Ibid.; "S. Glazyev."

35  Putin, "Poslanie federalnomy sobraniiu rossiiskii federatsii."

36  E.g., Kudrin, "Inflation."

37  Illarionov, "Kratkaia istoriia sozdaniia stabilizatsionnogo fonda."

38  Blank, Gurevich, and Uliukaev, "The Exchange Rate and Sectoral Competitiveness in the Russian Economy."

39  Kudrin, "Inflation," 36.

40  Ibid., 35.

41 Ibid., 47.
42 Ibid., 32.
43 Ibid., 49.
44 Ibid., 27.
45 Dabrowska and Zweynert, "Economic Ideas and Institutional Change," 13.
46 Kats, "Razgovory s Alekseem Kudrinym."
47 Qtd. in Gustafson, *Wheel of Fortune*, 361.
48 Glazyev, "Absurdnost denezhnoi politiki v Rossii."
49 Qtd. in Panina, "Tri goda ili deciat let."
50 "Glazyev: Stabilizatsionnii fond u nas lipovy," *Rosbalt*, June 6, 2006.
51 Qtd. in Belkin and Storozhenko, "Zolotovaliutnye rezervy Rossii i napravleniia ikh ratsional'nogo ispol'zovaniia."
52 Interview with Andrei Movchan, Moscow, December 17, 2015.
53 Qtd. in Panina, "Tri goda ili deciat let."
54 Kudrin, "Stabilization Funds," 9.
55 Ibid., 10.
56 Ibid., 8, 10.
57 Ibid., 8.
58 "Transcript: Interview with Nikolai Patrushev."
59 E.g., Belkin and Storozhenko, "The Rational Use of Russia's Foreign Exchange Reserves."

## Chapter 5

1 "Ofshory druga Putina glavnoe"; Harding, "Revealed: The $2 Billion Offshore Trail That Leads to Vladimir Putin"; Seddon, "Putin's Cellist Friend 'Interested Only in Musical Instruments.'"
2 Harding, "Revealed: The $2 Billion Offshore Trail That Leads to Vladimir Putin."
3 Qtd. in Seddon, "Putin's Cellist Friend 'Interested Only in Musical Instruments.'"
4 "Auction House Removes Details of Cello Bought by Putin's Friend Roldugin."
5 Kuzmina, Volchkova, and Zueva, "Foreign Direct Investment and Governance Quality in Russia," 3.
6 Zhukovskii, Twitter post, April 23, 2016.
7 Voskoboynikov, "New Measures of Output, Labour and Capital in Industries of the Russian Economy," 45.
8 Gaddy and Ickes, "Resource Rents and the Russian Economy," 566.
9 Ibid., 562.
10 Luong and Weinthal, *Oil Is Not a Curse*, 149.
11 Ahrend, "Russian Industrial Restructuring," 284.
12 Conference Board, "Growth Accounting and Total Factor Productivity."
13 Ibid.
14 OECD Stat, "Labor Productivity Levels in the Total Economy."
15 Ibid.; Conference Board, "Growth Accounting and Total Factor Productivity."
16 World Bank Group, "World Bank Open Data."

17 Timmer and Voskoboynikov, "Is Mining Fueling Long-Run Growth in Russia?";
Iradian, "Rapid Growth in Transition Economies"; Voskoboynikov, "New
Measures of Output, Labour and Capital in Industries of the Russian Economy."
18 E.g., Putin et al., *First Person*, 179.
19 Guriev and Rachinsky, "The Role of Oligarchs in Russian Capitalism." For a related
study of the Ukrainian case, see Gorodnichenko and Grygorenko, "Are Oligarchs
Productive?"
20 Hanson, "The Russian Economic Puzzle."
21 Bershidsky, "Putin May Be Tiring of His Cronies." $70,000 was at the exchange rate
at the time Yakunin said this.
22 Papchenkova, Starinskaya, and Serov, "Zarplaty Sechina, Yakunina i Millera
ostanutsia tainoi."
23 Lammey, "Russian Railways Won't Publish Yakunin's Pay Packet."
24 "Navalny Says Yakunin Owns Business Empire."
25 Ibid.
26 "The Making of a Neo-KGB State."
27 Dawisha, *Putin's Kleptocracy*, 99.
28 Yakunin, "Globalizatsia i kapitalizm."
29 Ragozin, "The Putin Adoration Society."
30 Yakunin, "Globalizatsia i kapitalizm."
31 "Navalny Says 'Patriot' Yakunin's Children Live in Foreign Luxury Homes."
32 For employment data, see Russian Railways, "Overview."
33 Thanks to Russell Pittman for sharing his understanding of the economics of railway
reform.
34 For a summary, see Pittman, "Blame the Switchman?"
35 Interview with industry stakeholder, July 2016; Reznik and Shatalova, "Russian
Railways Seeks to Fix 'Mistake' of Lost Monopoly."
36 Amos, "'Are You Mad?'"
37 Navalny, "How They Siphon at Russian Railways."
38 Hartog, "Yakunin Quit Russian Railways over Son's Wish to Become British Citizen";
"Navalny Says 'Patriot' Yakunin's Children Live in Foreign Luxury Homes."
39 "Navalny Says Yakunin Owns Business Empire."
40 They deny improprieties; Kim, "Putin's Judo Friend Says Premier Didn't Help Win
Gazprom Deals."
41 Sergey Aleksashenko, "Nota Bene," July 11, 2016, 5.
42 "Bright Spark"; Abdullaev, "Q&A."
43 For reviews of *reiderstvo*, see Hanson, "Reiderstvo"; Rochlitz, "Corporate Raiding
and the Role of the State in Russia"; and Levina et al., "Uncertainty as a Factor in
Investment Decisions."
44 Forthcoming research by Noah Buckley will provide quantitative evidence on this
question.
45 See, e.g., KPMG, "Investing in Russia."
46 Abdullaev, "Q&A."
47 Zimin, "Promoting Investment in Russia's Regions," 659.
48 Ibid., 663.

49  Bazenkova, "Why Foreign Investment in Russia's Regions Is Falling."
50  Abdullaev, "Q&A."
51  KPMG, "Investing in Russia," 30.
52  Agentsvo Strategicheskikh Intsiativ, "Natsionalnii reiting sostoianiia investitsionnogo klimata subektov Rossisski Federatsii," 7.
53  Kuzmina, Volchkova, and Zueva, "Foreign Direct Investment and Governance Quality in Russia."
54  KPMG, "Investing in Russia," 17.
55  Sonne, "How Looming Recession Is Unsettling One of Russia's Boom Cities."
56  Ibid.
57  Ibid.; "Russian Car Sales Down 36% in 2015."
58  "Volkswagen Bets on Long-Term Russian Growth with New Engine Plant."
59  Roston, "Nobody Knows How 21st-Century Russians Will Respond to Crisis."
60  "There's Light at the End of the Tunnel for Russia's Economy."
61  "President Receives Governor of Kaluga, Russia."
62  Conversation with Andrei Yakovlev, Moscow, July 2016.
63  Abdullaev, "Q&A."
64  Sonne, "How Looming Recession Is Unsettling One of Russia's Boom Cities."
65  Thanks to Alex Nice for this phrase.
66  "Food retailing," in Lewis and Palmeda, "Unlocking Economic Growth in Russia," 3.
67  Ibid., 4.
68  Ibid., 1.
69  Ibid., 1.
70  Ibid., exhibit 1.
71  "Food retailing," 5, in Lewis and Palmeda, "Unlocking Economic Growth in Russia."
72  Ibid.
73  Khrennikov, "No Ally of Putin, Retail Billionaire Pinched by Sanctions."
74  Appell, "Oligarch Angel," 42–47, 104.
75  Ibid.
76  Khrennikov, "No Ally of Putin, Retail Billionaire Pinched by Sanctions."
77  Qtd. in ibid.; Appell, "Oligarch Angel."
78  Magnitogorsk Iron & Steel Works, "History."
79  McKenzie and Dukeov, "Retail Strategy and Policy in Russia," 190.
80  "A Magnit for Investors."
81  Appell, "Oligarch Angel."
82  Khrennikov, "No Ally of Putin, Retail Billionaire Pinched by Sanctions."
83  Appell, "Oligarch Angel."
84  Bakatina et al., "Lean Russia," 61–82.
85  Ibid., 66.
86  Magnitogorsk Iron & Steel Works, "History."
87  Fortescue, "The Russian Steel Industry," 252.
88  World Steel Association, *Steel Statistical Yearbook*.
89  Fortescue, "The Russian Steel Industry," 253–54.
90  World Steel Association, *Steel Statistical Yearbook 1996*, 107.
91  Madar, *Big Steel*, 112.

92 Ibid., 113.
93 Magnitogorsk Iron & Steel Works, *Magnitogorsk Iron & Steel Works Annual Report 2014*, 11.
94 Buchanan, "Strong Revival at Magnitogorsk," 17.
95 "Russian Plantmakers Push for Market Share."
96 Buchanan, "MMK Accelerates," 16–18.
97 Fortescue, "The Russian Steel Industry," 255.
98 Gessen, "The Insatiable Mr. Putin."
99 Ibid.
100 Lewis and Palmeda, "Unlocking Economic Growth in Russia"; Bakatina et al., "Lean Russia," 50.
101 Bakatina et al., "Lean Russia," 45.
102 Ibid., 52.
103 Interview with steel industry analyst, Moscow, July 2016.
104 Madar, *Big Steel*, 113–14.

## Chapter 6

1 Qtd. in Artunyan, *The Putin Mystique*, 4; Kroll, "The World's Billionaires"; "Special Report: The World's Billionaires 2009."
2 Kroll, "The World's Billionaires"; "Special Report: The World's Billionaires 2009."
3 Elder, "Vladimir Putin Takes Oleg Deripaska to Task"; Stent, *The Limits of Partnership*, 185.
4 Myers, *The New Tsar*, 360–62.
5 Elder, "Vladimir Putin Takes Oleg Deripaska to Task."
6 Qtd. in ibid.
7 Artunyan, *The Putin Mystique*, chap. 4.
8 Qtd. in Crowley, "Monotowns, Economic Crisis, and the Politics of Industrial Restructuring in Russia."
9 Gaddy, *The Price of the Past*.
10 Gimpelson and Kapeliushnikov, "Labor Market Adjustment," 3.
11 Ibid.
12 Kozina, Vinogradova, and Cook, "Russian Labor," 219.
13 Crowley, "Monotowns, Economic Crisis, and the Politics of Industrial Restructuring in Russia," 17. Crowley notes that "9 out of 10 protest actions took place in forms not allowed by labor legislation," while "extreme forms of protest" such as hunger strikes were twice as frequent as legal protests.
14 Greene and Robertson, "Politics, Justice and the New Russian Strike."
15 A good discussion is Sil, "The Fluidity of Labor Politics in Postcommunist Transitions."
16 Gimpelson and Kapeliushnikov, "Labor Market Adjustment," 35.
17 Moffitt, "Unemployment Insurance and the Distribution of Unemployment Spells."
18 Gimpelson and Kapeliushnikov, "Labor Market Adjustment," 36.
19 Andrienko and Guriev, "Determinants of Interregional Mobility in Russia"; Gimpelson and Kapeliushnikov, "Labor Market Adjustment."

20 Crowley, "Monotowns, Economic Crisis, and the Politics of Industrial Restructuring in Russia," 15.
21 Commander, Nikoloski, and Plekhanov, "Employment Concentration and Resource Allocation," 12.
22 Russian businesspeople mention this regularly.
23 Qtd. in Crowley, "Monotowns, Economic Crisis, and the Politics of Industrial Restructuring in Russia," 7.
24 Gimpelson and Kapeliushnikov, "Labor Market Adjustment," 34.
25 Ibid., 8.
26 Sinitsina, "Experience in Implementing Social Benefits Monetization Reform in Russia," 9.
27 Ibid.
28 Ibid., 11.
29 Ibid., 12.
30 Ibid.
31 Ibid.
32 Ibid., 11.
33 Ibid., 56–57.
34 Putin et al., *First Person*, 180.
35 Sinitsina, "Experience in Implementing Social Benefits Monetization Reform in Russia," 10.
36 Ibid., 9.
37 Baker and Glasser, *Kremlin Rising*, 373.
38 Sinitsina, "Experience in Implementing Social Benefits Monetization Reform in Russia," 23.
39 Ibid., 24.
40 Ibid., 25.
41 "Putin Deplores Collapse of USSR."
42 Warren, "Putin Revives Soviet National Anthem."
43 Tsentr, "Praviteli v otechestvennoi istorii."
44 Remington, "Pension Reform in Authoritarian Regimes."
45 Madeva, "Chelovek v solidarnoi pensionnoi sisteme," 5.
46 Johnson, "Russia's Potential Growth Rate 'Close to Zero.'"
47 Hansl, Levin, and Shaw, "Searching for a New Silver Age in Russia."
48 Chandler, *Shocking Mother Russia*, 76.
49 Ibid., 79.
50 Ibid., 132.
51 Ibid., 135.
52 Ibid., 136.
53 Ibid., 138.
54 Piñera, "A Chilean Model for Russia."
55 Orenstein, *Privatizing Pensions*.
56 Chandler, *Shocking Mother Russia*, 142–43.
57 Ibid., 147, 152.
58 Ibid., 146–47.

59 Gurvich, "Printsipy novy pensionnii reform," table 2.

60 Madeva, "Chelovek v solidarnoi pensionnoi sisteme," 2.

61 Remington, "Pension Reform in Authoritarian Regimes," 14.

62 For a summary of debates, see ibid., 14. On Kudrin's view, see Kudrin and Gurvich, "Starenie naseleniia i ugroza biudzhetnogo krizisa."

63 Korsunskaya, Kelly, and Fabrichnaya, "Russia Considers Abolishing Mandatory Pension Savings."

64 Qtd. in Bershidsky, "Russian Pensions Paid for Putin's Crimea Grab."

65 Ostroukh, "Russia to Grab Pension Money, Temporarily." See also Remington, "Pension Reform in Authoritarian Regimes," 15.

### Chapter 7

1 For an overview of Russian foreign policy during the 2000s, see Mankoff, *Russian Foreign Policy*.

2 SIPRI Military Expenditure Database.

3 Wolf, "Cost of Lockheed's F-35 Fighter Soars."

4 For an overview of reforms intended in part to stem graft, see Bartles, "Defense Reforms of Russian Defense Minister Anatolii Serdyukov."

5 For an overview, see Asmus, *A Little War That Shook the World*.

6 Renz and Thornton, "Russian Military Modernization," 45.

7 Clover, "Russia Vows to Push Army Reform."

8 Oxenstierna and Westerlund, "Arms Procurement and the Russian Defense Industry," 2; Oxenstierna, "Russia's Defense Spending and the Economic Decline," 62.

9 Oxenstierna and Westerlund, "Arms Procurement and the Russian Defense Industry," 2. The 70 percent figure, it is worth noting, was never specifically defined.

10 Ibid., 7; "BOFIT Weekly Review."

11 Kuvshinova and Pismennaya, "Ekonomika sverkhoptimizma."

12 Hamilton, "Causes and Consequences of the Oil Shock of 2007–08."

13 "Vkratse."

14 "S novym rostom!"

15 "Vsyo podorozhaet."

16 "Inomarki ne pomeshali."

17 "Nauka konkurirovat."

18 Ibid.

19 Central Bank of Russia, "External Debt of the Russian Federation in National and Foreign Currency."

20 Federal State Statistics Service, "Indeksy potrebitelskikh tsen po Rossiiskoi Federatsii."

21 "Ot redaktsii."

22 Khutornikh, Grozovskii, and Baraulina, "FRS naoborot."

23 *Trading Economics*, "Russia MICEX Stock Market Index."

24 *Trading Economics*, "Brent Crude Oil."

25 Chechel and Pismennaya, "Vozvrascheniya v 1998 god."

26 Central Bank of Russia, "External Sector Statistics."

27 Aleksashenko, "Crisis 2008," 43.
28 Ibid.
29 Central Bank of Russia, "Protsentnye stavki v 2008 gody."
30 IMF, "Russian Federation 2009 Article IV Consultation," 13.
31 Fedorinova and Pismennaya, "Spasli Abramovicha"; Stolyarov et al., "Isklyuchitelnaya mera."
32 IMF, "Russian Federation: Financial System Stability Assessment," 11.
33 Interview with former Finance Ministry official, Moscow, 2015. Rutland, "The Impact of the Global Financial Crisis on Russia," 2–5.
34 Akindinova, Aleksashenko, and Yasin, "Scenarios and Challenges of Macroeconomic Policy," 23.
35 IMF, "Russian Federation 2000 Article IV Consultation," 13.
36 OECD Stat, "Government Deficit/Surplus as a Percentage of GDP."
37 Akindinova, Aleksashenko, and Yasin, "Scenarios and Challenges of Macroeconomic Policy," 22.
38 Ministry of Finance of the Russian Federation, "Amount of the Reserve Fund."
39 The government of Russia estimates the total amount of the fiscal stimulus plan as 1,212.6 billion rubles (about 3.1 percent of GDP in 2009), which corresponds to the amendments introduced into the law on the federal budget for 2009, but budget expenditures (with respect to the original plan) grew by just 667 billion rubles (1.7 percent of GDP 2009). The remainder was a result of redirecting expenses for 2009, mainly investments.
40 Guriev and Tsyvinski, "Challenges Facing the Russian Economy after the Crisis," 21.
41 Sergeev, "Biznes nedovolen pravitelstvom."
42 Qtd. in Mau, "Between Crises and Sanctions," 20.
43 Ibid.
44 Akindinova, Aleksashenko, and Yasin, "Scenarios and Challenges of Macroeconomic Policy," 35.
45 Ibid., 38.
46 Rutland, "Impact of the Global Financial Crisis," 3.
47 Ibid.
48 Treisman, *The Return*, 258.
49 The article title is also translated "Go, Russia!" I quote below from the official translation, online at http://en.kremlin.ru/events/president/news/5413.
50 Appell, "The Short Life and Speedy Death of Russia's Silicon Valley."
51 Ibid.; "Kremlin Picks Site for Russian 'Silicon Valley.'"
52 Appell, "The Short Life and Speedy Death of Russia's Silicon Valley."
53 "Russia's Sinking Ship."
54 For a good summary of the debate, see Gaddy and Ickes, "Resource Rents and the Russian Economy."
55 Qtd. in Clover and Belton, "Putin to Return as Russian President."
56 Qtd. in Walker, "Putin Announces Plan to Return as Russian President."
57 Qtd. in Clover and Weaver, "Russian Job Swap Sparks Kremlin Revolt."
58 Qtd. in ibid.
59 Ibid.

60 Qtd. in ibid.
61 Grove, "Russia's Chechnya."
62 Clover et al., "Tens of Thousands Protest against Putin."
63 Elder, "Russian Opposition Activist Jailed for Four and a Half Years."
64 Putin, "Stroitelstvo spravedlivosti."
65 Kotova, "Putin poruchil povysit dokhody naseleniya i snizit stoimost zhilya."
66 As forthcoming research from Bryn Rosenfeld will show.
67 Aris, "Another Tough Start for Russia before Return to Growth."

## Chapter 8

1 A.O., "A Global Elite Gathering in the Crimea."
2 A video of the panel, though not Glazyev's sideline comments, is here: https://www.youtube.com/watch?v=B1w-px4xBgk&list=PLR50ISXqKze9C1CvoFhF53N_KGAUDEyz6&index=10.
3 Thanks to Shaun Walker for speaking about the context of these comments. See Walker, "Ukraine's EU Trade Deal Will Be Catastrophic, Says Russia."
4 For a good summary, see Dabrowski, "The Systemic Roots of Russia's Recession."
5 IBT Staff Report, "Is Russia's APEC Summit a $21 Billion Waste?"
6 Anti-Corruption Foundation, "Azimut Hotel."
7 Ibid.
8 "VEB dogoforilsya o restrukturizatsii kreditov po Olimpiade." Dollar figure is 2014 prices.
9 Chevtayeva and Shebalina, "Pravitelstvo predostavilo 548 mlrd rubley garantii na podderzhku VEBa."
10 E.g., Shishkov, "SNG."
11 Aslund, "Russia's Accession to the World Trade Organization."
12 Ibid., esp. 296–300.
13 Dyker, "Russian Accession to the WTO"; Connolly and Hanson, "Russia's Accession to the World Trade Organization."
14 Obama, "Statement by the President on the Trans-Pacific Partnership."
15 Germany's failure in 2015–16 to convince other states to agree to a refugee distribution scheme is a good example of the limits of German power.
16 MacFarquhar, "Russia and 2 Neighbors Form Economic Union That Has a Ukraine-Size Hole."
17 Bordachev, "Russia and the Eurasian Economic Union."
18 International Republican Institute, "Public Opinion Survey: Residents of Ukraine," slide 10.
19 Sadowski, "Ukraine: Between the European Union and the Customs Union."
20 For a good summary, see Dragneva and Wolczuk, Ukraine between the EU and Russia.
21 Zinets and Balmforth, "Ukraine Parliament Deadlock on Tymoshenko Clouds EU Signing."
22 Englund and Lally, "Ukraine, under Pressure from Russia, Puts Brakes on E.U. Deal."
23 Davenport, "EU Rejects Russian Pressure on Ukraine, Seeks Trade Ties."

24  "Ukraine's Employers Federation: Russia's Customs Service Halts All Ukrainian Imports."
25  Aslund, "Oligarchs, Corruption, and European Integration," 65.
26  Englund and Lally, "Ukraine, under Pressure from Russia, Puts Brakes on E.U. Deal."
27  Walker, "Vladimir Putin Offers Ukraine Financial Incentives to Stick with Russia."
28  For a summary of the debate on the causes of Russia's intervention, see Mearsheimer, McFaul, and Sestanovich, "Faulty Powers." See also Miller, "What Putin Really Feared in Ukraine."
29  Yakovlev, "What Are the Russian Elites Going to Build?," 2.
30  Ibid., 3.
31  "Third Wave of Sanctions Slams Russian Stocks."
32  Council of the European Union, "Council Decision 2014/508/CFSP."
33  Oxenstierna and Olsson, *The Economic Sanctions against Russia.*
34  Mohsin, "Norway 'Ready to Act' as Putin Sanctions Spark Fallout Probe"; Swiss Federal Council, "Situation in Ukraine"; Takahashi and Reynolds, "Japan Steps Up Russia Sanctions"; Lewis, "Australia 'Working towards' Tougher Sanctions against Russia"; Global Affairs Canada, "Canadian Sanctions Related to Russia"; Croft, "EU Hawks Lead Calls for Tougher Sanctions on Russia."
35  This section draws on Miller, "Why Russia's Economic Leverage Is Declining."
36  Calus, "Russian Sanctions against Moldova."
37  Parshin, "Eyeing Tajikistan's Weak Spot, Russia Presses for Integration."
38  Miller, "Russia's Central Bank."
39  For a full assessment, see Gurvich and Prilepskiy, "The Impact of Financial Sanctions on the Russian Economy."
40  U.S. Department of Agriculture Foreign Agricultural Service, "Russia Bans Key U.S. Agricultural Exports."
41  European Commission Agriculture and Rural Development, "The Russian Ban on EU Agricultural Products."
42  Thanks to Koen Schoors and Bruno Merlevede for sharing their knowledge of this issue.
43  Radio Free Europe/Radio Liberty, "French Senate Urges Government to Lift Sanctions on Russia."
44  For an overview, see Connolly and Hanson, "Import Substitution and Economic Sovereignty in Russia."
45  Government of the Russian Federation, "Instructions on Additional Measures to Stimulate Economic Growth."
46  Gorst, "Russia Bans U.S., European Food and Agricultural Imports."
47  U.S. Energy Information Administration, "U.S. Field Production of Crude Oil."
48  Central Bank of Russia, "International Reserves of the Russian Federation."
49  World Bank, "Cash Surplus/Deficit (% of GDP)."
50  Kramer, "Russia Raises Key Interest Rate."
51  And on the record, too. See Kuvshinova, Prokopenko, and Papchenkova, "Ukreplenie rublya obespokoilo rossiiskie vlasti."
52  Galouchko, "Putin's Ruble Warning Puts Goldman Easing Bets on Shaky Ground."

53 Kelly and Kobzeva, "Putin Stands by Hawkish Russian Central Bank."
54 Data from Rosstat.
55 This section draws on Miller, "Russia's Central Bank."
56 Data on external borrowing comes from the Central Bank of Russia, "External Sector Statistics."
57 See Gazprom, "Bonds."
58 Neate, "Rosneft Takes over TNK-BP in $55bn Deal."
59 "Russia Central Bank Governor Cancels Visit to Davos Forum as Ruble Slides."
60 Data from the Central Bank of Russia.
61 Qtd. in "Deneg net, no vy derzhites: Medvedev otvetil pensioneram v Krimu."
62 International Trade Centre, "List of Products Exported by Russian Federation."
63 Qtd. in "Deneg net, no vy derzhites, eshe odin universalnii otvet na vse slychai zhizni"; Hobson, "RuNet Has a Field Day with Medvedev's 'No Money' Quote."
64 Pismennaya, "Putin's Once-Mighty Bank for Pet Projects Now on Chopping Block."
65 Ibid.
66 Ibid.
67 "Glava VEBa nashel v banke tolko 20% 'khoroshikh aktivov'"; Papchenkova, "Boleye 40% kreditov VEBa – problemnie."
68 For tax revenue as percentage of GDP, see World Bank, "Tax Revenue (% of GDP)."
69 Ministry of Finance of the Russian Federation, "Brief Information on the Execution of the Federal Budget."
70 For a summary, see "Russia's 2015 Budget Deficit Totals $25 Billion."

## Postscript

1 Frye, "Capture or Exchange," 1023.
2 Ernst & Young, *Russia 2013*.
3 E.g., Mikhail Fridman; see Thomas, "Billionaire Fridman Targets US and Europe in $16bn Telecoms Spree."
4 This section draws from Miller, "Russia Considers How to Impose Austerity in a Time of Recession."
5 Schreck, "Road Warriors."
6 Devitt and Kobzeva, "In Economic Crisis, Putin Helps a Mogul He Once Attacked."
7 "Putin uvelichil predelnuiu chislennosti shtata MVD pochti na 65,000 chelovek."
8 "Medvedev Says Russia Will Not Raise Taxes until at Least 2018."
9 See IMF, "Russian Federation 2016 Article IV Consultation."
10 Hansl, Levin, and Shaw, "Searching for a New Silver Age in Russia," 11.

# BIBLIOGRAPHY

Abalkin, Leonid. "Nesostoyatelnost programmy Grefa." *Nezavisimaya Gazeta*, August 18, 2000. http://www.ng.ru/economics/2000-08-18/4_gref.html.

Abdullaev, Nabi. "Q&A: How to Make Foreign Business Love Russia." *Moscow Times*, March 17, 2015. https://themoscowtimes.com/articles/qa-how-to-make-foreign-business-love-russia-44852.

Adomanis, Mark. "After Years of Crying Wolf, West Now Has Proof of Russia's Imminent Economic Collapse." *Business New Europe*, July 1, 2016. http://www.intellinews.com/comment-after-years-of-crying-wolf-west-now-has-proof-of-russia-s-imminent-economic-collapse-101125.

Afanasyev, M. "Instrumentarii stabilizatsionnogo fonda: Opyt i perspektvy." *Voprosy Ekonomiki* 3 (2004): 65–75.

Agentsvo Strategicheskikh Intsiativ. "Natsionalnii reiting sostoianiia investitsionnogo klimata subektov Rossiiski Federatsii." May 2014. http://www.asi.ru/upload_docs/Rating2014.pdf.

Ahrend, Rudiger. "Russian Industrial Restructuring: Trends in Productivity, Competitiveness and Comparative Advantage." *Post-communist Economies* 18, no. 3 (2006): 277–95.

Akindinova, N. V., S. V. Aleksashenko, and E. G. Yasin. "Scenarios and Challenges of Macroeconomic Policy." Report at XII International Conference on Economic and Social Development, 2011. http://hse.ru/data/2011/04/05/1211686377/Akindinova.engl.pdf.

Aleksashenko, Sergey. "Crisis 2008: Time to Make a Diagnosis." *Problems of Economic Transition* 51, no. 9 (2009): 33–50.

Alexeev, Michael, and Robert Conrad. "The Russian Oil Tax Regime: A Comparative Perspective." *Eurasian Geography and Economics* 50, no. 1 (2009): 93–114.

Alexeev, Michael, and Shlomo Weber, eds. *The Oxford Handbook of the Russian Economy*. Oxford: Oxford University Press, 2013.

"Almazy Rossii ukhodyat ot De Beers." *Kommersant*, October 2, 2001. http://www.kommersant.ru/doc/285277.

"Alternativnaia programma Vikotra Ishaeva." *Delovaia Pressa*, November 30, 2000. http://www.businesspress.ru/newspaper/article_mid_40_aid_44228.html.

Amos, Howard. "'Are You Mad?' Putin Orders Government to Restore Train Services." *Moscow Times*, February 4, 2015. https://themoscowtimes.com/articles/are-you-mad-putin-orders-government-to-restore-train-services-43581.

Andrienko, Yuri, and Sergei Guriev. "Determinants of Interregional Mobility in Russia." *Economics of Transition* 12, no. 1 (2004): 1–27.

Anti-Corruption Foundation. "Azimut Hotel." n.d. http://sochi.fbk.info/en/place/17.

Appel, Hilary. *Tax Politics in Eastern Europe: Globalization, Regional Integration, and the Democratic Compromise.* Ann Arbor: University of Michigan Press, 2011.

Appell, James. "Oligarch Angel." *Howler Magazine*, Spring 2016.

———. "The Short Life and Speedy Death of Russia's Silicon Valley." *Foreign Policy*, May 6, 2015. http://foreignpolicy.com/2015/05/06/the-short-life-and-speedy-death-of-russias-silicon-valley-medvedev-go-russia-skolkovo.

Aris, Ben. "Another Tough Start for Russia before Return to Growth." *bne IntelliNews*, December 22, 2015. http://www.intellinews.com/another-tough-start-for-russia-before-return-to-growth-87000.

Aron, Leon. "The Battle over the Debt." American Enterprise Institute, 2001. https://www.aei.org/publication/the-battle-over-the-debt.

Artunyan, Anna. *The Putin Mystique.* Northampton, Mass.: Olive Branch, 2014.

Aslund, Anders. *Building Capitalism: The Transformation of the Former Soviet Bloc.* Cambridge: Cambridge University Press, 2002.

———. *How Russia Became a Market Economy.* Washington, D.C.: Brookings Institution Press, 1995.

———. "Oligarchs, Corruption, and European Integration." *Journal of Democracy* 25, no. 3 (2014): 64–73. http://www.journalofdemocracy.org/sites/default/files/Aslund-25-3.pdf.

———. "Russia's Accession to the World Trade Organization." *Eurasian Geography and Economics* 48, no. 3 (2007): 289–305.

———. *Russia's Capitalist Revolution: Why Market Reforms Succeeded and Democracy Failed.* Washington, D.C.: Peterson Institute for International Economics, 2007.

Aslund, Anders, Sergei Guriev, and Andrew Kuchins. *Russia after the Global Economic Crisis.* Washington, D.C.: Peterson Institute for International Economics, 2010.

Asmus, Ronald. *A Little War That Shook the World: Russia and the Future of the West.* New York: Macmillan, 2010.

"Auction House Removes Details of Cello Bought by Putin's Friend Rodulgin." *Moscow Times*, April 22, 2016. https://themoscowtimes.com/news/auction-house-removes-details-of-cello-bought-by-putins-friend-roldugin-52650.

Bakatina, Daria, Jean-Pascal Duvieusart, Vitaly Klintsov, Kevin Krogmann, Jaana Remes, Irene Shvakman, Yermolay Solzhenitsyn, et al. "Lean Russia: Sustaining Economic Growth through Improved Productivity." McKinsey Global Institute, 2009.

Baker, Peter, and Susan Glasser. *Kremlin Rising: Vladimir Putin's Russia and the End of Revolution.* New York: Lisa Drew/Scribner, 2005.

Bank Rossii. *Russian Federation: Crude Oil Exports, 2000–15.* June 25, 2015. http://www.cbr.ru/Eng/statistics/print.aspx?file=credit_statistics/crude_oil_e.htm&pid=svs&sid=vt1.

Barnes, Andrew Scott. *Owning Russia: The Struggle over Factories, Farms, and Power.* Ithaca, N.Y.: Cornell University Press, 2006.

Bartles, Charles K. "Defense Reforms of Russian Defense Minister Anatollii Serdyukov." *Journal of Slavic Military Studies* 24, no. 1 (2011): 55–80.

Bazenkova, Anastasia. "Why Foreign Investment in Russia's Regions Is Falling." *Moscow Times*, April 27, 2015. https://themoscowtimes.com/articles/why-foreign-investment-in-russias-regions-is-falling-46146.

Bekker, Aleksandr. "Gref vo vtorom izdanii." *Vedemosti*, March 7, 2001. http://vedemosti .ru/newspaper/articles/2001/03/07/gref-vo-vtorom-izdanii.

Belkin, V., and V. Storozhenko. "The Rational Use of Russia's Foreign Exchange Reserves: The Structure of Foreign Exchange Reserves." *Problems of Economic Transition* 50, no. 9 (2008): 54–65.

———. "Zolotovaliutnye rezervy Rossii i napravleniia ikh ratsional'nogo ispol'zovaniia." *Voprosy Ekonomiki* 10 (2007): 41–51.

Berezovsky, Boris. "Our Reverse Revolution." *Washington Post*, October 16, 2000.

Berglof, Erik, Andrei Kunov, Julia Shvets, and Ksenia Yuaeva. *The New Political Economy of Russia*. Cambridge, Mass.: MIT Press, 2003.

Bershidsky, Leonid. "Putin May Be Tiring of His Cronies." *Bloomberg View*, August 18, 2015. https://www.bloombergview.com/articles/2015-08-18/putin-may-be-tiring-of-his-cronies.

———. "Russian Pensions Paid for Putin's Crimea Grab." *Bloomberg*, June 26, 2014. https://www.bloomberg.com/view/articles/2014-06-26/russian-pensions-paid-for-putin-s-crimea-grab.

Blank, A., E. Gurevich, and A. Uliukaev. "The Exchange Rate and Sectoral Competitiveness in the Russian Economy." *Problems of Economic Transition* 50, no. 1 (2007): 27–52.

Blasi, Joseph R., Maya Kroumova, and Douglas Kruse. *Kremlin Capitalism: The Privatization of the Russian Economy*. Ithaca, N.Y.: Cornell University Press, 1997.

Bobylev, Yuri. "Development Trends in Russia's Oil & Gas Sector." *Russian Economic Developments* 6 (2014): 19–23

"BOFIT Weekly Review." January 26, 2016. https://helda.helsinki.fi/bof/bitstream/handle/123456789/14554/w2016.pdf?sequence=1.

Bohlen, Celestine. "Rumors and Contradictions Fuel Russia Market Crisis." *New York Times*, August 16, 1998.

———. "Russia Acts to Fix Sinking Finances." *New York Times*, August 18, 1998.

Bordachev, Timofei. "Russia and the Eurasian Economic Union: The View from Moscow." European Council on Foreign Relations, January 21, 2015. http://www.ecfr .eu/article/commentary_russia_and_the_eurasian_economic_union_the_view _from_moscow403.

Boycko, Maxim, Andrei Shleifer, and Robert W. Vishny. *Privatizing Russia*. Cambridge, Mass.: MIT Press, 1997.

BP. "Rosneft and BP Complete TNK-BP Sale and Purchase Transaction." Press release, March 20, 2013. http://www.bp.com/en/global/corporate/media/press-releases/rosneft-and-bp-complete-tnk-bp-sale-and-purchase-transaction.html.

"Bright Spark." *Economist*, November 20, 2014. http://www.economist.com/news/briefing/21633814-some-russia-business-friendly-bright-spark.

Brym, Robert J., and Vladimir Gimpelson. "The Size, Composition, and Dynamics of the Russian State Bureaucracy in the 1990s." *Slavic Review* 63, no. 1 (2004): 90–112.

Buchanan, Sandra. "MMK Accelerates." *Metal Bulletin Monthly* 448 (May 2008): 16–18.

———. "Strong Revival at Magnitogorsk." *Metal Bulletin Monthly* 357 (September 2000): 17.

Bunin, Igor. *Biznesmeny Rossii: 40 istorii uspekha.* Moscow: OKO, 1994.

Burke, Justin. "How Russian Energy Giant Lost $300bn." *Guardian*, August 7, 2015. https://www.theguardian.com/world/2015/aug/07/gazprom-oil-company-share-price-collapse.

Calus, Kamil. "Russian Sanctions against Moldova." *OSW Commentary*, November 6, 2014. https://www.osw.waw.pl/en/publikacje/osw-commentary/2014-11-06/russian-sanctions-against-moldova-minor-effects-major-potential.

Central Bank of Russia. "External Debt of the Russian Federation in National and Foreign Currency." April 26, 2012. http://cbr.ru/eng/statistics/print.aspx?file=credit_statistics/debt-non_an_e.htm&pid=svs&sid=vdRF_nr_ap.http://cbr.ru/eng/statistics/print.aspx?file=credit_statistics/debt-non_an_e.htm&pid=svs&sid=vdRF_nr_ap.

———. "External Sector Statistics." http://www.cbr.ru/eng/statistics/?PrtId=svs.

———. "International Reserves of the Russian Federation." http://www.cbr.ru/eng/hd_base/Default.aspx?Prtid=mrrf_m.

———. "Protsentnye stavki v 2008 gody." http://www.cbr.ru/statistics/print.aspx?file=credit_statistics/interest_rates_08.htm&pid=cdps&sid=svodProcStav.

Chandler, Andrea. *Shocking Mother Russia: Democratization, Social Rights, and Pension Reform in Russia, 1990–2001.* Toronto: University of Toronto Press, 2004.

Charlton, Corey. "What More Does It Need? Chelsea Owner Roman Abramovich's £1.5 Billion Mega-yacht Which Is Twice the Length of a Football Pitch Is Renovated in Germany." *Daily Mail*, February 17, 2015. http://www.dailymail.co.uk/news/article-2957018/What-does-need-Chelsea-owner-Roman-Abramovich-s-1-5billion-mega-yacht-twice-length-football-pitch-renovated-Germany.html.

Chebankova, Elena. *Russia's Federal Relations: Putin's Reforms and Management of Regions.* London: Routledge, 2010.

Chebotareva, N. A. "The Structure of State Debt in Long-Term Perspective." *Problems of Economic Transition* 45, no. 1 (2002): 54–85.

Chechel, Alena, and Yevgeniy Pismennaya. "Vozvrascheniya v 1998 god." *Vedomosti*, December 17, 2008. http://www.vedomosti.ru/newspaper/articles/2008/12/17/vozvraschenie-v-1998-god.

Chevtayeva, Irina, and Yana Shebalina. "Pravitelstvo predostavilo 548 mlrd rubley garantii na podderzhku VEBa—Bloomberg." *Vedomosti*, February 3, 2017. https://www.vedomosti.ru/economics/articles/2017/02/03/676175-veb.

Chiodo, Abbigail, and Michael Owyang. "A Case Study of a Currency Crisis: The Russian Default of 1998." *Review, Federal Reserve Bank of St. Louis*, November/December 2002.

"Chronology of Russian Financial Crisis." *Reuters*, August 27, 1998.

Chung, Joanna. "Russia Pays Part of Paris Club Debt." *Financial Times*, July 6, 2005. https://www.ft.com/content/6c1a505a-edba-11d9-9ff5-00000e2511c8.

Chung, Joanna, and Neil Buckley. "Russia Finalises Paris Club Debt Deal." *Financial*

*Times*, June 23, 2006. http://www.ft.com/cms/s/0/aebacf66-0254-11db-a141-0000779e234o.html?ft_site=falcon&desktop=true.

Clover, Charles. "Russia Vows to Push Army Reform." *Financial Times*, December 4, 2012. https://www.ft.com/content/5abbb470-3e34-11e2-829d-00144feabdco.

Clover, Charles, and Catherine Belton. "Putin to Return as Russian President." *Financial Times*, September 24, 2011. https://www.ft.com/content/ea4f7162-e69c-11e0-8c5e-00144feab49a.

Clover, Charles, and Courtney Weaver. "Central Bank Succession Grips Russia." *Financial Times*, March 4, 2013. https://app.ft.com/content/ce8cbf42-84e4-11e2-88bb-00144feabdco.

———. "Russian Job Swap Sparks Kremlin Revolt." *Financial Times*, September 25, 2011. https://www.ft.com/content/594a509e-e78f-11e0-9da3-00144feab49a.

Clover, Charles, Courtney Weaver, Catherine Belton, and Isabel Gorst. "Tens of Thousands Protest against Putin." *Financial Times*, December 10, 2011. https://www.ft.com/content/991b6406-2330-11e1-af98-00144feabdco.

Commander, Simon, Zlatko Nikoloski, and Aleksander Plekhanov. "Employment Concentration and Resource Allocation: One-Company Towns in Russia." IZA Discussion Paper 6034 (October 2011): 1–32. http://ftp.iza.org/dp6034.pdf.

Conference Board. "Growth Accounting and Total Factor Productivity, 1990–2014." September 2015. http://www.conference-board.org/data/economydatabase/index.cfm?id=27762.

Connolly, Richard, and Philip Hanson. "Import Substitution and Economic Sovereignty in Russia." *Chatham House*, June 9, 2016. https://www.chathamhouse.org/sites/files/chathamhouse/publications/research/2016-06-09-import-substitution-russia-connolly-hanson.pdf.

———. "Russia's Accession to the World Trade Organization: Commitments, Processes, and Prospects." *Eurasian Geography and Economics* 53, no. 4 (2012): 479–501.

Cook, Linda J. *Postcommunist Welfare States: Reform Politics in Russia and Eastern Europe.* Ithaca, N.Y.: Cornell University Press, 2007.

Council of the European Union. "Council Decision 2014/508/CFSP." *EUR-Lex*, July 30, 2014. http://eur-lex.europa.eu/legal-content/EN/TXT/?uri=uriserv:OJ.L_.2014.226.01.0023.01.ENG.

Croft, Adrian. "EU Hawks Lead Calls for Tougher Sanctions on Russia." *Reuters*, January 26, 2015. http://www.reuters.com/article/us-ukraine-crisis-eu-idUSKBN0KZ2D320150126.

Crowley, Stephen. "Monotowns, Economic Crisis, and the Politics of Industrial Restructuring in Russia." https://www2.gwu.edu/~ieresgwu/assets/docs/Crowley_Monotowns_GW.pdf.

Dabrowska, Ewa, and Joachim Zweynert. "Economic Ideas and Institutional Change: The Case of the Russian Stabilization Fund." IOS Working Papers 339 (2014).

Dabrowski, Marek. "The Systemic Roots of Russia's Recession." *Bruegel Policy Contribution*, October 16, 2015. http://www.bruegel.org/2015/10/the-systemic-roots-of-russias-recession.

Daigle, Katy. "Warnings by Soros Send Markets into Panic." *Moscow Times*, August 14, 1998.

Dallek, Robert. *Franklin D. Roosevelt and American Foreign Policy, 1932–1945*. New York: Oxford University Press, 1979.

Davenport, Claire. "EU Rejects Russian Pressure on Ukraine, Seeks Trade Ties." *Reuters*, September 11, 2013. https://www.reuters.com/article/us-eu-ukraine-russia-idUSBRE 98A0KV20130911.

Dawisha, Karen. *Putin's Kleptocracy: Who Owns Russia?* New York: Simon and Schuster, 2015.

Delyagin, Mikhail. "Krizis prezidenta." *Vedemosti*, June 30, 2000. http://www.vedemosti .ru/newspaper/articles/2000/06/30/krizis-prezidenta.

"Deneg net, no vy derzhites, eshe odin universalnii otvet na vse slychai zhizni." *Meduza*, May 24, 2016.

"Deneg net, no vy derzhites: Medvedev otvetil pensioneram v Krimu." *RBK*, May 24, 2016. http://styler.rbc.ua/rus/zhizn/deneg-net-derzhites-medvedev-otvetil-pensioneram-1464075469.html.

Denisova, Irina, and Judith Shapiro. "Recent Demographic Developments in the Russian Federation." In *The Oxford Handbook of the Russian Economy*, edited by Michael Alexeev and Shlomo Weber, 800–826. Oxford: Oxford University Press, 2013.

De Silva, Migara, Galina Kurlyandskaya, Elena Andreeva, and Natalia Golovanova. *Intergovernmental Reforms in the Russian Federation: One Step Forward, Two Steps Back?* Washington, D.C.: World Bank, 2009.

Devitt, Polina, and Oksana Kobzeva. "In Economic Crisis, Putin Helps a Mogul He Once Attacked." *Reuters*, July 14, 2016. http://www.reuters.com/article/ us-russia-mechel-rescue-insight-idUSKCN0ZU0XL.

Dmitriev, Mikhail. "Strategiia—2010: Itogi realizatsii 10 let spustia." www.iep.ru/files/ text/policy/2010_3/dmitriev.pdf.

Dragneva, Rilka, and Kataryna Wolczuk. *Ukraine between the EU and Russia: The Integration Challenge*. London: Palgrave Macmillan, 2015.

Duhamel, Luc. *The KGB Campaign against Corruption in Moscow, 1982–1987*. Pittsburgh: University of Pittsburgh Press, 2010.

Dyker, David A. "Russian Accession to the WTO—Why Such a Long and Difficult Road?" *Post-communist Economies* 16, no. 1 (2004): 3–20.

Easter, Gerald M. *Capital, Coercion, and Postcommunist States*. Ithaca, N.Y.: Cornell University Press, 2012.

Elder, Miriam. "Fradkov Named Foreign Spymaster." *Moscow Times*, October 8, 2007.

———. "Russian Opposition Activist Jailed for Four and a Half Years." *Guardian*, November 9, 2012. https://www.theguardian.com/world/2012/nov/09/russian-opposition-activist-jailed-years.

———. "Vladimir Putin Takes Oleg Deripaska to Task." *Telegraph*, June 4, 2009. http:// www.telegraph.co.uk/news/worldnews/europe/russia/5446293/Vladimir-Putin-takes-Oleg-Deripaska-to-task.html.

Englund, Will, and Kathy Lally. "Ukraine, under Pressure from Russia, Puts Brakes on E.U. Deal." *Washington Post*, November 21, 2013. https://www.washingtonpost .com/world/europe/ukraine-under-pressure-from-russia-puts-brakes-on-eu-deal/2013/11/21/46c50796-52c9-11e3-9ee6-2580086d8254_story.html.

Ernst & Young. *Russia 2013: Shaping Russia's Future.* http://www.ey.com/Publication/
vwLUAssets/2013-Russia-attractiveness-survey-Eng/$FILE/2013-Russia-
attractiveness-survey-Eng.pdf.

European Commission Agriculture and Rural Development. "The Russian Ban on EU
Agricultural Products—12 Months On." August 7, 2015. https://ec.europa.eu/agri
culture/newsroom/218_en.

Everett, Burgess. "McCain: Russia Is a 'Gas Station.'" *Politico,* March 26, 2014.

"Executive Profile: Sergey A. Sulimov." *Bloomberg.* https://www.bloomberg.com/
research/stocks/private/person.asp?personId=14553428&privcapId=9681745.

Federal State Statistics Service. "Indeksy potrebitelskikh tsen po Rossiiskoi Federatsii."
July 10, 2017. http://www.gks.ru/free_doc/new_site/prices/potr/tab-potr1.htm.

Fedorin, Vladimir. "Mozhem i bez profitsita." *Vedomosti,* August 16, 2002. http://www
.vedomosti.ru/newspaper/articles/2002/08/16/mozhem-i-bez-proficita.

Fedorinova, Yuliya, and Yevgeniya Pismennaya. "Spasli Abramovicha." *Vedomosti,*
November 24, 2008. http://www.vedomosti.ru/newspaper/articles/2008/11/24/
spasli-abramovicha.

Fetisov, G. "Russia's Monetary Policy." *Problems of Economic Transition* 51, no. 9 (2009):
3–32.

Fortescue, Stephen. "The Russian Steel Industry, 1990–2009." *Eurasian Geography and
Economics* 50, no. 3 (2009): 252–74.

———. *Russia's Oil Barons and Metal Magnates: Oligarchs and the State in Transition.*
London: Palgrave Macmillan UK, 2007.

Freeland, Chrystia. *Sale of the Century: Russia's Wild Ride from Communism to Capitalism.*
New York: Crown Business, 2000.

Frye, Timothy. *Building States and Markets after Communism: The Perils of Polarized
Democracy.* Cambridge: Cambridge University Press, 2010.

———. "Capture or Exchange: Business Lobbying in Russia." *Europe-Asia Studies* 54,
no. 7 (2002): 1017–36.

Gaddy, Clifford. *The Price of the Past: Russia's Struggle with the Legacy of a Militarized
Economy.* Washington, D.C.: Brookings Institution Press, 1996.

Gaddy, Clifford, and Barry Ickes. "Resource Rents and the Russian Economy." *Eurasian
Geography and Economics* 46, no. 8 (2005): 559–83.

Galaktionova, Aleksandra, and Elena Miazina. "Rotenburg poluchil bez konkursa
podriadi Gazproma pochti na 200 mlrd rub." *RBK,* December 23, 2015.

Galouchko, Ksenia. "Putin's Ruble Warning Puts Goldman Easing Bets on Shaky
Ground." *Bloomberg,* July 27, 2016. http://www.bloombergquint.com/business
/2016/07/28/putin-s-ruble-warning-puts-goldman-easing-bets-on-shaky-ground-
ir5dkkum.

Gazprom. "Bonds." http://www.gazprom.com/investors/creditor-relations/bonds.

"Gazprom teriaet tarifnoe lobbi." *Kommersant,* July 30, 2015. http://kommersant.ru/
doc/2778371.

Gehlbach, Scott. *Representation through Taxation, Revenue, Politics, and Development in
Postcommunist States.* Cambridge: Cambridge University Press, 2008.

Germanovich, Aleksei. "Oligarkhov poprosiat ne bespokoitsya." *Vedomosti,* July 28,

2000. http://www.vedemosti.ru/newspaper/articles/2000/07/28/oligarhov-poprosyat-ne-bespokoitsya.

———. "Trebuetsya novoe slovo." *Vedemosti*, July 31, 2000. http//www.vedemosti.ru/newspaper/articles/2000/07/31/trebuetsya-novoe-slovo.

Gessen, Masha. "The Insatiable Mr. Putin." *Sydney Morning Herald*, March 31, 2012. http://www.smh.com.au/world/the-insatiable-mr-putin-20120330-1w34b.html.

———. *The Man without a Face: The Unlikely Rise of Vladimir Putin.* New York: Riverhead, 2013.

———. "The Wrath of Putin." *Vanity Fair News*, March 31, 2012.

Gilman, Martin. *No Precedent, No Plan: Inside Russia's 1998 Default.* Cambridge, Mass.: MIT Press, 2010.

Gimpelson, Vladimir, and Rostislav Kapeliushnikov. "Labor Market Adjustment: Is Russia Different?" IZA Discussion Papers 5588 (March 2011): 1–36. Reprinted in Alexeev and Weber, *The Oxford Handbook of the Russian Economy.*

"Glava VEBa nashel v banke tolko 20% 'khoroshikh aktivov.'" *Forbes*, July 5, 2016. http://www.forbes.ru/news/324285-glava-veba-nashel-v-banke-tolko-20-khoroshikh-aktivov.

Glazyev, Sergey. "Absurdnost denezhnoi politiki v Rossii." *Promyshlennie Vedomosti*, no. 4 (April 2006). http://promved.ru/articles/article.phtml?id=7648&nomer=28.

Global Affairs Canada. "Canadian Sanctions Related to Russia." March 18, 2016. http://www.international.gc.ca/sanctions/countries-pays/Russia-Russie.aspx?lang=eng.

"Godfather of the Kremlin? Power. Politics. Murder. Boris Berezovsky Could Teach the Guys in Sicily a Thing or Two." *Forbes*, December 30, 1996.

Goldman, Marshall. *Petrostate: Putin, Power, and the New Russia.* New York: Oxford University Press, 2008.

———. *The Piratization of Russia: Russian Reform Goes Awry.* London: Routledge, 2003.

Gorodnichenko, Yuriy, and Yegor Grygorenko. "Are Oligarchs Productive? Theory and Evidence." IZA Discussion Papers 3282 (January 2008). http://ftp.iza.org/dp3282.pdf.

Gorst, Isabel. "Russia Bans U.S., European Food and Agricultural Imports." *Los Angeles Times*, August 6, 2014. http://www.latimes.com/world/europe/la-fg-russia-bans-us-european-food-20140806-story.html.

Government of the Russian Federation. "Instructions on Additional Measures to Stimulate Economic Growth." Documents, May 14, 2014. http://en.kremlin.ru/acts/news/23900.

Granville, Brigitte. "Farewell, Ruble Zone." In *Russian Economic Reform at Risk*, edited by Anders Aslund, 65–87. New York: Pinter, 1995.

———. "The IMF and the Ruble Zone: Response to Odling-Smee and Pastor." *Comparative Economic Studies* 44, no. 4 (2002): 59–80.

Greene, Samuel A., and Graeme B. Robertson. "Politics, Justice and the New Russian Strike." *Communist and Post-communist Studies* 43, no. 1 (2010): 73–95.

"Gref prizyvaet borotsya s gollandskoi bolezniu v rossiiskoi ekonomike." *RIA Novosti*, August 23, 2004. http://www.ria.ru/economy/20040823/660781.html.

Grey, Stephen, Tom Bergin, Sevgil Musaieva, and Roman Anin. "Special Report: Putin's Allies Channeled Billions to Ukraine Oligarch." *Reuters*, November 26, 2014.

Grove, Thomas. "Russia's Chechnya: How Did Putin's Party Win 99 Percent?" *Reuters*, December 22, 2011. http://www.reuters.com/article/us-russia-chechnya-elections-idUSTRE7BK1CA20111221.

Guriev, Sergei, and Andre Rachinsky. "The Role of Oligarchs in Russian Capitalism." *Journal of Economic Perspectives* 19, no. 1 (Winter 2005): 131–50.

Guriev, Sergei, and Aleh Tsyvinski. "Challenges Facing the Russian Economy after the Crisis." In *Russia after the Global Economic Crisis*, edited by Anders Aslund, Sergei Guriev, and Andrew Kuchins, 9–38. Washington, D.C.: Peter G. Peterson Institute for International Economics and Center for Strategic and International Studies, 2010.

Gurvich, E. "Printsipy novy pensionnii reform." *Voprosy Ekonomiki* 4 (April 2011): 4–31. http://www.dlib.eastview.co/browse/doc/24582433-table-2.

Gurvich, Evsey, and Ilya Prilepskiy. "The Impact of Financial Sanctions on the Russian Economy." *Russian Journal of Economics* 1, no. 4 (2015): 359–85.

Gustafson, Thane. *Wheel of Fortune: The Battle for Oil and Power in Russia*. Cambridge, Mass.: Harvard University Press, 2012.

Hamilton, James. "Causes and Consequences of the Oil Shock of 2007–08." National Bureau of Research Working Paper 15002 (May 2009). http://www.nber.org/papers/w15002.pdf.

Hansl, Birgit, Victoria Levin, and William Shaw. "Searching for a New Silver Age in Russia: The Drivers and Impacts of Population Aging—Overview Report." World Bank Group Working Paper 99487 (2015).

Hanson, Philip. "Reiderstvo: Asset-Grabbing in Russia." *Chatham House*, March 2014. https://www.chathamhouse.org/sites/files/chathamhouse/home/chatham/public_html/sites/default/files/20140300AssetGrabbingRussiaHanson1.pdf.

———. *The Rise and Fall of the Soviet Economy*. Harlow, U.K.: Longman, 2003.

———. "The Russian Economic Puzzle: Going Forwards, Backwards, or Sideways?" *International Affairs* 83, no. 5 (2007): 869–89.

Harding, Luke. "Revealed: The $2 Billion Offshore Trail That Leads to Vladimir Putin." *Guardian*, April 3, 2016. https://www.theguardian.com/news/2016/apr/03/panama-papers-money-hidden-offshore.

Hartog, Eva. "Yakunin Quit Russian Railways over Son's Wish to Become British Citizen—Report." *Moscow Times*, October 11, 2015. https://themoscowtimes.com/articles/yakunin-quit-russian-railways-over-sons-wish-to-become-british-citizen-report-50185.

Henderson, James. *Non-Gazprom Gas Producers in Russia*. Oxford: Oxford Institute for Energy Studies, 2010.

Henderson, James, and Simon Pirani. *The Russian Gas Matrix: How Markets Are Driving Change*. Oxford: Oxford University Press, 2014.

Hill, Fiona, and Clifford G. Gaddy. *Mr. Putin: Operative in the Kremlin*. Washington, D.C.: Brookings Institution Press, 2013.

———. *The Siberian Curse: How Communist Planners Left Russia Out in the Cold*. Washington, D.C.: Brookings Institution Press, 2003.

Hobson, Peter. "RuNet Has a Field Day with Medvedev's 'No Money' Quote." *Moscow Times*, May 25, 2016. https://themoscowtimes.com/articles/runet-has-a-field-day-with-medvedevs-no-money-quote-52999.

Hoffman, David E. *The Oligarchs: Wealth and Power in the New Russia*. New York: PublicAffairs, 2001.

———. "Russia Devalues the Ruble to Prop Up Banking System." *Washington Post*, August 18, 1998.

Iasin, E. and E. Gavrilenkov. "The Problem of Settling Russia's Foreign Debt." *Problems of Economic Transition* 45, no. 5 (2000): 86–95.

IBT Staff Report. "Is Russia's APEC Summit a $21 Billion Waste?" *International Business Times*, September 5, 2012. http://www.ibtimes.com/russias-apec-summit-21-billion-waste-761551.

———. "Russia's Virtual Economy." *Foreign Affairs*, September/October 1998, 53–67.

Illarionov, Andrei. "Kratkaia istoriia sozdaniia stabilizatsionnogo fonda." Blog entry, December 26, 2009. http://aillarionov.livejournal.com/149236.html.

IMF (International Monetary Fund). "Russian Federation: Financial Stability Assessment." September 2011. http://imf.org/external/pubs/ft/scr/2011/cr11291.pdf.

———. "Russian Federation 2000 Article IV Consultation." https://www.imf.org/external/pubs/ft/scr/2000/cr00145.pdf.

———. "Russian Federation 2009 Article IV Consultation." https://www.imf.org/external/pubs/ft/scr/2009/cr09246.pdf.

———. "Russian Federation 2016 Article IV Consultation." http://www.imf.org/external/pubs/ft/scr/2016/cr16229.pdf.

"Inomarki ne pomeshali." *Vedomosti*, January 9, 2008. http://www.vedomosti.ru/newspaper/articles/2008/01/09/inomarki-ne-pomeshali.

International Republican Institute. "Public Opinion Survey: Residents of Ukraine." August 27–September 9, 2013. http://www.iri.org/sites/default/files/IRI_Ukraine_August-September_2013_Edited%20Poll.pdf.

Iradian, Garbis. "Rapid Growth in Transition Economies: Growth-Accounting Approach." IMF Working Paper, July 2007. https://www.imf.org/external/pubs/ft/wp/2007/wp07170.pdf.

Ivanova, Anna, Michael Keen, and Alexander Klemm. "The Russian Flat Tax Reform." IMF Working Paper, 2005.

Johnson, Juliet. *A Fistful of Rubles: The Rise and Fall of the Russian Banking System*. Ithaca, N.Y.: Cornell University Press, 2000.

Johnson, Steve. "Russia's Potential Growth Rate 'Close to Zero.'" *Financial Times*, April 13, 2016. https://www.ft.com/content/96d6bbea-00bd-11e6-ac98-3c15a1aa2e62.

Kaiser, Robert. "One Entrepreneur's Adventures Illustrates Hopes, Frustrations." *Washington Post*, July 18, 1999.

Kats, Maks. "Razgovory s Alekseem Kudrinym—stabilizatsionny fond." *Ekho Moskvy*, December 12, 2013. http://echo.msk.ru/blog/maxkatz/1216823-echo.

Kelly, Lidia, and Oksana Kobzeva. "Putin Stands by Hawkish Russian Central Bank—For Now." *Reuters*, November 23, 2014. http://www.reuters.com/article/russia-cenbank-independence-idUSL6N0TB40W20141124.

Khodorkovsky, Anatolii. "Forum kritikov pravitelstva." *Vedomosti*, June 16, 2000. http://www.vedemosti.ru/newspaper/articles/2000/06/16/forum-kritikov-pravitelstva.

———. "Ned—biudzhetu." *Vedomosti*, July 10, 2000. http://www.vedomosti.ru/newspaper/articles/2000/07/10/net-byudzhetu.

Khrennikov, Ilya. "No Ally of Putin, Retail Billionaire Pinched by Sanctions." *Bloomberg*, November 20, 2014. https://www.bloomberg.com/news/articles/2014-11-20/no-ally-of-putin-retail-billionaire-pinched-by-sanctions.

Khutornikh, Elena, Boris Grozovskii, and Anna Baraulina. "FRS naoborot." *Vedomosti*, February 4, 2008. http://www.vedomosti.ru/newspaper/articles/2008/02/04/frs-naoborot.

Kim, Lucian. "Putin's Judo Friend Says Premier Didn't Help Win Gazprom Deals." *Bloomberg*, April 28, 2010. http://www.bloomberg.com/news/articles/2010-04-28/putin-s-judo-playing-friend-says-premier-didn-t-help-him-win-gazprom-deals.

Kochetov, Sergey. "Moda na malenkie nalogi." *Vedemosti*, May 11, 2000. http://www.vedemosti.ru/newspaper/articles/2000/05/11/moda-na-malenkie-nalogi.

Kondrashov, Alexey. "Taxation in the Russian Oil Sector: Learning from Global Fiscal Perspectives." July 2015. http://www.ey.com/Publication/vwLUAssets/ey-taxation-in-the-russian-oil-sector-learning-from-global-fiscal-perspectives/$FILE/ey-taxation-in-the-russian-oil-sector-learning-from-global-fiscal-perspectives.pdf.

Korsunskaya, Darya, Lidia Kelly, and Elena Fabrichnaya. "Russia Considers Abolishing Mandatory Pension Savings." *Reuters*, March 15, 2016. http://www.reuters.com/article/us-russia-pensions-idUSKCN0WH19M.

Kotova, Yuliya. "Putin poruchil povysit dokhody naseleniya i snizit stoimost zhilya." *Vedomosti*, May 8, 2012. http://www.vedomosti.ru/realty/articles/2012/05/08/putin_poruchil_povysit_dohody_naseleniya_i_snizit_stoimost.

Kovalyova, Svetlana. "Duma Calls for Loan to Cover Paris Club Debt." *Moscow Times*, January 24, 2001. http://old.themoscowtimes.com/news/article/tmt/255831.html.

Kozina, Irina, Elena Vinogradova, and Linda Cook. "Russian Labor: Quiescence and Conflict." *Communist and Post-communist Studies* 45, no. 3 (September–December 2012): 219–31.

KPMG. "Investing in Russia: An Overview of the Current Investment Climate in Russia." April 2013.

Kramer, Andrew. "Rem Vyakhirev, Former Chief of Gazprom, Dies at 78." *New York Times*, February 17, 2003.

———. "Russia Raises Key Interest Rate." *New York Times*, December 11, 2014. https://www.nytimes.com/2014/12/12/business/international/russia-raises-key-lending-rate.html.

"Kremlin Picks Site for Russian 'Silicon Valley.'" *Reuters*, March 18, 2010. http://www.reuters.com/article/us-russia-siliconvalley-idUSTRE62H33S20100318.

Kroll, Luisa. "The World's Billionaires." *Forbes*, March 5, 2008. https://www.forbes.com/2008/03/05/richest-people-billionaires-billionaires08-cx_lk_0305billie_land.html.

Kronick, Dorothy. "Why Only Half of Venezuelans Are in the Streets." *FiveThirtyEight*, March 17, 2014. https://fivethirtyeight.com/features/why-venezeulas-middle-class-is-taking-to-the-streets.

Kudrin, Alexei. "Inflation: Russian and Global Trends." *Problems of Economic Transition* 50, no. 9 (2008): 27–53.

———. "O stabilizatsionnom fonde RF." http://www.akudrin.ru/achievements/stabfond.

———. "Stabilization Funds: International and Russian Experience." *Problems of Economic Transition* 50, no. 1 (2007): 6–26.

Kudrin, Alexei, and E. Gurvich. "Starenie naseleniia i ugroza buidzhetnogo krizisa." *Voprosy ekonomiki* 3 (2012): 52–79.

Kuvshinova, Olga, and Yevgenia Pismennaya. "Ekonomika sverkhoptimizma." *Vedomosti*, April 15, 2008. http://www.vedomosti.ru/newspaper/articles/2008/04/15/jekonomika-sverhoptimizma.

Kuvshinova, Olga, Aleksandra Prokopenko, and Margarita Papchenkova. "Ukreplenie rublya obespokoilo rossiiskie vlasti." *Vedomosti*, July 20, 2016. http://www.vedomosti.ru/finance/articles/2016/07/21/649999-ukreplenie-rublya.

Kuzmina, Olga, Natalya Volchkova, and Tatiana Zueva. "Foreign Direct Investment and Governance Quality in Russia." *New Economic School*, April 2014, 1–37.

Lammey, Mark. "Russian Railways Won't Publish Yakunin's Pay Packet," *Moscow Times*, June 19, 2014.

Ledeneva, Alena V. *Can Russia Modernize? Sistema, Power Networks and Informal Governance*. Cambridge: Cambridge University Press, 2013.

———. *How Russia Really Works: The Informal Practices That Shaped Post-Soviet Politics and Business*. Ithaca, N.Y.: Cornell University Press, 2006.

Levada Tsentr. "Praviteli v otechestvennoi istorii." March 1, 2016. http://www.levada.ru/2016/03/01/praviteli-v-otechestvennoj-istorii.

Levina, Irina A., Gregory V. Kisunko, Israel I. Marques, and Andrei A. Yakovlev. "Uncertainty as a Factor in Investment Decisions." World Bank Group Policy Research Working Paper 7806 (August 2016). http://documents.worldbank.org/curated/en/666331472570249124/pdf/WPS7806.pdf.

Lewis, Bill, and Vincent Palmeda. "Unlocking Economic Growth in Russia." In *Russia's Uncertain Economic Future*, edited by John P. Hardt, 47–80. New York: Routledge, 2015.

Lewis, Rosie. "Australia 'Working towards' Tougher Sanctions against Russia: Abbott." *Australian*, August 8, 2014. http://www.theaustralian.com.au/national-affairs/australia-working-towards-tougher-sanctions-against-russia-abbott/news-story/a304707f23a51f8b20fcb6551f0a2510?nk=7e7b4549152d528c050fc5023352ccf1-1488983425.

Luhn, Alec. "Gennady Timchenko Denies Putin Links Made Him One of Russia's Top Oligarchs." *Guardian*, March 21, 2014.

Luong, Pauline Jones, and Erika Weinthal. *Oil Is Not a Curse: Ownership Structure and Institutions in Soviet Successor States*. Cambridge: Cambridge University Press, 2010.

MacFarquhar, Neil. "Russia and 2 Neighbors Form Economic Union That Has a Ukraine-Size Hole." *New York Times*, May 29, 2014. https://www.nytimes.com/2014/05/30/world/europe/putin-signs-economic-alliance-with-presidents-of-kazakhstan-and-belarus.html.

Madar, Daniel. *Big Steel: Technology, Trade, and Survival in a Global Market*. Vancouver: UBC Press, 2010.

Madeva, Tatyana. "Chelovek v solidornoi pensionnoi sisteme." *Konferentsiya ANTSEA*, October 3, 2014. http://pensionreform.ru/files/84111/Maleva%2520presentation%25202014-10-03.pdf.

Magnit. "Klyuchevyie pokazateli." http://ir.magnit.com/ru/klyuchevyie-pokazateli.

"A Magnit for Investors." *Economist*, June 6, 2013. http://www.economist.com/news/business/21579023-retailer-doing-well-business-unfriendly-country-magnit-investors.

Magnitogorsk Iron & Steel Works. "History." http://en.mmk.ru/about/history.

———. *Magnitogorsk Iron & Steel Works Annual Report 2014*. http://eng.mmk.ru/
upload/iblock/eda/Annex_to_annual_report_MMK_2014_eng2.pdf.

"The Making of a Neo-KGB State." *Economist*, August 3, 2007. http://www.economist
.com/node/9682621.

Mankoff, Jeffrey. *Russian Foreign Policy: The Return of Great Power Politics*. Lanham, Md.:
Rowman and Littlefield, 2009.

Markus, Stanislav. *Property, Predation, and Protection*. Cambridge: Cambridge University
Press, 2015.

Martinez-Vasquez, Jorge, Mark Rider, and Sally Wallace. *Tax Reform in Russia*. London:
Edward Elgar, 2008.

Mau, Vladimir. "Between Crises and Sanctions: Economic Policy of the Russian
Federation." *Post-Soviet Affairs* 32, no. 4 (2016): 350–77.

———. "Economic and Political Results for 2001 and Prospects of Strengthening
Economic Growth." Institute for the Economy in Transition. http://www.iep.ru/
files/persona/MAU/results2001en.pdf.

McDermott, Roger N., Bertil Nygren, and Carolina Vendil Pallin, eds. *The Russian
Armed Forces in Transition: Economic, Geopolitical and Institutional Uncertainties*.
London: Routledge, 2012.

McKenzie, Brent, and Igor Dukeov. "Retail Strategy and Policy in Russia." In *Retailing
in Emerging Markets: A Policy and Strategy Perspective*, edited by Malabi Mukherjee,
Richard Cuthbertson, and Elizabeth Howard, 176–99. New York: Routledge, 2014.

Mearsheimer, John, Michael McFaul, and Stephan Sestanovich. "Faulty Powers:
Who Started the Ukraine Crisis?" *Foreign Affairs*, November/December 2014.
https://www.foreignaffairs.com/articles/eastern-europe-caucasus/2014-10-17
/faulty-powers.

"Medvedev Says Russia Will Not Raise Taxes until at Least 2018." *Reuters*, April 19, 2016.
http://www.reuters.com/article/russia-economy-medvedev-idUSR4N17G058.

Mehdi, Ahmed. "How the Kremlin Accidentally Liberalized Russia's Natural Gas
Market." *Foreign Affairs*, May 6, 2012.

Miller, Chris. "Russia Considers How to Impose Austerity in a Time of Recession."
*Business New Europe*, March 23, 2016. http://www.intellinews.com/comment-
russia-considers-how-to-impose-austerity-in-a-time-of-recession-93528.

———. "Russia's Central Bank—Giving Credit where Credit Is Due." *bne IntelliNews*,
May 16, 2016. http://www.intellinews.com/comment-russia-s-central-bank-giving-
credit-where-credit-is-due-97502.

———. *The Struggle to Save the Soviet Economy*. Chapel Hill: University of North
Carolina Press, 2016.

———. "What Putin Really Feared in Ukraine." *FPRI E-Notes*, September 17, 2014.
http://www.fpri.org/article/2014/09/what-putin-really-feared-in-ukraine.

———. "Why Russia's Economic Leverage Is Declining." Transatlantic Academy
2015–16 Paper Series 7 (2016). http://www.transatlanticacademy.org/publications/
why-russia%E2%80%99s-economic-leverage-declining.

Ministry of Finance of the Russian Federation. "Amount of the Reserve Fund." http://
old.minfin.ru/en/reservefund/statistics/amount/index.php?id_4=5817.

———. "Brief Information on the Execution of the Federal Budget." April 28, 2017. http://old.minfin.ru/en/statistics/fedbud/execute.

Moffitt, Robert. "Unemployment Insurance and the Distribution of Unemployment Spells." *Journal of Econometrics* 28 (1985): 85–101.

Mohsin, Saleha. "Norway 'Ready to Act' as Putin Sanctions Spark Fallout Probe." *Bloomberg*, August 12, 2014. https://www.bloomberg.com/news/articles/2014-08-12/norway-ready-to-act-as-russian-sanctions-trigger-fallout-probe.

Munter, Paivi, and Nicholas George. "Russian Fund Highlights Dependence on Oil." *Financial Times*, October 4, 2004. https://www.ft.com/content/3df6592a-1620-11d9-b835-00000e2511c8.

Myers, Steven Lee. *The New Tsar: The Rise and Reign of Vladimir Putin.* New York: Simon and Schuster, 2015.

"Nauka konkurirovat." *Vedomosti*, January 16, 2008. http://www.vedomosti.ru/newspaper/articles/2008-01-16/nauka-konkurirovat.

Navalny, Alexei. "How They Siphon at Russian Railways." Blog post, July 24, 2013. http://navalny-en.livejournal.com/93479.html.

"Navalny Says 'Patriot' Yakunin's Children Live in Foreign Luxury Homes." *Moscow Times*, October 8, 2013. https://themoscowtimes.com/articles/navalny-says-patriot-yakunins-children-live-in-foreign-luxury-homes-28417.

"Navalny Says Yakunin Owns Business Empire." *Moscow Times*, July 16, 2013. https://themoscowtimes.com/articles/navalny-says-yakunin-owns-business-empire-25891.

Neate, Rupert. "Rosneft Takes Over TNK-BP in $55bn Deal." *Guardian*, March 21, 2013.

Nichols, Bill. "Doubts Riddle Optimism of Young Russians." *USA Today*, November 15, 1999.

Noren, James. "The Controversy over Western Measures of Soviet Defense Expenditures." *Post-Soviet Affairs* 11, no. 3 (1995): 238–76.

Nove, Alec. "Agriculture." In *Soviet Policy for the 1980s*, edited by Archie Brown and Michael Kaser, 171. London: St. Anthony's, 1982.

O., A. "A Global Elite Gathering in the Crimea." *Economist*, September 24, 2013. http://www.economist.com/blogs/easternapproaches/2013/09/other-yalta-conference.

Obama, Barack. "Statement by the President on the Trans-Pacific Partnership." October 5, 2015. https://obamawhitehouse.archives.gov/the-press-office/2015/10/05/statement-president-trans-pacific-partnership.

Odling-Smee, John. "The IMF and Russia in the 1990s." IMF Staff Papers 53, vol. 1 (2006). https://www.imf.org/External/Pubs/FT/staffp/2006/01/pdf/odling.pdf.

OECD Stat. "Government Deficit/Surplus as a Percentage of GDP." May 6, 2014. http://www.oecd-ilibrary.org/economics/government-deficit_gov-dfct-table-en.

———. "Labor Productivity Levels in the Total Economy." OECD Dataset. http://www.stats.oecd.org/index.aspx?DatasetCode=LEVEL.

"Ofshory druga Putina glavnoe." *Novaia Gazeta*, April 3, 2016. http://www.meduza.io/feature/2016/04/03/ofshory-druga-putina-glavnoe.

Olson, Mancur. "Dictatorship, Democracy, and Development." *American Political Science Review* 87, no. 3 (1993): 567–76.

———. *The Rise and Decline of Nations: Economic Growth, Stagflation, and Social Rigidities.* New Haven, Conn.: Yale University Press, 1984.

Orenstein, Mitchell A. *Privatizing Pensions: The Transnational Campaign for Social Security Reform*. Princeton, N.J.: Princeton University Press, 2008.

Ostroukh, Andrey. "Russia to Grab Pension Money, Temporarily." *Wall Street Journal*, October 3, 2013. http://blogs.wsj.com/emergingeurope/2013/10/03/russia-to-grab-pension-money-temporarily.

"Otchet Tsentralnogo Banka Rossiiskii Federatsii za 1992." In *Gosudarstvenny Arkhiv Rossiiskii Federatsii*, f.10026, o. 1, d. 1080, l. 119.

"Ot redaktsii: Zapozdalaya pobeda." *Vedomosti*, February 1, 2008. http://www.vedomosti.ru/opinion/articles/2008/02/01/ot-redakcii-zapozdalaya-pobeda.

Owen, David, and David Robinson. *Russia Rebounds*. Washington, D.C.: International Monetary Fund, 2003.

Oxenstierna, Susanne. "Russia's Defense Spending and the Economic Decline." *Journal of Eurasian Studies* 7, no. 1 (2016): 60–70.

Oxenstierna, Susanne, and Per Olsson. *The Economic Sanctions against Russia: Impact and Prospects of Success*. Swedish Defense Research Agency, September 2015. https://www.foi.se/report-search/pdf?fileName=D:%5CReportSearch%5CFiles%5Cb247e9be-8972-4bff-9643-b7afdc239946.pdf.

Oxenstierna, Susanne, and Fredrik Westerlund. "Arms Procurement and the Russian Defense Industry: Challenges up to 2020." *Journal of Slavic Military Studies* 26, no. 1 (2013): 1–24.

Panin, Alexander. "Gazprom's Grip on Russian Gas Exports Weakens as Novatek Gets Export License." *Moscow Times*, September 7, 2014.

Panina, Tatiana. "Tri goda ili deciat let." *Rossiiskaia Gazeta*, January 12, 2006. http://www.rg.ru/2006/01/12/yasin-glaziev.html.

Papchenkova, Margarita. "Boleye 40% kreditov VEBa–problemnie." *Vedomosti, May 29, 2017*. https://www.vedomosti.ru/finance/articles/2017/05/30/692009-kreditov-veba-problemnie.

Papchenkova, Margarita, Galina Starinskaya, and Mikhail Serov. "Zarplaty Sechina, Yakunina i Millera ostnutsia tainoi." *Vedomosti*, March 30, 2015. http://www.vedomosti.ru/economics/articles/2015/03/30/zarplati-sechina-yakunina-i-millera-ostanutsya-tainoi.

Parshin, Konstantin. "Eyeing Tajikistan's Weak Spot, Russia Presses for Integration." *Moscow Times*, January 15, 2015. https://themoscowtimes.com/articles/eyeing-tajikistans-weak-spot-russia-presses-for-integration-42941.

Paterson, Lea, Helen Womack, and Stephen Vines. "Russia Rebuffs Soros on Call for Devaluation." *Independent*, October 23, 2011.

Paxton, Robin. "Reindeer Herders Battle Alcohol on Russia's Edge." *Reuters*, August 13, 2009.

Petrov, Nikolai. "The Security Dimension of the Federal Reforms." In *The Dynamics of Russian Politics: Putin's Reform of Federal-Regional Relations*, vol. 11, edited by Peter Reddaway and Robert W. Orttung, 7–32. Lanham, Md.: Rowman and Littlefield, 2005.

Piñera, José. "A Chilean Model for Russia." *Foreign Affairs*, September/October 2000. https://www.foreignaffairs.com/articles/russia-fsu/2000-09-01/chilean-model-russia.

Pismennaya, Evgenia. "Putin's Once-Mighty Bank for Pet Projects Now on Chopping Block." *Bloomberg*, June 14, 2016. https://www.bloomberg.com/news/articles/2016-06-15/putin-s-once-mighty-bank-for-pet-projects-now-on-chopping-block.

Pittman, Russell. "Blame the Switchman? Russian Railways Restructuring after Ten Years." In *The Oxford Handbook of the Russian Economy*, edited by Michael Alexeev and Shlomo Weber, 490–513. Oxford: Oxford University Press, 2013.

"Pravitelstvo predlagaet otmenit litsenzirovanie po 49 vidam deyatelnosti." *Vedomosti*, August 27, 2004. http://www.vedomosti.ru/library/news/2004/08/27/pravitelstvo-predlagaet-otmenit-licenzirovanie-po-49-vidam-deyatelnosti.

"President Receives Governor of Kaluga, Russia." *Viet Nam News*, March 24, 2016. http://vietnamnews.vn/politics-laws/294246/president-receives-governor-of-kaluga-russia.html.

"Prezident obelil vyvoz kapitala." *Kommersant*, June 6, 2001.

"Putin Deplores Collapse of the USSR." *BBC News*, April 25, 2005. http://www.news.bbc.co.uk/2/hi/4480745.stm.http://www.kommersant.ru/doc/269848.

"Putin uvelichil predelnuiu chislennosti shtata MVD pochti na 65,000 chelovek." *Vedomosti*, July 7, 2016. http://www.vedomosti.ru/politics/news/2016/07/07/648353-putin-shtata-mvd.

Putin, Vladimir. "Address to the Federal Assembly." May 26, 2004. http://archive.kremlin.ru/text/appears/2004/05/71501.shtml.

———. "Priamaia liniia." December 18, 2003. http://www.linia2003.ru.

———. "Speech to the Federal Assembly." July 8, 2000. http://archive.kremlin.ru/eng/speeches/2000/07/08/0000_type70029type82912_70658.shtml.

———. "Stroitelstvo spravedlivosti: Sotsialnaya politika dlya Rossii." *Komsomolskaia Pravda*, February 13, 2012. http://www.kp.ru/daily/3759/2807793.

———. "Vystuplenie v davose." January 9, 2009. http://www.vesti.ru/doc.html?id=246949.

Putin, Vladimir, Nataliya Gevorkyan, Natalya Timakova, and Andrei Kolesnikov. *First Person: An Astonishingly Frank Self-Portrait by Russia's President*. Translated by Catherine A. Fitzpatrick. New York: PublicAffairs, 2000.

Radio Free Europe/Radio Liberty. "French Senate Urges Government to Lift Sanctions on Russia." June 9, 2016. https://www.rferl.org/a/27787635.

Ragozin, Leonid. "The Putin Adoration Society." *Politico*, October 11, 2015. http://www.politico.eu/article/the-putin-adoration-society.

Reeves, Phil. "Russia Is Down but Not Out." *Independent*, April 6, 1999.

Remington, Thomas F. "Pension Reform in Authoritarian Regimes: Russia and China Compared." July 31, 2015. https://ai2-s2-pdfs.s3.amazonaws.com/af16/3f68c90759c32c9942e843bc8eb865e7cfc5.pdf.

Renz, Bettina, and Rod Thornton. "Russian Military Modernization: Cause, Course, and Consequences." *Problems of Post-communism* 59, no. 1 (2012): 44–54.

Reynolds, Maura. "Putin Reaches Out to Oligarchs." *Los Angeles Times*, July 29, 2000.

Reznik, Irina, and Ekaterina Shatalova. "Russian Railways Seeks to Fix 'Mistake' of Lost Monopoly." *Bloomberg*, September 19, 2013. https://www.bloomberg.com/news/articles/2013-09-19/russian-railways-chief-seeks-to-fix-mistake-of-lost-monopoly.

Robinson, Neil, ed. *The Political Economy of Russia*. Lanham, Md.: Rowman and Littlefield, 2012.

Rochlitz, Michael. "Corporate Raiding and the Role of the State in Russia." *Post-Soviet Affairs* 30 (2014): 89–114.

Romanova, Olga. "Bratya po razumu." *Vedemosti*, July 28, 2000. http://www.vedemosti .ru/newspaper/articles/2000/07/28/bratya-po-razumu.

Roston, Eric. "Nobody Knows How 21st-Century Russians Will Respond to Crisis." *Bloomberg*, December 17, 2014. http://www.bloomberg.com/news/articles/2014- 12-17/nobody-knows-how-21st-century-russians-will-respond-to-crisis.

"Russia Central Bank Governor Cancels Visit to Davos Forum as Ruble Slides." *Reuters*, January 21, 2016. http://www.reuters.com/article/us-russia-cenbank-davos- cancellation-idUSKCN0UZ25V.

"Russia Improves Position in International Corruption Rating." *Moscow Times*, January 27, 2016. https://themoscowtimes.com/articles/russia-improves-position- in-international-corruption-rating-51595.

"Russian Car Sales Down 36% in 2015." *Moscow Times*, January 14, 2016. https:// themoscowtimes.com/articles/russian-car-sales-down-36-in-2015-51454.

Russian Legal Information Agency. "Decision to Deny Rosneft Access to Sakhalin-II Pipeline Upheld." June 25, 2015. http://rapsinews.com/judicial _news/20150625/274009152.html.

"Russian Plantmakers Push for Market Share." *Metal Bulletin Monthly* 390 (June 2003): 13–14, 16.

Russian Railways. "Overview." http://eng.rzd.ru/statice/public/en?STRUCTURE_ID =4223. http://eng.rzd.ru/statice/public/en?STRUCTURE_ID=4223.

"Russia's Magnit Raises Forecast for New Store Openings." *Reuters*, July 23, 2015. http:// www.reuters.com/article/russia-crisis-magnit-outlook-idUSL5N1034YQ20150723.

"Russia's Quiet Loan." *Wall Street Journal*, March 11, 1998.

"Russia's Shrinking Options: John Thornill Explains Why Russia Has Devalued the Ruble and Asks Whether It Will Work." *Financial Times*, August 19, 1998.

"Russia's Sinking Ship." *Moscow Times*, July 13, 2010. http://old.themoscowtimes.com/ sitemap/free/2010/7/article/russias-sinking-ship/410271.html.

"Russia's 2015 Budget Deficit Totals $25 Billion." *Moscow Times*, January 25, 2016. https:// themoscowtimes.com/articles/russias-2015-budget-deficit-totals-25-billion-51559.

Rutland, Peter. "The Impact of the Global Financial Crisis on Russia." In "Russia and the Financial Crisis," special issue, *Russian Analytical Digest* 48 (2008): 2–5.

Sadowski, Rafal. "Ukraine: Between the European Union and the Customs Union." *OSW*, December 12, 2012. https://www.osw.waw.pl/en/publikacje/analyses/ 2012-12-12/ukraine-between-european-union-and-customs-union.

Sakwa, Richard. *Putin and the Oligarchs: The Khodorkovsky-Yukos Affair*. London: I. B. Tauris, 2014.

———. *Putin: Russia's Choice*. London: Routledge, 2004.

———. *The Quality of Freedom: Khodorkovsky, Putin and the Yukos Affair*. Oxford: Oxford University Press, 2009.

Samoylenko, Vladimir. *Special Report: Government Policies in Regard to Internal Tax Havens in Russia*. Moscow: International Tax and Investment Center, 2003.

Sanders, Katie. "Did Vladimir Putin Call the Breakup of the USSR 'the Greatest Geopolitical Tragedy of the 20th Century'?" *PolitiFact*, March 6, 2014. http://www .politifact.com/punditfact/statements/2014/mar/06/john-bolton/did-vladimir-putin-call-breakup-ussr-greatest-geop.

Sanko, Vladimir. "Rossiiskii variant gollandskoi bolezni." *Nezavisimaia Gazeta*, June 10, 2001. http://www.ng.ru/economics/2001-06-10/4_variant.html.

Schoors, Koen, and Ksenia Yudaeva. "Russian Banking as an Active Volcano." In *The Oxford Handbook of the Russian Economy*, edited by Michael Alexeev and Shlomo Weber, 544–73. Oxford: Oxford University Press, 2013.

Schreck, Carl. "Road Warriors: Russia Yields on New Transport Tax after Long-Haul Truckers Protests." Radio Free Europe/Radio Liberty, November 20, 2015. https:// www.rferl.org/a/27378046.html.

Seddon, Max. "Putin's Cellist Friend 'Interested Only in Musical Instruments.'" *Financial Times*, April 7, 2016. https://www.ft.com/content/5fd894fa-fcd6-11e5-b5f5-070dca6d0a0d.

Sergeev, Mikhail. "Biznes nedovolen pravitelstvom." *Nezavisimaia Gazeta*, October 10, 2008. http://ng.ru/economics/2008-10-10/4_rspp.html.

Serov, Mikhail. "Gazprom potraril 2.4 trin rublei na nevostrebovannie proekti." *Vedomosti*, July 29, 2015. http://vedomosti.ru/business/articles/2015/07/29/602559-gazprom-potraril-24-trin-rub-na-nevostrebovannie-proekti.

Serov, Mikhail, and Margarita Papchenkova. "Chinovniki ne budut otbirat u Gazproma trubu." *Vedomosti*, September 1, 2015. http://vedomosti.ru/business/articles/2015/09/01/606994-chinovniki-ne-budut-otbirat-u-gazproma-trubu.

"S. Glazyev: Po vine TsB Rossia kazhdy god teriaet po $30–40 mlrd." *RBK*, June 4, 2012. http://www.rbc.ru/economics/04/06/2012/653628.shtml.

Shatalov, Sergey. "Tax Reform in Russia." International Tax and Investment Center, Economic Policy Distinguished Lecture, February 2006.

Shishkov, Iu. "SNG: Poltora desiatiletiia tshchetnykh usilii." *Voprosy Ekonomiki* 4 (2007): 113–26.

Shleifer, Andrei. *A Normal Country: Russia after Communism*. Cambridge, Mass.: Harvard University Press, 2005.

Shleifer, Andrei, and Daniel Treisman. "A Normal Country." *Foreign Affairs*, March/April 2004.

———. *Without a Map: Political Tactics and Economic Reform in Russia*. Cambridge, Mass.: MIT Press, 2001.

Sil, Rudra. "The Fluidity of Labor Politics in Postcommunist Transitions: Reconfiguring the Narrative of Russian Labor Quiescence." In *Political Creativity: Reconfiguring Institutional Order and Change*, edited by Gerald Berk, Dennis C. Galvan, and Victoria Hattam, 188–209. Philadelphia: University of Pennsylvania Press, 2013.

Sinitsina, Irina. "Experience in Implementing Social Benefits Monetization Reform in Russia: Literature Review." *CASE Network Studies and Analyses* 381 (2009): 1–45.

SIPRI Military Expenditure Database. https://www.sipri.org/databases/milex.

Smirnov, Konstantin. "Zhizn i smert programma Grefa." *Kommersant*, July 4, 2000. http://www.kommersant.ru/doc/17157.

"S novym rostom!" *Vedomosti*, January 9, 2008. http://www.vedomosti.ru/newspaper/articles/2008/01/09/s-novym-rostom.

Soldatkin, Vladimir. "How Gazprom's $1 Trillion Dream Has Fallen Apart." *Reuters*, June 28, 2013.

———. "Russian Oil Output Hits Post-Soviet Record High." *Reuters*, January 2, 2016. http://www.reuters.com/article/us-russia-energy-production-idUSKBN0UG02S20160102.

———. "Russia Oil Output Forecast to Rise Next Year despite Low Prices: Reuters Poll." *Reuters*, December 23, 2015.

Soldatov, Andrei, and Irina Borogan. *The New Nobility: The Restoration of Russia's Security State and the Enduring Legacy of the KGB*. New York: PublicAffairs, 2010.

Sonne, Paul. "How Looming Recession Is Unsettling One of Russia's Boom Cities." *Wall Street Journal*, March 16, 2015. http://www.wsj.com/articles/how-looming-recession-is-unsettling-one-of-russias-boom-cities-1426559403.

Spears and Associates. *Petroleum Equipment and Service Needs of the CIS*. Tulsa, Okla.: Spears and Associates, 1992.

"Special Report: The World's Billionaires 2009." *Forbes*, March 11, 2009. https://www.forbes.com/lists/2009/10/billionaires-2009-richest-people_The-Worlds-Billionaires_Rank_7.html.

Stent, Angela E. *The Limits of Partnership: US-Russian Relations in the Twenty-First Century*. Princeton, N.J.: Princeton University Press, 2015.

Stern, Jonathan P. *The Future of Russian Gas and Gazprom*. Oxford: Oxford University Press, 2005.

Stolyarov, Gleb, Irina Reznik, Kirill Khripunov, and Evgeniya Pismennaya. "Isklyuchitelnaya mera." *Vedomosti*, October 30, 2008. http://www.vedomosti.ru/newspaper/articles/2008/10/30/isklyuchitelnaya-mera.

Sutela, Pekka. *The Political Economy of Putin's Russia*. London: Routledge, 2013.

Swiss Federal Council. "Situation in Ukraine: Federal Council Decides on Further Measures to Prevent the Circumvention of International Sanctions." August 27, 2014. https://www.admin.ch/gov/en/start/dokumentation/medienmitteilungen.msg-id-54221.html.

Takahashi, Maiko, and Isabel Reynolds. "Japan Steps Up Russia Sanctions, Protests Island Visit." *Bloomberg*, September 24, 2014. https://www.bloomberg.com/news/articles/2014-09-24/japan-to-protest-russian-official-s-visit-to-disputed-islands.

"There's Light at the End of the Tunnel for Russia's Economy." *Moscow Times*, December 3, 2015. http://old.themoscowtimes.com/guides/eng/doing-business-in-russia-2015/551141/theres-light-at-the-end-of-the-tunnel-for-russias-economy/551144.html.

"Third Wave of Sanctions Slams Russian Stocks." *Moscow Times*, July 17, 2014. https://themoscowtimes.com/articles/third-wave-of-sanctions-slams-russian-stocks-37409.

Thomas, Daniel. "Billionaire Fridman Targets US and Europe in $16bn Telecoms Spree." *Financial Times*, April 5, 2015. https://www.ft.com/content/f0a1579a-d876-11e4-ba53-00144feab7de.

Thornill, John. "Russia's Moment of Truth." *Financial Times*, August 14, 1998.

Timmer, Marcel P., and Ilya B. Voskoboynikov. "Is Mining Fueling Long-Run Growth in

Russia? Industry Productivity Growth Trends since 1995." BOFIT Discussion Papers 19 (2013).

Tompson, William. "The Russian Economy under Vladimir Putin." In *Russian Politics under Putin*, edited by Cameron Ross, 114–32. Manchester, U.K.: Manchester University Press, 2004.

*Trading Economics*. "Brent Crude Oil." http://www.tradingeconomics.com/commodity/brent-crude-oil.

———. "Russia MICEX Stock Market Index, 1997–2016." http://www.tradingeconomics.com/russia/stock-market.

"Transcript: Interview with Nikolai Patrushev." *Financial Times*, June 21, 2015. https://www.ft.com/content/b81bbd70-17f0-11e5-a130-2e7db721f996.

Treisman, Daniel. *After the Deluge: Regional Crises and Political Consolidation in Russia.* Ann Arbor: University of Michigan Press, 2001.

———. "Putin's Silovarchs." *Orbis* 51, no. 1 (Winter 2007): 141–53.

———. *The Return: Russia's Journey from Gorbachev to Medvedev*. New York: Simon and Schuster, 2012.

———. "Ruble Politics: Evaluating Exchange Rate Management in 1990s Russia." In *The State after Communism: Governance in the New Russia*, edited by Timothy J. Colton and Stephen Holmes, 187–224. Lanham, Md.: Rowman and Littlefield, 2006.

"Ukraine's Employers Federation: Russia's Custom Service Halts All Ukrainian Imports." *Kyiv Post*, August 14, 2013. https://www.kyivpost.com/article/content/ukraine-politics/ukraines-employers-federation-russias-customs-service-halts-all-ukrainian-imports-328360.html.

U.S. Department of Agriculture Foreign Agricultural Service. "Russia Bans Key U.S. Agricultural Exports." *International Agricultural Trade Reports*, August 8, 2014. https://www.fas.usda.gov/data/russia-bans-key-us-agricultural-exports.

U.S. Energy Information Administration. "U.S. Field Production of Crude Oil." http://www.eia.gov/dnav/pet/hist/LeafHandler.ashx?n=PET&s=MCRFPUS1&f=A.

Vatansever, Adnan. *The Political Economy of Allocation of Natural Resource Rents and Fighting the Resource Curse: The Case of Oil Rents in Putin's Russia*. Baltimore: Johns Hopkins University, 2009.

"VEB dogoforilsya o restrukturizatsii kreditov po Olimpiade." *Rossiya Segodnya*, July 5, 2016. http://www.ria.ru/economy/20160705/1459032189.html.

Vernikov, Andrei. "Russian Banking: The State Makes a Comeback?" December 31, 2009, BOFIT Discussion Paper No. 24/2009. https://ssrn.com/abstract=1539988.

"Vkratse." *Vedomosti*, April 9, 2008. http://www.vedomosti.ru/newspaper/articles/2008/01/09/vkratse2.

"Vladivostok Holds Its Breath for Life after APEC." *Moscow Times*, September 5, 2012. https://themoscowtimes.com/articles/vladivostok-holds-its-breath-for-life-after-apec-17520.

Volkov, Vladim. "The Political Economy of Coercion, Economic Growth, and the Consolidation of the State." *Problems of Economic Transition* 43, no. 4 (2000): 24–40.

"Volkswagen Bets on Long-Term Russian Growth with New Engine Plant." *Moscow Times*, September 4, 2015. http://www.reuters.com/article/volkswagen-russia-engines-idUSL5N11A1A920150904.

Voskoboynikov, Ilya. "New Measures of Output, Labour and Capital in Industries of the Russian Economy." *Groningen Growth and Development Centre Research Memorandum* GD-123 (2012).

"Vospitanie chuvstv." *Vedemosti*, March 30, 2005. http://www.vedemosti.ru/opinion/articles/2005/03/30/ot-redakcii-vospitanie-chuvstv.

"Vstupil v silu zakon 'o valyutnom regulirovanii i valyutnom kontrole." *Vedemosti*, June 18, 2004. http//www.vedemosti/library/news/2004/06/18/vstupil-o-valyutnom-regulirovanii-i-valyutnom-kontrole.

"Vsyo podorozhaet." *Vedomosti*, January 9, 2008. http://www.vedomosti.ru/newspaper/articles/2008/01/09-vsyo-podorozhaet.

Wagstyl, Stefan. "Deripaska Calls for Changes at 'Ridiculous' Central Bank." *Financial Times*, April 20, 2012. https://www.ft.com/content/6a92416d-cc78-3d3f-910c-228f4b6cd359.

Walker, Shaun. "Putin Announces Plan to Return as Russian President." *Independent*, September 24, 2011. http://www.independent.co.uk/news/world/europe/putin-announces-plan-to-return-as-russian-president-2360639.html.

———. "Ukraine's EU Trade Deal Will Be Catastrophic, Says Russia." *Guardian*, September 22, 2013. https://www.theguardian.com/world/2013/sep/22/ukraine-european-union-trade-russia.

———. "Vladimir Putin Offers Ukraine Financial Incentives to Stick with Russia." *Guardian*, December 18, 2013. https://www.theguardian.com/world/2013/dec/17/ukraine-russia-leaders-talks-kremlin-loan-deal.

Warren, Marcus. "Putin Revives Soviet National Anthem." *Telegraph*, December 9, 2000. http://www.telegraph.co.uk/news/worldnews/europe/russia/1377685/Putin-revives-Soviet-national-anthem.html.

Weaver, Courtney. "Debt Sale Seen as Triumph for Moscow." *Financial Times*, April 23, 2010. https://www.ft.com/content/292f861c-4e3a-11df-b48d-00144feab49a.

Wegren, Stephen K. *Land Reform in Russia: Institutional Design and Behavioral Responses.* New Haven, Conn.: Yale University Press, 2014.

Weiss, Andrew S. "Five Myths about Vladimir Putin." *Washington Post*, March 2, 2012. https://www.washingtonpost.com/opinions/five-myths-about-vladimir-putin/2012/02/29/gIQAchg8mR_story.html?utm_term=.39963888d7b4.

Wengle, Susanne, and Michael Rasell. "The Monetisation of L'goty: Changing Patterns of Welfare Politics and Provision in Russia." *Europe-Asia Studies* 60, no. 5 (2008): 739–56.

Wolf, Jim. "Cost of Lockheed's F-35 Fighter Soars." *Reuters*, March 11, 2007.

Woodruff, David. *Money Unmade: Barter and the Fate of Russian Capitalism.* Ithaca, N.Y.: Cornell University Press, 2000.

World Bank. "Cash Surplus/Deficit (% of GDP)." http://databank.worldbank.org/data/reports.aspx?source=2&series=GC.BAL.CASH.GD.ZS&country.

———. *Russian Economic Reform: Crossing the Threshold of Structural Change.* Country Study. Washington, D.C.: World Bank, 1992.

———. *Russian Federation: Promoting Equitable Growth: A Living Standards Assessment.* Washington, D.C.: World Bank, 2008.

———. "Tax Revenue (% of GDP)." http://data.worldbank.org/indicator/GC.TAX.TOTL.GD.ZS

World Bank Group. "World Bank Open Data," 2017. http://data.worldbank.org/.

World Steel Association. *Steel Statistical Yearbook*. http://www.worldsteel.org/statistics/statistics-archive/yearbook-archive.html.

———. *Steel Statistical Yearbook 1996*. https://www.worldsteel.org/en/dam/jcr:81073f61-10b6-464f-83cd-1d4cb740a9d0/Steel+statistical+yearbook+1996.pdf.

Yaffa, Joshua. "Oligarchy 2.0: Putin's Shadow Cabinet and the Bridge to Crimea." *New Yorker*, May 29, 2017.

Yakovlev, Andrei. "What Are the Russian Elites Going to Build?" *Russian Analytical Digest* 187 (2016): 2–3. http://www.css.ethz.ch/content/dam/ethz/special-interest/gess/cis/center-for-securities-studies/pdfs/RAD187.pdf.

Yakunin, Vladimir. "Globalizatsia i kapitalizm." *Razvitie i Ekonomika* 13 (July 2015): 6. http://www.devec.ru/almanah/13/1846-vladimir-jakunin-globalizatsija-i-kapitalizm.html.

Yasin, Yevgeny. "Putin's Undercover Liberalism." *Project Syndicate*, May 24, 2001. http://www.project-syndicate.org/commentary/putin-s-undercover-liberalism#4hC5Er54mtvm5Jz4.99.

Zhavoronkov, S., V. Mau, D. Chernyi, and K. Yanovskiy. "The Deregulation of the Russian Economy." *Problems of Economic Transition* 45, no. 5 (2002): 5–66. Translation of "Deregulirovanie rossiiskoiekonomiki." Academic Works, no. 32R. Moscow: Institute for Economic Transition, 2001.

Zhukovskii, Vladislay. Twitter post, April 23, 2016. http://www.twitter.com/vlad_zhukovskiy/status/723803288504819712.

Zimin, Dmitry. "Promoting Investment in Russia's Regions." *Eurasian Geography and Economics* 51, no. 5 (2010): 653–68.

Zinets, Natalia, and Richard Balmforth. "Ukraine Parliament Deadlock on Tymoshenko Clouds EU Signing." *Reuters*, November 13, 2013. https://www.reuters.com/article/us-ukraine-eu-idUSBRE9AC0EZ20131113.

Zolotareva, A., S. Drobyshevskii, S. Sinel'nikov, and P. Kadochnikov. "The Prospects for Creating a Stabilization Fund in the Russian Federation." *Problems of Economic Transition* 45, no. 2 (2002): 5–85.

Zubkov, Valentin. "Vremennoe okno dlya Rossii mozhet zaklopnutsya." *Russkoe Voskresenie*. http://www.voskres.ru/interview/ishaev_printed.htm.

# INDEX

Index | 215

on natural gas, 55; on oligarchs, 34–35; oligarchs and, 44–46; on pensions, 107; protests against, 134; Sobchak and, 8; on Soviet collapse, 107; St. Petersburg and, 8; Vyakhirev *and, 48–49

Quality of life: defense spending and, 10; increasing, 99; inflation and, 151

Rachinsky, Andrei, 83
"Raider attacks," 88
Red Directors, 94–95
Regulatory compliance, 32–33
Rents: energy companies and, 44–45
Reserve funds, 59–60, 64–68, 65, 73–78, 74, 125
Resource extraction tax, 41, 58
Retail industry, 90–93
Revolutions, 115–16
Rodina (party), 71
Roldugin, Sergei, 79, 80
Roosevelt, Franklin Delano, 30
Rose Revolution, 115–16, 117, 146
Rosneft, 18, 46, 52, 56, 138–39, 152
Rosselkhozbank, 123
Rotenberg, Arkady, 51, 87, 160
Rotenberg, Boris, 87
Ruble: in 1998 financial crisis, 2, 18–19; in 2008 financial crisis, 126–27; in 2014 oil crash, 148–49; devaluation, 18–19, 81–82, 127–28, 149–50, 152; "gold," 68; oligarchs and, 12–13. *See also* Currency
"Rule of the Seven Boyars," 13–14
Russian Railways, 83, 85–86
Rutskoi, Aleksandr, 28
Rybolovlev, Dmitri, 82

Saakashvili, Mikheil, 115, 117
Safety net, 104–7. *See also* Social programs
St. Petersburg, 7–9
Sakhalin Island, 56
Sakharov, Andrei, 134
Sanctions, 145–48
Saudi Arabia, 82
Savings, 59–60, 64–68, 65, 73–78, 74

Sberbank, 152
Sechin, Igor, 46, 52
Security Council (Russia), 26
Security services: expansion of influence of, 11; Putin's control of, 26. *See also* KGB
*Semiboyarschina*, 13–14
September 11 attacks, 115
Serdyukov, Anatoly, 117–18
Sevastopol, 111
Severstal, 95
Shadow economy. *See* Black market
Shamalov, Nikolai, 84
Shell companies, 80, 84
Shevardnadze, Eduard, 115
Shokhin, Alexander, 61
Shuvalov, Igor, 47
Sibneft, 40, 51
Siluanov, Anton, 111
Skolkovo Innovation Center, 130
Slovakia, 82
Sobchak, Anatoly, 7–9
Sochi Olympics, 139–40, 155
Social contract, 99–100, 104, 111–13, *112, 113*
Social programs, 27–28, 42–43, 104–7
Social welfare, 27
Soros, George, 17
South Africa, 115
South Korea, 1
South Ossetia, 117
Spears, Richard, 175n1
Spending cuts, 10, 14–15, 20, 155–56, 160–61. *See also* Austerity
Stabilization Fund, 64–65, 67–68, 73, 74–77
Stalin, Joseph, 37, 68, 93
Standard of living, 99
State property, 11, 12
State-run firms, 83–87
Statism, 23
Steel industry, 93–95, 96–97
Stock prices, 120
"Strategy for the Development of Russia through 2010," 31
Stroigazmontazh, 86
Stroitransgaz, 48, 86
Stroyev, Ygor, 28

Subsidies: 1998 financial crisis and, 3, 4;
    corruption and, 88; energy sector, 126;
    farm, 142; Gref and, 27–28; inflation
    and, 6–7, 71, 73; rail, 86; Yeltsin and, 6
Supermarkets, 91–93
Surgutneftegaz, 48

Tatarstan, 24–25
Taxation: 2008 financial crisis and, 125; of
    black market, 8–9; corporate, 33; cuts
    in, 66–67; debt and, 62; "Dutch disease"
    and, 67; of energy companies, 15, 54–55,
    57; energy companies and, 40, 41; feder-
    alism and, 25; flat, 34, 64; Gazprom and,
    16–17; highway, 160; individual income,
    33, 64; inflation as, 69; by mafias, 11;
    as obstacle to development, 157, 158;
    of oligarchs, 34–37; Putin on reforms
    for, 22; rates, 33; resistance to, 15–16; of
    resource extraction, 41, 58; Temporary
    Extraordinary Commission and, 16
Tax havens, 80
Tech firms, 80
Temporary Extraordinary Commission,
    15–16
Terrorism, 115
Thailand, 1, 2
Timchenko, Gennady, 51, 86, 87
TNK-BP, 52, 55, 56, 138–39
Trans-Pacific Partnership, 141, 142
Turnover tax, 33

Ukraine, 5, 115–16, 137–38, 141, 143–46,
    153–54
Ulyukaev, Alexey, 72
Unemployment, 99, 100–101, 102–3, 160–61
Union of Right Forces, 31
Unions, 101
United Russia, 45, 132, 133–34
United States, 52, 85, 91, 102, 141, 145–46
Uralkali, 82
Uralvagonzavod, 161

VEB (bank), 80, 110, 123, 140, 152, 154–55
Vedomosti (newspaper), 102–3, 119

Vekselberg, Viktor, 55
Venezuela, 82
Vertical power, 24–27
Veterans, bonuses for, 134
Virgin Islands, 80
VKontakte, 80
Vladivostok, 19
Vote rigging, 133–34
VTB (bank), 124, 145, 152
Vyakhirev, Rem, 11–12, 17, 48
Vyakhirev, Yuri, 48
Vyakhireva, Tatiana, 48

Wage arrears, 98–99, 103
Wage decline, 150
Wage growth, 100, 112, 113
Wage stagnation, 160–61
Wealth: accumulation of, 30–31, 59–60,
    79, 84
Welfare, 27, 42–43, 104–7
World Bank, 33, 82
World Economic Forum, 125
World Trade Organization (WTO), 33,
    141–42
World War II, 137

Yakovlev, Vladimir, 9, 83–85
Yakunin, Andrei, 86
Yakunin, Vladimir, 83–85
Yalta Conference (1945), 137
Yalta Conference (2013), 137–38
Yandex, 80
Yanukovych, Viktor, 144
Yasin, Yevgeny, 31, 61
Yeltsin, Boris: 1998 financial crisis and, 1–2;
    market prices and, 5–6; oligarchs and,
    12–13; Primakov and, 21
Yeltsin, Tatiana, 12, 98
Yevtushenkov, Vladimir, 162
Youth League, 42
Yuganskneftegaz, 46
Yukos, 40, 42–43, 45–48, 52. See also
    Energy companies

Zyuganov, Gennady, 13, 17, 19, 45, 61, 109

CPSIA information can be obtained
at www.ICGtesting.com
Printed in the USA
LVHW041936100322
713134LV00013B/1646